Identity in the 21st Century

Identity Studies in the Social Sciences

Titles include:

Ben Rogaly and Becky Taylor
MOVING HISTORIES OF CLASS AND COMMUNITY
Identity, Place and Belonging in Contemporary England

Margaret Wetherell (*editor*)
IDENTITY IN THE 21ST CENTURY
New Trends in Changing Times

Margaret Wetherell (*editor*)
THEORIZING IDENTITIES AND SOCIAL ACTION

Identity Studies in the Social Sciences
Series Standing Order ISBN 978–0–230–20500–0
(*outside North America only*)

You can receive future titles in this series as they are published by placing a standing order. Please contact your bookseller or, in case of difficulty, write to us at the address below with your name and address, the title of the series and the ISBN quoted above.

Customer Services Department, Macmillan Distribution Ltd, Houndmills, Basingstoke, Hampshire RG21 6XS, England

Identity in the 21st Century

New Trends in Changing Times

Edited by

Margaret Wetherell
Open University, UK

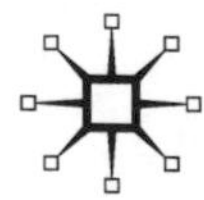

First published 2009 by
PALGRAVE MACMILLAN

Palgrave Macmillan in the UK is an imprint of Macmillan Publishers Limited, registered in England, company number 785998, of Houndmills, Basingstoke, Hampshire RG21 6XS.

Palgrave Macmillan in the US is a division of St Martin's Press LLC, 175 Fifth Avenue, New York, NY 10010.

Palgrave Macmillan is the global academic imprint of the above companies and has companies and representatives throughout the world.

Palgrave® and Macmillan® are registered trademarks in the United States, the United Kingdom, Europe and other countries.

ISBN-13: 978–0–230–58087–9 hardback

This book is printed on paper suitable for recycling and made from fully managed and sustained forest sources. Logging, pulping and manufacturing processes are expected to conform to the environmental regulations of the country of origin.

A catalogue record for this book is available from the British Library.

A catalog record for this book is available from the Library of Congress.

Printed and bound in Great Britain by
CPI Antony Rowe, Chippenham and Eastbourne

Contents

List of Tables

Series Editors' Preface

The concept of identity has had a long and chequered history in the social sciences – many chafe at its ambiguity and frustrating complexity – yet it remains the pivotal site for exploring the relations between social life and subjectivity. Who we are is always complicated – a matter of social classifications, shifting social categorisations and group memberships, and a matter, too, of the ways in which social and cultural materials are organised as psychology and taken on as personal projects. Identity draws attention to 'names' and 'looks'. It is lived out in grand narratives and performances which construct sometimes passionately invested 'imagined' routes and destinies as well as in the more mundane arenas of everyday interaction, inter-subjective relations and in social institutions. Identity guides and predicts social action. It highlights positions and intelligibility defining what is possible and liveable and what is unthinkable and excessively troubled.

We suggest, in short, that identity is one of the most interesting points at which the trajectories of post-colonial societies, globalisation and assumptions about 'liquid modernity' come into focus along with new formations of social class, gender relations and issues of inequality, rights and social justice. Identity is at the heart of some of the most intractable and troubling contemporary social problems – community conflict, racism, discrimination, xenophobia and marginalisation.

It is the key laboratory, too, for any social psychologist focused on the interface of personal lives and social lives.

Identity Studies in the Social Sciences brings together psychologists, sociologists, anthropologists, geographers, social policy researchers, education researchers and political scientists to address this territory. The interdisciplinary reach of the series is matched by the degree of theoretical diversity. The books reflect on and take inspiration from the many 'theory wars' in the social sciences which have used identity as their hinge and also develop new theory and critique for current times, including new ontologies and new politics to do justice to contemporary amalgams of practices and subjectivities. The series includes empirical work, scholarly debate and research reviews on the core social categories and the intersections of these including 'race', ethnicity, social class, gender, generation, disability, nationality and sexuality along with less easily nameable social and institutional categorisations and affiliations.

Identity Studies in the Social Sciences highlights the ways in which identities are formed, managed and mobilised in contexts and spaces such as schools, work-places, clinics, homes, communities and streets. We welcome you to this rich collection of accounts from the various front-lines of identity studies.

Margaret Wetherell, Valerie Hey and Stephen Reicher

Acknowledgements

Genuinely collaborative work is becoming an unusual and fraught experience in academia, but this book and the ESRC Programme *Identities and Social Action* which funded the research were an exception and a delight. I am very grateful to all the researchers in the programme for their companionship, good will and stamina. Their achievements were remarkable and will persist. I want to particularly acknowledge those who authored the chapters in the two published collections for their willingness to revise and re-shape their chapters to find the themes and tell the stories.

Collectively, we owe an enormous debt to Kerry Carter, the Programme Administrator, who put together this manuscript and managed the book projects. As we know, administrating academics is never easy and Kerry bit her lip, got on with it and did a superb job putting together the infrastructure for our activities. I am grateful for her skills and for all the great times during the six years we worked together. In the ESRC, I want to thank the managers assigned to the programme – Joy Todd and, then, Dr Chris Wyatt – for their support and hard work. *Identities and Social Action* was commissioned by the ESRC's Strategic Research Board. Prof. David McCrone was responsible for initiating this large investment in identities research and Gabriel Channan, Prof. Satnam Virdee and Prof. John Solomos acted as the nominated Board members for the programme. I am extremely grateful to them and to the members of the Programme Advisory Committee (chaired by David McCrone) who mentored the work and advised me at all stages – Anjana Ahuja (The Times), Jabeer Butt (Deputy Chief Executive, Race Equality Foundation), Mark Carroll (formerly Department of Communities and Local Government), Prof. Paul Du Gay (Warwick University), Prof. Valerie Hey (Sussex University), Michelynn Lafleche (Director of the Runnymede Trust), Ben Page (Managing Director of Ipsos MORI Public Affairs), Prof. Stephen Reicher (St Andrews University), Prof. Steve Vertovec (COMPAS) and Claire Tyler (Chief Executive Relate).

Finally, I want to thank Philippa Grand, our Editor at Palgrave Macmillan who has made the task easy and enjoyable, my colleagues at the Open University in the Psychology Department and in the Faculty of Social Sciences for their forbearance in the years I disappeared, my husband, Pete Williams, and my son, Sam Wetherell, for their unfailing good spirits, great meals and critical reading.

Margaret Wetherell
Open University

List of Contributors

Phoebe Beedell is a Research Fellow at the University of the West of England, Bristol.

Andrew Bengry-Howell is a Research Fellow based in the Psychology Department at the University of Bath.

Simon Clarke is Professor of Psycho-Social Studies and Director of the Centre for Psycho-Social Studies at the University of the West of England, Bristol.

Rosie Cox is Senior Lecturer in Geography and Gender Studies at Birkbeck, University of London.

Gill Crozier is Professor of Education and Assistant Dean Research at Roehampton University.

John Curtice is Professor of Politics and Director of the Social Statistics Laboratory in the Department of Government at the University of Strathclyde.

Rod Earle is Lecturer in Youth Justice at the Open University.

Gabriella Elgenius is a British Academy Research Fellow at Nuffield College, Oxford University.

Steve Garner is Senior Lecturer in Sociology in the School of Languages and Social Science at Aston University.

Rosie Gilmour is a Research Fellow at the University of the West of England, Bristol.

Christine Griffin is Professor of Social Psychology and Head of the Psychology Department at the University of Bath.

Chris Hackley is Professor of Marketing at Royal Holloway, University of London.

Lucy Hadfield is a Research Fellow in the Faculty of Health and Social Care at the Open University.

Roxy Harris is Senior Lecturer in Language in Education in the Department of Education and Professional Studies at King's College London.

Anthony Heath is Professor of Sociology at the University of Oxford, a Fellow of Nuffield College and a Fellow of the British Academy.

Sumi Hollingworth is a Research Fellow at the Institute for Policy Studies in Education at London Metropolitan University.

Sue Jackson is Professor of Lifelong Learning and Gender at Birkbeck, University of London and Director of the Birkbeck Institute for Lifelong Learning.

David James is Professor of Education at the University of the West of England, Bristol.

Fiona Jamieson is a Research Fellow in Education at the University of Sunderland.

Mary Jane Kehily is Senior Lecturer in Childhood and Youth Studies at the Open University.

Meena Khatwa is a Research Fellow at Birkbeck, University of London.

Dina Kiwan is Lecturer in Citizenship Education at Birkbeck, University of London.

Willm Mistral manages the Mental Health R&D Unit, a joint unit of the University of Bath and Avon and Wiltshire Mental Health Trust.

Coretta Phillips is Senior Lecturer in Social Policy at the London School of Economics and Political Science.

Ben Rampton is Professor of Applied and Socio-Linguistics and Director of the Centre for Language, Discourse and Communication at King's College, London.

Diane Reay is Professor of Education at the University of Cambridge.

Ben Rogaly is Senior Lecturer in Human Geography at the University of Sussex.

Sue Sharpe is a freelance social researcher and Visiting Fellow at London South Bank University.

Beverley Skeggs is Professor of Sociology at Goldsmiths, University of London.

Deborah Sporton is Senior Lecturer in Geography at the University of Sheffield.

Isabelle Szmigin is Professor of Marketing at the Business School, University of Birmingham.

Becky Taylor is Lecturer in History at Birkbeck, University of London.

Rachel Thomson is Professor of Social Research in the Faculty of Health and Social Care at the Open University.

Gill Valentine is Professor in the School of Geography, University of Leeds.

Valerie Walkerdine is Professor in the School of Social Sciences, Cardiff University.

Margaret Wetherell is Professor of Social Psychology at the Open University and Director of the ESRC Identities and Social Action Programme.

Katya Williams is a Research Fellow based at Institute for Policy Studies in Education, London Metropolitan University.

Helen Wood is Reader in Media Studies at De Montfort University.

Introduction: Negotiating Liveable Lives – Identity in Contemporary Britain

Margaret Wetherell

Who can we be in the 21st century? The chapters in this book explore this question. Focusing on trends in Britain, the authors examine the current patterning of identities based on class and community, gender and generation, 'race', faith and ethnicity, and derived from popular culture. We look at how people locate themselves now, how they make sense of their biographies and trajectories, and tell their stories. The chapters examine the forms of 'we' and wider social categorisations available as resources for identity work, and the various kinds of trouble which seem to emerge, as people struggle to align themselves with, or resist, contemporary prescriptions.

These are interesting times for the study of identity. It has been suggested, for example, that stable identities based on familiar social class hierarchies have been replaced with multiple, fragmented and more uncertain identity projects based on 'life-style' and consumer choices. But is that the case – are traditional commitments, family and workplace loyalties breaking down in the ways commentators diagnose? Are 'liquid' senses of self, and volatile and dynamic forms of identity politics, becoming more salient? Upsurges of intense solidarities based on religious, ethnic and national identities are also seen as characteristic of contemporary life. But current times are described, too, as a period of even greater mobility and 'mixing' than previously where ethnic diversity has become banal and commonplace. In social and psychological theory, the term 'identity' is itself the locus of controversy – what is its value and currency? It seems to suggest illusory fixity, it seems to separate the social from the personal and its range is surely too large and its definition ambiguous; yet the empirical territory 'identity' marks out is too important to dismiss or neglect.

Our credentials for attempting to address these issues and give a robust sense of identity trends in changing times rest on five years of collective research through an Economic and Social Research Council (ESRC) Programme (see http://www.identities.org.uk/). This book and its companion volume, Theorizing Identities and Social Action, also published by Palgrave/Macmillan, summarise the findings and conclusions from extensive, systematic and empirically rich investigations. The 25 projects which made up the Identities and Social Action Programme worked with over 12,000 participants across the UK using quantitative surveys, in-depth qualitative interviews, focus groups, ethnography, oral history, textual analysis and studies of natural interaction (see Appendix A for a list of the 12 research projects informing this collection).

Each chapter presents a snapshot of a particular sample, site or context for identity making. These accounts from Sheffield and South Wales, from London and Norwich, from ethnically diverse metropolitan contexts and homogeneous, provincial communities are more than the sum of the parts. They allow thought about directions of social change, along with critical reflection on the validity of some of the meta-narratives guiding current policy and found in social theory and in political life. The research in this volume does not exhaust the play of identity by any means. No one collection could be complete and there are many obvious absences. But this set of snapshots focused around class, community, ethnicity, gender and generation is intended to provoke thought about some core aspects of contemporary identities, their nature, shape and form, the possibilities and resources for people's identity stories, the limits on these and about the puzzle of identity itself.

The book is divided into three parts. Part I examines class and community and engages with grand social theories of change, especially the claims of the individualisation theorists (e.g. Beck, 1992; Beck and Beck-Gernsheim, 2002; Giddens, 1991) and claims about the new technologies for work on the self found in these globalised and neo-liberal times (e.g. Bauman, 2001; 2005; Rose, 1989; 1997; 1999). Part II focuses on ethnicity and migration and considers the complex multicultures (Gilroy, 2005; 2006) emerging in metropolitan contexts and the claims of new ethnicities theorists (Hall, 1992), as well as examining white majority communities. Part III takes up intimate identities based on gender and generation and presented in popular culture. The chapters in this Part return from a different direction to debates about the individualising tendencies in contemporary life. This introduction will pre-review each of these Parts and will try to summarise the main points across the chapters. First, however, I want to identify some of the over-arching themes which inform the book as a whole.

Threads

The ESRC programme which inspired this collection was profoundly inter-disciplinary including, for example, sociologists, psychologists, geographers, anthropologists, social policy and education researchers, media and business studies researchers, criminologists and sociolinguists. Of course, there were deep theoretical and methodological disagreements but a surprising level of shared focus. Most of us agreed that in some sense studying identity involved studying the conditions and practices of 'social intelligibility'. Not all of us had read Judith Butler (1990; 2004; 2006), would concur that she was a suitable interlocutor, or would turn automatically first to her philosophy, but her work does perhaps express this shared interest best. This became an interest, too, in how people in very different circumstances and with very different trajectories manage to negotiate 'liveable' as opposed to 'unliveable' lives.

When we talk about identity, we are describing, in part, communicative practices. F. Scott Fitzgerald is reputed to have said, for example, that identity is a 'series of successful gestures' (Leith, 2009). In many ways, this is a facile comment but it does draw attention to the ways in which identity involves a 'gathering together', a communicative embodiment, encapsulation and stylisation. This gathering together is a 'presentation of self' (Goffman, 1959) designed for an audience, even if that audience is only there in imagination or fantasy, or consists of a self observing itself. Identity, in other words, is about becoming intelligible to oneself and to others. And being intelligible, as Butler (2004) argues, involves engaging with current forms of social recognition. It also requires repetition over time – one gesture alone would be insufficient to count as characteristic – as Fitzgerald states, a series is required.

There is a lot at stake in the intelligibility practices of identity, as Butler points out. What counts as a successful series of gestures is ambiguous, and indeed success can be a mixed blessing. Being recognised as a particular kind of 'someone' can entail engaging with normative expectations of identity which demean, oppress and blight, resulting in what Butler (2006) describes as literally 'unliveable' situations and precarious lives. The chapters try to outline the 'conditions of intelligibility' characteristic of these times. They discuss how people construct (and fail to construct) liveable paths from the social, cultural and material resources available to them. There are stories here which are 'for identities' and stories which are 'against identities', narratives of perceived 'identity theft', of conviviality, dismay, collective disgust and celebration.

A second thread which unites the book is our collective recognition of the complexity of identity and a commitment to following that complexity, mostly as it knots together and unravels in ordinary rather than spectacular life. The years from 2004 to 2008 were turbulent ones with some vivid identity displays provoking huge amounts of commentary and evaluation in the media and elsewhere. These were the years of the Iraq War, the bombings on London tube trains, the emerging salience of faith and the election of Barack Obama. These and other events often rightly demand simple and strategic responses and the request to researchers from policy-makers similarly tends to be for one page answers. But, in contrast, what emerges most strongly in the research collected here is the ways in which lived experience in the UK cannot be reduced in line with conventional images, for example, of divided, homogeneous and culturally coherent communities. The research highlights the intersectional nature of identity, the entangled affiliations people articulate across identity categories, the diversity of standpoints in response to ethnicised and other classifications, as well as the importance of understanding the variable geography of these things. Above all, as the chapters in Part II particularly demonstrate, the dramatic and the pressure to find the simple can be radically misleading.

Finally, the chapters in this collection push forward theory in identity studies. In both theory and in empirical investigations, explicit and implicit distinctions are often made between social identity and personal identity. These are assigned to different disciplines, have their own traditions of scholarship and their own investigative histories. The study of social identities focuses on what is given by group memberships, participation in social movements and acquired through belonging to large social categories, while investigations of personal identity lead to studies of biographical narratives, emotional investments and the kinds of repetitions that most interest psychology and psychoanalysis. The chapters in this collection show how arbitrary these distinctions are. The authors certainly reveal different forms of social relations – from more intimate and interpersonal to more collective – but also that intelligibility practices interweave personal biography and collective practices.

Following this thread, the chapters develop new ways of thinking about and investigating identity as both contingent and yet organised, open and predictable. Butler again expresses this standpoint well in her notion of performativity as a 'practice of improvisation within a scene of constraint' (2004: 1). The chapters indicate, too, how relationality, affect and memory pervade identity, exemplifying the new emphases on these topics in identity studies (c.f. Blackman et al., 2008).

Class and community

The first Part of the book consists of four chapters examining current configurations of identity, social class and community. It is on this ground that arguments about changing risk environments, individualisation effects and the new 'liquidity' of identity bite hardest and these chapters help evaluate these claims. The individualisation thesis (Beck, 1992; Beck and Beck-Gernsheim, 1995; 2002; Beck et al., 1994; Giddens, 1991) is a set of arguments about the nature of social and technological changes combined with a claim about the effects of these on identity, people's psychology, their social relations with each other and their everyday practices. It is suggested that neo-liberal labour markets, the increased casualisation of work, changing patterns of family life and new pressures for reflexivity have disrupted traditional communities, identifications and affiliations. Individuals are becoming disembedded from older, communal ways of life, and must now develop their own life worlds unanchored by tradition, constructing identities that are more negotiable, looser, reflexive and autonomous. People's senses of self are thought to be more provisional as a consequence, less firmly rooted in the ethics of duty, responsibility and self-sacrifice, dominated instead by 'the religion of me'. Life as a result is said to have become more risky and uncertain, although exposure to this risk remains highly unevenly distributed.

Individualisation is said to undermine perceptions of common fate, mutual dependence, trust and long-term commitments, along with robust associations between class consciousness, sense of identity and collective action. Indeed individualisation is thought to undermine any form of social relation which is at odds with market-oriented exchange. Individual choice instead is thought to become the cornerstone in these new worlds and the ability to display skilful choices and high levels of agency becomes the marker of a successful person. Current economic conditions, it is argued, demand work on the self to develop an identity that can be more mobile, more enterprising, flexible and responsive to competition with others, in situations 'without guarantees'.

What did our empirical work in this area find? It is notoriously difficult to draw firm conclusions about individualisation effects. As Brannen and Nielsen (2005) note, the concepts and claims derived from the individualisation thesis are sweeping, crude and imprecise. They rely on numerous questionable assumptions about historical patterns. All manner of translations seem to be required to move from a pattern embedded in a particular local context with its own local determinants to a claim about broader identity trends. Part I opens, however, with a chapter which does attempt to assess the broad descriptive and explanatory power of individualisation claims.

Anthony Heath, John Curtice and Gabriella Elgenius conducted the first longitudinal comparative study of individualisation predictions about social class identity, examining people's affiliations across the period from the 1960s to 2005. Systematic and rigorous longitudinal work is one of the few methods attempting to deliver a useful and valid empirical verdict. As they describe in their chapter, Heath et al. found a mixed pattern. On the one hand, identity changes were broadly in the direction that the individualisation thesis predicts but not nearly of the magnitude suggested. Change was, in fact, 'glacial', apparently dependent on immediate, strategic (and perhaps contingent) changes in the political landscape with little strong support for the claim that people are now 'forced' to choose their own identities unanchored by tradition, community and family history. Their chapter is full of fascinating detailed findings. Here I note just a couple. First, they found, that the actual incidence of people identifying with any particular social class has remained pretty much constant since the 1960s, although people are more likely to describe themselves as middle class now. Second, and more in line with individualisation predictions, traditional 'identity packages' seem to be less important than they once were in the sense that a reliable and predictable relationship between factors, such as senses of class belonging, voting preferences and political attitudes, is disappearing. To the extent that social class remains a powerful normative frame of reference, it is likely then to operate in very different ways.

Quantitative survey analysis establishes the general picture. The second chapter in Part I then moves us on to different ground and reports on the experience of negotiating class positions and community from the inside. Ben Rogaly and Becky Taylor present an intensive qualitative case study of the oral histories produced by a mother and daughter (Lily and Lorna) describing their struggles and the challenges of life on a stigmatised and deprived estate in Norwich. Here what is most salient is the continued and unrelenting power of class positioning as a salient frame for self-understanding and the complex and contradictory forms of recognition, allegiance, loyalty and shame entailed. In this context, Judith Butler's (2004) exploration of liveable and unliveable lives, noted earlier, becomes highly applicable and the ways in which some dominant forms of intelligibility can imperil the development of a viable identity. If, as individualisation theorists suggest, individuals are increasingly floating free of traditional communities, affiliations and identifications, then Rogaly and Taylor's chapter is a reminder of the compromises, pain, losses and gains that might be involved in such a process. Their chapter raises questions about just who can be an individualised subject, when and in what cross-generational chronologies.

Chapter 3 from Valerie Walkerdine continues this emphasis and begins to investigate the causes of uneven responses to individualising pressures. Her chapter develops the theoretical thread mentioned above which runs through this book – the importance of taking account of the affective practices mediating responses to understand variations. Walkerdine describes a research project analysing a classic, litmus test, situation for the individualisation thesis. Again, the findings from this research disconfirm expectations. Walkerdine's focus is on one community, SteelTown, in South Wales which has lost its main employer and where the employment options available to redundant workers exemplify the features of new kinds of jobs within neo-liberalism. It turns out, however, that the workers in SteelTown, unlike the similar workers Walkerdine and her colleagues studied in Sydney, Australia, do not buy individualised scripts. The workers in Sydney did very visibly recast themselves in terms of discourses of entrepreneurial self-management. (An account of the Australian data can be found in Walkerdine and Bansel, in press.) But in SteelTown, some time after the closure, people continue to be deeply connected to their community and continue to act collectively. A number of residents found success in the new work regimes available but with little evidence that they have fundamentally altered their identity narratives or re-modeled themselves to do so. Walkerdine concludes that the difference lies in the nature of the traditional working-class community in South Wales. The dominant affective practices, and what she calls the 'community of affect' created by residents, prove resilient, motivating and sustaining and thus the community continues as a powerful point of reference.

Any reader who has casually flicked through the pages of this book up to this point and read, for example, Shelia's account of the trials around the Christmas lights in SteelTown in Chapter 3 or Lily and Lorna's narratives in Chapter 2 might begin to wonder whether anyone anywhere in the UK could ever be described in individualised terms. Critics of the individualisation thesis such as Skeggs (2004) and Savage (2000) have argued that one of the main problems with individualisation theories are their universalising. Very particular kinds of identity work – which are in fact quite specific – are overly generalised as a global new identity trend. Skeggs argues that the entrepreneurial, mobile and self-managing characters diagnosed by individualisation theorists represent in fact a highly classed identity. Middle-class academic theorists, she maintains, are guilty of reading the general from their own particular subjectivities.

Chapter 4 confirms this suspicion. Finally, the voices, methods of self-accounting and ways of configuring the world seen as characteristic of individualised times begin to appear. The last chapter in Part I from David James, Diane Reay, Gill Crozier, Fiona Jamieson, Phoebe Beedell, Sumi Hollingworth and Katya Williams reports on research investigating the identity work of the white urban middle class. James et al. focus on a particular and quite unusual class fraction – white middle class parents who against the usual practices of those in their social class position have chosen socially diverse comprehensive schools with average or below average examination results for their children. Those interviewed regard this as a risky strategy and their motivations, as the chapter illustrates, are a complex mix of social justice concerns and lie in family educational histories. The chapter presents a fascinating account of this group's identity stories, and what is particularly interesting is how their identity work exemplifies middle-class habitus and its forms of capital and maintains these as they disrupt it.

The material in Part I confirms both the particularity of individualised identity discourses and their uneven take-up. In common with others working on individualisation in neighbourhood, class and community contexts (e.g. Butler with Robson, 2003; Crow et al., 2002; Forrest and Kearns, 2001; Savage, 2000; Savage et al., 2005; Skeggs, 2004; Webb, 2004), the research reported in Part I finds that individualisation turns out to be a 'now you see it, now you don't' phenomenon. The 'identity story' over time is clearly much more complicated than a transition to 'new autonomous individuals' from 'individuals embedded in old style solidary social relations'. We do not see, for example, the kind of demise of social class and community as an organising point for identity in the way predicted. Instead we see that interpellation through individualised ways for making sense of oneself is patchy varying geographically, mediated by local affective practices, by context and by initial class position.

Individualisation predictions about class and community need substantial qualification. But this is only part of the story of identity in changing times. Reading the qualitative material, I am struck by how 'psychologised' people's narratives and accounts appear. They display, in other words, the very broad 'psychological make-over' and 'compulsory individuality' effects described by Nikolas Rose (1989; 1997) and others (Cronin, 2000; Strathern, 1992). Arguably, 'interesting individuality' is now a mandatory part of 'doing a good interview'. We will return to this issue of the more general contemporary requirements for 'telling the self' in Part III.

Ethnicities and encounters

Part I focuses on class, community and identity and claims about new, emerging conditions of intelligibility for making sense of oneself and others. Part II turns to contemporary intelligibility practices around race and ethnicity, examining these in intersection with identities articulated through gender, nationality, social class, age, faith, geographical locations and migration status. The chapters report research findings from three current crucial staging posts for ethnicised and racialised identities – post-colonial London, white English working-class and middle-class estates and refugee settlement in Sheffield and, also, from two institutions (the prison and the urban metropolitan classroom) where 'mixing' is mandatory.

If one looks at contemporary political discourse, then race and ethnic identities and their intelligibility become simple matters. In one of his last speeches before he left office, the British Prime Minister Tony Blair, for example, sketched out a basic vision. This speech, given in December, 2006, and entitled 'a duty to integrate', describes a relatively straightforward social world of 'divided communities', 'inter-cultural dialogue', the 'tolerant majority', 'extremists' and 'law-abiding, moderate ethnic minorities', along with the need for 'living harmoniously together across racial and religious divides', 'defining common values' and 'peaceful co-existence'. As I have argued elsewhere (Wetherell, 2008), the contemporary hegemonic view in British politics and policy interprets ethnic relations through a particular and perhaps now outdated sociological lens. It is assumed that society divides neatly into homogeneous cultures, communities and groups with clearly marked external boundaries, where these communities are distinguished by a large number of shared and essential characteristics and clearly marked cultural traditions. Ethnic groups are assumed to act like a set of mini states or uni-minority cultures against the backdrop of the majority uni-culture. Relations between groups are conceptualised, therefore, as rather like relations between nation-states where crossing from one community to another might involve major acts of translation. The culture which characterises these divided communities similarly tends to be understood in static terms defined by outward symbols such as rituals, festivals, distinctive emblems and religious observances rather than in terms of more ordinary, unmarked, daily activities. Equally, identity and identification tend to be presented as relatively straightforward processes. Group and large-scale social categories confer unambiguous identities; ethnic identity is generally singular and these singular identities reliably predict behaviour, attitudes and values.

As Stuart Hall (2001) has argued, reflecting on his experience as a member for the Runnymede Commission on the Future of Multi-Ethnic Britain (Parekh, 2000), there are indeed still places, moments or contexts in the UK which are culturally homogeneous in the way generally assumed but, increasingly, this is only part of the story. Hall suggests that there remain places, moments and contexts which are relatively unchanging, where group culture can be summarised and meaningfully defined in terms of race and ethnic differences and where what remains most evident to people is the traditions they share and their strong group identities based on common life circumstances. As a whole, however, Britain is moving away from this pattern. Recent theory (e.g. Gilroy, 2006) diagnoses the UK as a set of complex and vibrant multicultures in contrast, for instance, to the much more segregated situation in the States. In particular, the lives of young people on No 10's doorstep in large metropolitan cities such as London are thought now to be distinguished by 'an unruly, untidy and convivial mode of interaction where differences have to be negotiated' (Gilroy, 2005: 438). Gilroy argues that the differences which divide young people are no longer automatically those of ethnicity, culture or race but often involve issues of life-style, music choices, consumption patterns, values and politics.

The chapters in Part II directly investigate these claims and the current ordering of identity around ethnicity, faith and race. These empirical investigations traverse the paradox that social categories and the classifications of ethnicity and race are both exceptionally powerful ways of making sense and often entirely slippery in the actual identity scenarios and situations of everyday life. Group-based modes of understanding community and identity still have purchase (see Modood, 2007, for a defence of this point of view), and certainly there is substantial evidence of the persistence of inequality and racism (e.g. see Heath and

Cheung's, 2006, report on work-based discrimination), yet in ordinary life, as we shall see, the identity situation is also open, fluid, 'hybridised' and extremely complicated.

The first chapter in Part II from Roxy Harris and Ben Rampton analyses a riveting, relatively long, piece of peer interaction recorded in an urban comprehensive school using radio microphones. Harris and Rampton's argument based on data of this kind is both methodological and substantive. They found that the patterns they observed in the highly diverse urban comprehensive schools they studied confirmed Gilroy's analysis. Race and ethnicity featured for the most part as subsidiary issues, conforming to the 'unruly convivial mode' Gilroy identifies. There was a great deal of unselfconscious 'rubbing along'. Harris and Rampton also argue, however, that there is a danger that this 'success', in terms of the way the political debate is usually framed, will be invisible to policy not least because traditional methodologies such as interviews tend to over-emphasise essentialised and more categorical accounts as people struggle to be intelligible, find the story to tell and 'achieve' identity. They outline the advantages of linguistic ethnography as a method for revealing the 'jostling, allusive, multi-voiced' flavour of actual mixing and the positioning of self and others in ordinary life.

Chapter 6 then reports on the ethnography of a second institution – a prison for young offenders (HMYOI Rochester) – which equally throws together young people from very diverse ethnic backgrounds. Rod Earle and Coretta Phillips argue that here, too, conviviality, culture-swapping and mixing are an important part of young prisoners' attempts to manage proximity and build a kind of liveable life in what they describe as the austere, semi-permanent and semi-public spaces of the prison. Earle and Phillips argue that racialised antagonism was not entirely absent and social relations were slightly wary, but racism was not a central organising identity discourse. For the white prisoners, it became a private and equivocal resource. One important finding among many in this subtle and careful account is the centrality of locality and territoriality in the young men's identities, expressed through what the authors call 'postcode pride'. The young men displayed the kind of 'neighbourhood nationalism' others have detected in young working-class men's cultures (e.g. Back, 1996). Earle and Phillips discuss the functions of this as resistance and as status claims, and the complex ways it intersects with local organisations of ethnicities and friendship groups.

Earle and Phillips describe how young white prisoners mostly disavowed ethnicity or understandings of themselves as a 'social group with a culture' on a par with other 'culture-rich' groups. The authors, following Nayak (2003) describe how white prisoners articulate an 'ethnicity that is not one'. What, then, in more detail is happening to whiteness and white identities in these new times? The next chapter in Part II addresses this issue. Simon Clarke, Stephen Garner and Rosie Gilmour chose to work with precisely those groups which Blair seemed to have in mind when organising the rhetorical shape of his 2006 speech – the majority 'we', unfamiliar with diversity on a daily basis, supposedly anxious and restless. As Clarke et al. note, the vast majority of UK nationals live in electoral wards with fewer than 5% black and ethnic minority residents. Clarke et al. find that the people they worked with living in white working class and middle-class estates in Bristol and Plymouth consistently expressed the same kinds of information deficits and confusions about migration and asylum seeking. At odds with the image of the white working class as the 'owner' of racism in Britain, the content of people's concerns did not vary by class, although middle-class respondents described these in more abstracted and less immediate terms. What is particularly important in this work is the impression of the 'fragility' of white English identity which emerges. The talk among the sample is of identity injustice and identity theft, the predominant emotion is one of being beleaguered and in this context, respondents find it difficult to construct an imagined, sustaining, inclusive, national English community which could be unambivalently endorsed and celebrated.

Chapter 8, the fourth chapter in Part II, extends the analysis through an examination of the young Somali community in Sheffield. Gill Valentine and Deborah Sporton describe the complex negotiations of these recent migrants around several possible identity categories and narratives – 'Somali', 'British', 'Black', 'Muslim'. Valentine and Sporton focus in particular on the identity work of young Somali in disavowing being 'British' and 'Black'. Yet, this disavowal does not mean that alternative categorisations such as 'Somali' can be easily embraced. Awareness of emerging differences from those Somali who live in Somaliland, and often extremely complicated histories of mobility, make 'countries' an ambivalent point of identification. In these contexts, being Muslim often provides the only or main source of continuity and emotional investment.

Valentine and Sporton's chapter precisely shows the importance of intelligibility, avowal and disavowal for identity and adds transnationalism as a further dimension of identity work in contemporary Britain. This theme is taken up, too, in the final chapter in Part II from Rosie Cox, Sue Jackson, Meena Khatwa and Dina Kiwan. The authors describe the process of constructing belonging among South Asian and white women living in post-colonial London. Again, this negotiation turns out to be about liveability in Judith Butler's (2004) sense – how can a viable life emerge, how do women want to be recognised and what forms of recognition are affirming and which debilitating? The authors describe a fascinating series of negotiations through multiculturalist discourses and how 'London' itself becomes an actor in the performativities of the women observed and interviewed. This is London understood to multiply as a series of concrete spaces, as an imagined place and as a historical and material site. Cox et al. reveal plural layerings of belonging and the ways in which women carve out 'homelands' as they negotiate these spaces.

Popular culture and relationality

Part III of the book turns from the negotiation of ethnicised and racialised identities to popular culture and to a more explicit focus on gender and generation. This Part contains three chapters which in different ways describe subjectively and emotionally intense engagements with popular cultural and narrative resources and thus with the intelligibility conditions for 'telling' identities. The chapters examine the identity work involved in the transition to first-time motherhood, young people's drinking groups and the identities found on reality television and their reception by female viewers. They chart not just the ways in which people engage with cultural narratives and material objects such as advertisements, new kinds of alcoholic drinks, televisions, programmes and notions of ideal motherhood but some of the new relational cultures currently emerging and the identity slots these allow. Part III returns to the general territory of the individualisation claims reviewed above, and particular arguments within that tradition for the 'transformation of intimacy' (e.g. Giddens, 1993) and for new shapes to biographies. In addition, these last chapters continue to carry forward the theoretical agenda of the book. Along with earlier chapters, they illustrate the creative blurring which is occurring in recent research as investigations of subjectivity and personal identity intertwine with investigations of group-based identities, material and cultural resources and social locations. Their methodologies, including some highly innovative modes of investigation, focused on memory, narrative, affect, symbolic value, embodiment, textual production and relationality demonstrate how social intelligibility and personal intelligibility interweave.

As we saw, individualisation theory and writings about social trends and identity change include not only some relatively specific claims about the demise of social class and traditional communities but also some broader attempts to identify changing relational practices and the flavour of family life, relationships and friendships, identity narratives and self and other evaluations. These are in part changes in what Skeggs and Wood describe in their chapter as the 'moral economy' or the kinds of symbolic value placed on particular ways of being in the world. They are also changes, too, to the social organisation of intimate family lives, friendships and social relationships. Giddens (1993), for example, described what he saw as the rise of the 'pure relationship' or relationships for their own sake, so that romantic and sexual partnerships, for instance, become justified through the intrinsic pleasures they offer, becoming an aspiration in themselves rather than in terms of their strategic, traditional or practical value.

Carol Smart (2007) reviewing these debates wisely concludes that such grand theories and claims of identity change serve a useful purpose even if their initial 'excessive popularity' has by now given way to qualification, caveat and stale over-familiarity. She notes that individualisation claims about changing relationship patterns (especially in Beck and Beck-Gernsheim's work) remain irritatingly non-specific. As she describes (p. 18), individualisation theories create a special moment in history which can then be compared with the present in a way that highlights maximum difference while neglecting existing, careful family historical research showing the much more complicated progression and patterning of change. The chapters in Part III concur with the general critical assessment of individualisation claims offered by scholars of family life and relationships (e.g. Jamieson, 1998; 1999; Roseneil and Budgeon, 2004; Williams, 2004), and with the class specificity of individualisation described in the Part I of the book, but they also show that there are new identity phenomena to explain and considerable evidence for 'compulsory individuality' and the requirement to be an 'extraordinary subject'.

Chapter 10 opens Part III with the transition to first-time motherhood and discusses two case studies of women presenting very different 'conception stories'. This chapter from Rachel Thomson, Mary Jane Kehily, Lucy Hadfield and Sue Sharpe examines how the emergent identity of 'mother' takes shape and the kind of 'memorial' work involved in developing more or less coherent accounts selecting, including and excluding from the flux of events. Thomson et al. describe how women's accounts of this key biographical moment indicate the social and economic resources organising the telling, the differential narrative capitals women possess as well as the current forms of social intelligibility for gender. One main contrast is between the accounts of older middle-class mothers in their wider sample which do often illustrate the kind of careful biographical planning individualisation theorists suggest and the more 'chaotic' accounts of younger, less well-resourced, mothers.

The next chapter from Christine Griffin, Andrew Bengry-Howell, Chris Hackley, Willm Mistral and Isabelle Szmigin explores young people's drinking practices and collective identifications. It describes how young people's drinking activities have become hedged around by the moralistic identity categories (e.g. 'binge drinker') found in health education discourses and in disparaging, common sense accounts of 'youth today'. In the face of these, young people have evolved drinking cultures which, as Griffin et al. describe, are based on 'determined drunkenness', 'the controlled loss of control' and 'calculated hedonism'. Yet, the independence which comes from being 'against official identities', and from rejecting outsider accounts, is itself a key form of identity address and interpellation used by other powerful identity-ascribing institutions such as the alcohol industry. Alcohol advertisements offer subject positions of rebellion and independence as well as scripts around the pleasures and excitements of belonging to social groups of drinkers.

Like the previous chapter, the authors note a mixed pattern in relation to individualisation. There is evidence for it in the increasing prevalence of consumption and life-style as a marker of identity and in the key role friendship groups play for these young people compared to the former centrality of family. Yet, the picture Griffin et al. paint of young drinkers' collective identifications is very far removed from Beck and Beck-Gernsheim's (2002: 46) assumption that people are 'now forced to live their own life'. Collective identities mutate all the time and forms of solidarity are certainly different these days. Belonging may be only patchily experienced (as it probably always was); but, overall, the young people Griffin et al. study show high levels of social solidarity and mutual support. Their identity performances, and associated self-fashioning through consumption patterns, produce and are achieved through intense group bonding. Similarly, even the poorly resourced first-time mothers Thomson et al. investigated hardly seem unanchored. As Thomson et al. conclude, a life which appears difficult in comparison to carefully planned middle-class trajectories is not automatically unliveable or indeed without its own subtle and sustaining forms of validation and recognition. Again, then, this is clear evidence that the key empirical question is not whether individualisation has occurred as a universal social phenomenon but who can draw on individualised accounts of identity. When and in what contexts do individualised narratives work, seem appropriate, valuable and normatively encouraged?

The final chapter in Part III from Beverley Skeggs and Helen Wood reports on an innovative study of the identity scenarios found in reality television and the affect, evaluation and judgements they incite in groups of women viewing these programmes. Reality television has become a dominant genre and includes programmes that feature first person accounts from ordinary members of the public of biographical events, and participation in games of self-transformation, make-over and involvement in 'journeys' of self-exploration. Skeggs and Wood argue convincingly that the identity and ethical scenarios constructed in these programmes do substantiate the hypothesised shift in public life to what Lauren Berlant (2000) calls 'intimate citizenship'. Citizens are required to perform 'extraordinary subjectivity' and, in general, the identity performances show the kind of self-authorising and 'religion of me' features diagnosed in contemporary social theory.

Skeggs and Wood, however, question the novelty of this shift, seeing parallels with earlier requirements for self-revealing, reflexive, 'respectability narratives' from working-class claimants for poor relief. As ever, what is crucial is who is encouraged to perform, who gets to watch and judge and what general values get applied as they judge. Skeggs and Wood describe the classed nature of reality television – working-class participants predominate, they are set up to perform in ways that will fascinate and horrify and which encourage strong affective reactions in audiences. The new self-reflexivity described by theorists is thus not universally performed and universally equivalently valued. It is made manifest and, then, regulated in very different ways. For middle-class audiences, evaluating participants in reality television can be a moment of asserting what Skeggs and Wood call, following Savage (2003), the 'particular-universal' aspirations of their class through affective contempt towards the participants and insistence on more 'seemly' ways of self-display. Skeggs and Wood provide an absorbing account of an emerging relational and identity circuit in popular culture as 'the many watch the many' on reality television, pulled into responding to carefully constituted ethical scenarios and thus into self-surveillance, judgement and various normative roundabouts.

References

Back, L. (1996) *New Ethnicities and Urban Culture: Racisms and Multiculture in Young Lives*. London: UCL Press.
Bauman, Z. (2001) *The Individualized Society*. Cambridge: Polity.
Bauman, Z. (2005) *Liquid Life*. Cambridge: Polity.
Beck, U. (1992) *Risk Society: Towards a New Modernity*. London: Sage.
Beck, U. and Beck-Gernsheim, E. (1995) *The Normal Chaos of Love*. Cambridge: Polity.
Beck, U. and Beck-Gernsheim, E. (2002) *Individualization*. London: Sage.
Beck, U., Giddens, A. and Lash, S. (1994) *Reflexive Modernisation: Politics, Tradition and Aesthetics in the Modern Social Order*. Cambridge: Polity.
Berlant, L. (2000) The Subject of True Feeling: Pain, Privacy, Politics. In S. Ahmed, J. Kilby, C. Lury, M. McNeil and B. Skeggs (eds.) *Transformations: Thinking Through Feminism*. London: Routledge.
Blackman, L., Cromby, J., Hook, D., Papadopoulos, D. and Walkerdine, V. (2008) Creating Subjectivities. *Subjectivity: International Journal of Critical Psychology* 22, 1–27.
Brannen, J. and Nielsen, A. (2005) Individualization, Choice and Structure: A Discussion of Current Trends in Sociological Analysis. *Sociological Review* 53 (3), 412–28.
Butler, J. (1990) *Gender Trouble: Feminism and the Subversion of Identity*. New York: Routledge.
Butler, J. (2004) *Undoing Gender*. New York: Routledge.
Butler, J. (2006) *Precarious Life: The Powers of Mourning and Violence*. London: Verso.
Butler, T. with Robson, G. (2003) *London Calling: The Middle Classes and the Remaking of Inner London*. Oxford: Berg.
Cronin, A.M. (2000) Consumerism and 'Compulsory Individuality': Women, Will and Potential. In S. Ahmed, J. Kilby, C. Lury, M. McNeil and B. Skeggs (eds.) *Transformations: Thinking Through Feminism*. London: Routledge.
Crow, G., Allan, G. and Summers, M. (2002) Neither Busybodies nor Nobodies: Managing Proximity and Distance in Neighbourly Relations. *Sociology* 36 (1), 127–45.
Forrest, R. and Kearns, A. (2001) Social Cohesion, Social Capital and the Neighbourhood. *Urban Studies* 38 (12), 2125–43.
Giddens, A. (1991) *Modernity and Self-Identity: Self and Society in the Late Modern Age*. Cambridge: Polity.
Giddens, A. (1993) *The Transformation of Intimacy*. Cambridge: Polity.
Gilroy, P. (2005) Multiculture, Double Consciousness and the 'War on Terror'. *Patterns of Prejudice* 39 (4), 431–43.
Gilroy, P. (2006) *Postcolonial Melancholia*. New York: Columbia University Press.
Goffman, E. (1959) *The Presentation of Self in Everyday Life*. Harmondsworth: Penguin.
Hall, S. (1992) New Ethnicities. In J. Donald and A. Rattansi (eds.) *'Race', Culture and Difference*. London: Sage.
Hall, S. (2001) The Multicultural Question. *Pavis Papers in Social Research*, No. 4, Open University.

Heath, A. and Cheung, S.Y. (2006) *Ethnic Penalties in the Labour Market: Employers and Discrimination.* Department of Work and Pensions, Research Report No. 341.

Jamieson, L. (1998) *Intimacy: Personal Relationships in Modern Societies.* Cambridge: Polity.

Jamieson, L. (1999) Intimacy Transformed?: A Critical Look at the 'Pure Relationship'. *Sociology* 33 (3), 477–94.

Leith, S. (2009) Comment Piece. *The Guardian*, 8th of January, p. 9.

Modood, T. (2007) *Multiculturalism.* Oxford: Polity.

Nayak, A. (2003) *Race, Place and Globalisation: Youth Cultures in a Changing World.* Oxford: Berg.

Parekh, B. (2000) *The Future of Multi-Ethnic Britain.* London: Runnymede Publications.

Rose, N. (1989) *Governing the Soul: The Shaping of the Private Self.* London: Routledge.

Rose, N. (1997) Assembling the Modern Self. In R. Porter (ed.) *Rewriting the Self: Histories from the Renaissance to the Present.* London: Routledge.

Rose, N. (1999) *Powers of Freedom: Reframing Political Thought.* Cambridge: Cambridge University Press.

Roseneil, S. and Budgeon, S. (2004) Beyond the Conventional Family: Intimacy, Care and Community in the 21st Century. *Current Sociology* 52 (2), 135–59.

Savage, M. (2000) *Class Analysis and Social Transformation.* Buckingham: Open University Press.

Savage, M. (2003) A New Class Paradigm? Review Article. *British Journal of Sociology of Education* 24 (4), 535–41.

Savage, M., Bagnall, G. and Longhurst, B. (2005) *Globalization and Belonging.* London: Sage.

Skeggs, B. (2004) *Class, Self and Culture.* London: Routledge.

Smart, C. (2007) *Personal Life.* Cambridge: Polity.

Strathern, M. (1992) *After Nature: English Kinship in the Late 20th Century.* Cambridge: Cambridge University Press.

Walkerdine, V. and Bansel, P. (in press) Neoliberalism, Work and Subjectivity: Towards a More Complex Account. In M. Wetherell and C. Talpade Mohanty (eds.) *The Sage Handbook of Identities.* London: Sage.

Webb, J. (2004) Organisations, Self-Identities and the New Economy. *Sociology* 38 (4), 719–39.

Wetherell, M. (2008) Speaking to Power: Tony Blair, Complex Multicultures and Fragile White English Identities. *Critical Social Policy* 28 (3), 299–319.

Williams, F. (2004) *Rethinking Families.* London: Calouste Gulbenkian Foundation.

Part I
Class and Community

1
Individualization and the Decline of Class Identity

Anthony Heath, John Curtice and Gabriella Elgenius

Introduction

Many writers have suggested that as we move from an industrial to a post-industrial society, traditional social identities such as class will decline in social significance (Clark and Lipset, 1991; Pakulski and Waters, 1996; though compare Hout et al., 1993). Clark and Lipset, for example, have posed the question, 'Are classes dying?', while in a book entitled *The Death of Class* Pakulski and Waters have penned what is in effect an obituary of the concept. The idea is particularly prominent in the work of writers such as Ulrich Beck who have spoken of the individualization of modern society. For Beck, class is a 'zombie category': 'the idea lives on even though the reality to which it corresponds is dead' (Beck and Willms, 2004: 51–52 cited in Atkinson, 2007: 354). On this account, individuals are no longer members of stable social communities whose members all share in the same distinctive 'life-world', but instead are people 'condemned to choose' their own life-worlds.

These writers do not necessarily claim that class inequalities *per se* have disappeared; 'the structure of social inequality ... displays a surprising *stability*,' note Beck and Beck-Gernsheim (2001: 30; although Beck, for example, does argue that instead of being concentrated in the working class, risks are now much more evenly spread across the different classes). Their concern is not with 'objective' inequalities; rather, their arguments are about classes as social formations that have a sense of group belonging and solidarity. In other words, the focus is on *subjective* class identities and their allegedly declining significance in post-industrial society. Many, including Clark and Lipset and Pakulski and Waters, concentrate specifically on the decline of class identity and of class as a social formation, while for others such as Beck, Giddens, or

Bauman the decline of class is part of a more general thesis about the decline of all kinds of social identities rooted in traditional, inherited, social groups. The key claim in Beck's account is that individuals are no longer so firmly rooted in 'given' social identities that provide social bases for what people think or how they behave. Thus so far as class in particular is concerned Beck draws on Marx's distinction between class 'in itself' and class 'for itself': 'There emerges a capitalism without classes, more precisely: without classes *for themselves*. Individualization uncouples class culture from class position' (Beck, 2007: 686, italics in the original). As Scott has summarized the thesis: 'Class relations may not have disappeared completely, but they have become less corporate, less collective and less communal in character' (Scott, 2002: 32).

There is however remarkably little empirical research that systematically investigates the decline of class communities. To be sure there has been a large volume of empirical research on the declining (or otherwise) relationship between 'objective' class and voting behaviour that addresses some of the themes advanced by Clark and Lipset (see, for example, Evans, 1999; Heath et al., 1985; Lee and Turner, 1996). But to our knowledge there has not been any systematic empirical enquiry into how the subjective aspects of class have changed over time. There are many notable recent studies of class identity, such as Savage et al. (2001), whose findings suggest that class identities nowadays are weak. But all of these studies look at the position at a single point in time and therefore cannot convincingly demonstrate that class identities have *weakened* over time. Our aim in this chapter is to fill this gap and to provide a more rigorous empirical evaluation of the main claims about the decline of class as a social identity.[1]

There are four distinct claims that we can derive from the two sets of theoretical accounts described above. The first two flow from both sets of literatures, while the remaining two are specific to the wider literature on individualization. First, it is argued that social class no longer provides as strong a basis of social identity as it once did. Even if individuals still use the language of social class, and agree to locate themselves as members of a particular social class, they are now less likely to have a strong sense of belonging to that class. As Savage has suggested, while individuals may still use the terminology of social class, 'class position no longer generates a deep sense of identity and belonging' (Savage, 2000: 37, 111–16).

Secondly, both sets of accounts assume that, even among those who still adhere to them, collective class identities have reduced force and are less influential for social action. One way of translating this kind of claim into testable sociology is to treat it as a claim about the declining role of social classes as normative reference groups (Merton, 1957). Do people who feel a sense of community with other members of their group also follow their group in their attitudes and behaviour? The implication of the accounts of Clark and Lipset, Pakulski and Waters, and of Beck or Scott is that these older forms of identity are no longer such powerful stimuli to collective or indeed to individual action as they once were, and no longer constitute significant reference points for values and action. 'The attachment of people to a social class (in Max Weber's sense) has nevertheless become weaker. It now has much less influence on their actions' (Beck, 1992: 92).

A third claim that is particularly prominent in Beck's thesis of individualization is that because people now choose their own life-worlds and biographies, social identities are no longer inherited in the way they once were. This implies that class identity is now related more weakly to one's social class origins than it once was. Earlier accounts of the formation of class identity suggested that it was learned through socialization in one's family of origin (Reissman, 1960: 234). While it was assumed that class identities would change over time if one experienced social mobility, the standard sociological literature suggested that class origins would have a lasting legacy on one's identity, albeit declining in force across the life cycle. In contrast, Beck suggests that in today's post-modern 'risk society', class identities, 'become relatively independent of inherited or newly formed ties (e.g. family, neighbourhood, friendship, or partnership). By becoming independent from traditional ties, people's lives take on an independent quality which, for the first time, makes possible the experience of a personal destiny' (Beck and Beck-Gernsheim, 2001: 33).

Fourthly, Beck is quite clear that one's own current occupational position will be more weakly related to class identity. 'The argument of the individualization theorists is that objective features (income, position in the hierarchy) and subjective features (consciousness, lifestyle, leisure interests, political attitudes) *diverge*.' (Beck, 2007: 686, italics in original). Because the occupations in which people are employed are now the product of individual decisions and attributes rather than collective forces over which they have little control, those in the same class position no longer necessarily think of themselves as sharing a common life trajectory. We expect to find, therefore, a de-coupling of the so-called objective and subjective aspects of class.

Although both sets of accounts point towards the first two claims about the declining strength and power of class identity, there are, however, some differences in the processes that are thought to be responsible. For writers such as Clark and Lipset or Pakulski and Waters, strong social classes are features of an earlier stage of industrial development centred on traditional manufacturing industry. Thanks to the decline of heavy industries and their associated stable communities, together with increasing affluence, social mobility, and the decline of trade unions this world no longer exists. So in essence these arguments focus on general long-term processes of economic growth and development and the associated process of industrial restructuring.

Beck in contrast emphasizes the way in which certain institutional features of post-modern society, especially the organization of the labour market and the welfare state, undermine class cohesion and ensure that life chances depend on decisions made by individuals. Success – or failure – in the (post-)modern highly competitive labour market depends on individuals' ability to acquire educational qualifications (a process which in itself undermines traditional forms of thinking) and the personal career choices they subsequently make. As Beck puts it: 'as soon as people enter the labour market... they are forced to take charge of their own life. The labour market... reveals itself as a driving force behind the individualization of people's lives' (Beck and Beck-Gernsheim, 2001: 32–33).[2] The welfare state, meanwhile, increasingly assigns rights and responsibilities to people on the basis of the decisions they make as individuals rather than on account of their membership of collective groups or social institutions such as the family. In such a world, according to Beck's famous aphorism, 'Community is dissolved in the acid bath of competition' (1992: 94).

However, there is a third possible explanation for the decline of class identities, one that we ourselves have previously developed in the British context. This points to top-down changes and in particular New Labour's deliberate attempt to move away from its traditional electoral territory and to cultivate the centre ground.[3] On this account (the intellectual origins of which can be traced back to Karl Marx), class identities are not simply spontaneous grass-roots occurrences but can be stimulated, or inhibited, by political organization. For a long period in Britain, Labour was seen as the party of the working class, followed a programme designed more or less overtly to protect working-class interests, and actively organized in working-class constituencies. Under the pressure of electoral failure and recognizing the declining size of the working class, Labour, first under Neil Kinnock and then much more dramatically under Tony Blair, deliberately cut loose from its working-class image and became a catch-all party of the centre ground. Thus whereas in 1987, no less than 46% of people believed that Labour looked 'very closely' after the interests of working-class people, and as many as 33% still did so in 1997, by 2005, the figure had fallen to just 10% (Curtice, 2007). So, with working-class identity no longer being promoted by Labour, fewer people may have come to feel the impetus to acknowledge or feel attached to a class, or to regard their class identity as a cue as to what attitudes they should adopt towards political issues.

These three sets of explanations not only differ in their explanation of the decline of class identities, but also when the change is expected to have occurred. The decline of heavy industry and rising affluence that lie at the heart of the 'death of class' thesis occurred gradually throughout most of the second half of the twentieth century (although perhaps accelerating in the 1970s), and so this argument suggests that class identities have declined over the same extended period. In contrast, the individualizing role of the labour market is likely to have been given added impetus, at least in Britain, by the Thatcherite reforms of the 1980s which deregulated the labour market. So the individualization thesis points to the 1980s as the time when the decline of class identities would have accelerated. Meanwhile, Tony Blair rebranded Labour as New Labour in the mid-1990s before securing power in 1997. So if the top-down political thesis is correct, then any change should only date from the mid-1990s.

Our key research aims in this chapter, therefore, are

- To establish whether there has been decline in the proportions adhering to a traditional class identity and/or a decline in the strength of belonging to social class;
- To examine whether class identities are decreasingly inherited from one's family;
- To examine whether they are increasingly uncoupled from one's current occupation;
- To explore whether there has been decline in the relationship between adherence to a class identity and individuals' political attitudes and partisanship.
- To investigate the timing of any changes which have occurred.

Empirical material

To investigate these research questions, we draw on the series of British Election Surveys (BES), which have been conducted after every general election since 1964 together with the 2005 British Social Attitudes (BSA) survey. Social class identity was one of the central concerns of the political scientists who designed the first BES (Butler and Stokes, 1974) and the 1964 BES (together with a pre-election survey conducted in 1963) included a number of questions on class identity that subsequently have been administered in the election studies on a regular basis. Thus by replicating a number of these questions on the 2005 BSA we can not only look at long-term changes over a period of 40 years, but also look at the timing of any changes that have occurred.

Of course, it would be even better if we had readings from the 1950s. However, it is still the case that Britain in 1963/1964, when our time series begins, remained very similar to the Britain of the 1950s: class voting was still at a very high level just as it had been in the 1950s (see Weakliem and Heath, 1999) and the restructuring of industry, the decline of traditional manufacturing, the rise of the knowledge-based service economy, and the expansion of professional and managerial occupations were only just in their very early stages (see Halsey and Webb, 2000). Our time series does then arguably go back to a period (just) before Britain's transformation into a post-industrial society.

The BESs are all nationally representative probability samples, designed to provide coverage of the electorate living in private households, though until 1970 this meant those aged 21 and over rather than 18 or above. Note that, in response to increasing disparity between the adult resident population and those included on the electoral register, the sampling frame was switched in 1997 from the electoral register to the Postcode Address File. The 1992 and 1997 BESs included oversamples in Scotland, and these have been down-weighted in order to make these samples as a whole representative of Great Britain. Our key measure of class identity was included in the 1964, 1970, 1974 (October election), 1983, 1987, 1992, and 1997 BESs and hence these are the years that we include in our analysis, together with the 2005 BSA. Note that in 1964, 1970, and 2005, the measure of class identity we use was only asked of half samples of the relevant survey; this means that the sample sizes for 1964 and 1970 in particular are relatively small.

Like the BES, the BSA is a representative probability sample of individuals living in private households in Great Britain. It also uses the Postcode Address File as its sampling frame. The BSA series began in 1983, but in earlier years it used a different measure of class identity from the one used in the BES. The data are weighted to take into account both differential probability of selection and known patterns of non-response.

We use the time series provided by these two survey series to answer our five key research questions. We begin by looking at the incidence of class identity, then move on to look at the de-coupling of class identity from one's class origins and from one's own occupation and turn finally to the role of class as a normative reference group.

Incidence of class identity

Our first task is to establish whether there has been a decline in the proportions adhering to traditional class identities and/or a decline in the strength of belonging to social class. The early BESs experimented with a number of ways of asking about class identity. One version in particular has stood the test of time and been repeated in many subsequent studies. Respondents were asked

> Do you ever think of yourself as belonging to any particular class?
> IF YES Which one is that?
> IF NO (or YES but other than middle or working class) Most people say they belong to either the middle class or to the working class. Do you ever think of yourself as being in one of these classes?

We can think of the first, unprompted, question as tapping respondents' own identities and it is perhaps the key question from our point of view. Respondents were of course free to volunteer the name of any class that they wished but the great majority volunteered 'middle class' or 'working class'. The follow-up question, addressed to those who did not respond 'middle' or 'working class' to the initial question and which prompts respondents to choose one of those two labels, is likely to tap a more superficial recognition of class differences. It thus might identify, as Savage suggests, people who are happy to use the language of social class but for whom the term has no deeper significance. Table 1.1 shows the trends over time in both prompted and unprompted responses.

The table suggests that there has not been any move away from class identity generally or from unprompted class identity in particular. Even at the beginning of our series in 1964, only a little under half the respondents declared unprompted that they were either middle or working class, and the position was much the same in 2005. The percentages giving unprompted responses bumped around somewhat, rising to a peak in 1983, when issues of social class were perhaps particularly salient as party politics polarized between a middle-class-oriented Conservative party under Margaret Thatcher and a working-class-oriented 'Old'

Table 1.1 Prompted and unprompted class identity, 1964–2005

	Column percentages							
	1964	**1970**	**1974**	**1983**	**1987**	**1992**	**1997**	**2005**
Unprompted: middle class	14	16	17	20	16	16	20	20
Unprompted: working class	34	25	25	33	30	29	31	25
Total unprompted	48	41	41	53	46	45	51	45
Prompted: middle class	16	17	17	14	18	18	17	17
Prompted: working class	31	38	38	27	31	30	30	32
Did not identify with any class	4	4	4	6	5	6	2	6
N	832	731	2329	3637	3795	2672	2906	2102

Notes: The 1974 survey is the one following the October general election. 1992 and 1997 are weighted to correct for over-sample in Scotland, and 2005 is weighted to account for differential refusal. DK/refused are included with the category 'did not identify with any class'. Respondents aged 21 and over in 1964.
Sources: 1964–1997 British Election Studies; 2005 BSA.

Labour Party under Michael Foot, though they were almost as high when class-consensual New Labour won the 1997 election. But in any event, there is clearly no underlying downward movement of the sort expected by some theorists.

What has changed is the balance between those calling themselves 'middle class' and those claiming to be 'working class'. In 1964, for every person calling themselves middle class there were over two who said they were working class. In 2005, the ratio was closer to 2:3. In short, while the incidence of class identities overall has not declined, but that of working-class identities has – we clearly should not mistake the latter for the former. The decline in working-class identity almost certainly reflects the changes over the period in the shape of the 'objective' class structure, as defined by the actual numbers of people in manual and non-manual jobs.

Even so, it is notable that whereas sociologists typically claim that the proportion of manual jobs has now declined to much less than 50% of the labour force, the proportion who (either prompted or unprompted) identify themselves as working class is still clearly in a considerable majority. Even in 2005, 57% of respondents in total defined themselves as working class while only 37% defined themselves as middle class. One possible explanation for this, in line with the socialization theories mentioned in the introduction, is that class identities are learned in childhood and thus reflect one's class origins. The net upward mobility that has occurred in Britain over much of our period (see e.g. Goldthorpe and Mills, 2004; Heath and Payne, 2000) means that the proportion of people with working-class origins greatly exceeds the proportion currently in working-class situations.

So Table 1.1 provides little support therefore for the claim that class as a social identity has died or disappeared. However, there is a further question, asked in the 1963 pre-election wave of the BES, that more explicitly taps the key aspect of a deeper sense of belonging. In that wave, respondents were asked in respect of the class with which they said they identified

> Some people feel they have a lot in common with other people of their own class, but others don't feel this way so much. How about you? Would you say you feel... READ OUT...
> pretty close to other [middle/working] class people,
> or, that you don't feel much closer to them than you do to people in other classes?

We replicated this question in 2005, but it is available only in these two years and hence we cannot look at the intermediate years. The results for 1963 and 2005 are given in Table 1.2.

Table 1.2 The strength of belonging to one's social class

	Column percentages	
	1963	**2005**
Class identity		
Close to middle class	14	14
Middle class but not close	13	22
Neither	6	6
Working class but not close	29	35
Close to working class	37	22
N	1938	2102

Note: The direction of class identity was obtained in 1963 from a question worded differently from that asked in 2005. For details, see Butler and Stokes (1974: 476).
Sources: BES 1963 and BSA 2005.

In replication of the results of Table 1.1, we see an increase in the percentage defining themselves as middle class and a decline in the percentage regarding themselves as working class. In contrast to what we would have anticipated from Table 1.1, however, the table also shows a clear change in the sense of closeness to one's class. In 1963, rather more than half of each class felt close to their class, but by 2005, this proportion had fallen, in both classes, to around two fifths. This is not perhaps a very dramatic change when we consider that the table covers a time span of 42 years; if it reflects a gradual change, then it is indeed a rather slow, almost 'glacial', rate of change. But it is at least in the direction predicted by the theorists.

It is also worth noting moreover that, even in 1963, the sense of class belonging was not all that strong, and was only slightly stronger in the working class than it was in the middle class. (Again, this mirrors the picture from the prompted/unprompted class identity distinction in Table 1.1.) This suggests that our theorists may well have been exaggerating the extent of class solidarity that existed in Britain before the country embarked on its transformation into a post-industrial society. Indeed, Marshall et al. (1988) have previously drawn attention to this tendency among theorists to (mis)remember and perhaps romanticize the class solidarity of their youth.

The answer to our first question is therefore somewhat ambivalent. We see no sign of a decline in the willingness to use the language of class but there is some evidence of relatively modest decline in the strength of belonging to one's class over the 42 years since 1963. We next move on to consider whether the evidence on the claimed 'de-coupling' of subjective class from own or father's occupational position is any more encouraging for our theorists.

In Table 1.3, we classify respondents according to their father's class, using a classification that is widely used in sociological research and which distinguishes the professional and managerial positions of the 'salariat' from lower-level routine non-manual workers, the petty bourgeoisie of small employers and the self-employed, the skilled working class (including supervisors of manual workers), and the lower grades of semi- and unskilled workers (including routine personal service workers).[4] (For details of this scheme and its theoretical rationale see Goldthorpe, 2007.)

Since much of the theoretical literature implicitly focuses on the decline of working-class solidarity and identity in particular, in Table 1.3 we show the percentage from each social class origin who defined themselves as working class (grouping together both the prompted and

Table 1.3 Fathers' class and respondents' class identity: Percentage giving a working-class identity (prompted and unprompted combined)

Father's class	**Cell percentages**							
	1964	**1970**	**1974**	**1983**	**1987**	**1992**	**1997**	**2005**
Salariat	28	34	28	32	31	37	37	35
Routine non-manual	54	27	46	52	48	39	51	51
Petty bourgeoisie	53	50	53	50	53	50	53	53
Supervisors or skilled manual	73	66	72	64	73	67	70	71
Semi- and unskilled manual	78	78	72	72	75	74	77	69
All	66	62	62	59	62	59	62	58
Gap	50	44	44	40	44	37	40	34

Gap: Percentage semi- and unskilled manual saying they are working class minus the proportion of the salariat doing so.
Sources: BES 1964–1997, BSA 2005.

unprompted responses described earlier). As it happens similar patterns are evident for middle-class identity and for unprompted working-class identity on its own.

The key question we have to ask of these data is whether there has been any convergence over time in the proportions from each class origin who espouse a working-class identity. If Beck is right to suppose that class identity is decreasingly inherited, then the association between father's class and respondent's identity would be expected to weaken over time. In Table 1.3, this would most obviously show up as a narrowing of the gap in the proportion claiming a working-class identity between respondents from salariat backgrounds and those from working-class origins. We show this gap in the bottom row of the table.[5]

As we can see, there is some bumpiness in the trends, almost certainly reflecting sampling error, which can be especially large in some of the smaller classes such as the routine non-manual class. But there are two clear findings. First, in all years, there is a definite gradient with respondents from salariat origins being much less likely to define themselves as working class than are respondents from the skilled or semi-/unskilled classes. Family background is persistently associated with current class identity. Secondly, however, the gap between people from salariat and working-class origins has shrunk over time, down from a 50 percentage point difference in 1964 to a 34 point difference in 2005. It seems that family background makes rather less difference than it once did.

Still, the change is hardly on a revolutionary scale – less than half a point change each year – and should lead us to be sceptical about some of the more dramatic claims of Beck and Giddens. Moreover, the readings for the period between 1970 and 1997 barely show any change at all. But even leaving that aside, much of the change had occurred by 1983, that is, before the liberalization of the labour market which we see as such a key part of Beck's explanation of individualization.

Table 1.4 presents a parallel analysis of the changing relationship over time between one's own occupational class and subjective class identity.[6] It shows a similar picture to the previous table. Those in manual occupations are consistently more likely to have a working-class identity; those in the salariat are least likely to do so. Equally, however, the gap appears to have declined over time, though again much of the decline seems to have occurred by 1983, before the Thatcherite liberalization of the labour market had taken effect.

However, we should exercise some caution in drawing conclusions from such bivariate analysis. Both in Table 1.4 and in our previous analysis of father's class one reason why the gap might have fallen is because of changes in the pattern of social mobility. Perhaps, for example, the difference between those in the salariat and those in semi- and unskilled occupations in terms of the occupations pursued by their fathers has

Table 1.4 Own occupational class and subjective class identity: Percentage giving a working-class identity

Own class	**Cell percentages**							
	1964	**1970**	**1974**	**1983**	**1987**	**1992**	**1997**	**2005**
Salariat	32	36	36	38	38	36	41	42
Routine non-manual	53	55	53	53	58	59	63	58
Petty bourgeoisie	45	49	53	48	60	53	62	58
Supervisors or skilled manual	81	81	78	71	78	74	79	77
Semi- and unskilled manual	85	81	78	74	76	75	76	72
All	66	62	62	59	62	59	61	57
Gap	53	45	42	36	38	39	35	30

Gap: Percentage semi- and unskilled manual saying they are working class minus the proportion of the salariat doing so.
Sources: BES 1964–1997, BSA 2005.

narrowed. Equally, perhaps father's class is likely to be strongly related nowadays to respondent's class. Such changes would reduce the strength of the bivariate relationships in Tables 1.3 and 1.4 even if the independent impact of father's class on class identity after controlling for the effect of respondent's class was unchanged, as was the independent effect of respondent's class on class identity after controlling for father's class. And if the independent effect of the two classes on class identities is largely unchanged, then it is far from clear that individuals have become more likely to choose their own class identities.

There was, indeed, some sign in our data series that the relationship between father's and respondent's class has weakened over time (see also Heath and Payne, 2000).[7] Indeed when we took this into account in a multivariate analysis – and also took into account the possibility that the relationship between objective and subjective class may differ between men and women – we found that there was no consistent evidence that the relationship between subjective class and either father's class or respondent's class has weakened (see Heath et al., 2009, Appendices 1 and 2 for this material). In fact in the case of women respondents, class seems to have come to matter more as partner's class has declined, evidence perhaps of individualization within the family of the kind Beck would anticipate but not of de-coupling of the link between class position and class identity.

We can also obtain a slightly different perspective on whether class identities have become de-coupled from occupation-based class position from a further question that was asked in 1963 and replicated in 2005 (but was not asked in the intermediate years). Respondents were asked an open-ended question

> What sort of people would you say belong to the middle class?
> What sort of people would you say belong to the working class?

If indeed occupation is now less likely to influence class identity, then one might anticipate that fewer people would define class membership in occupational terms in response to these questions. The outcome is shown in Table 1.5. In 1963, over half of the sample said that they thought that middle-class people were ones with white-collar (or similar) jobs, while two-thirds said that they thought working-class people were ones with blue-collar (or similar) jobs. In 2005, the type of occupation someone was in remained the primary characteristic associated with class membership, but the proportion linking occupation with class was around fifteen points below what it had been 40 years earlier.

Table 1.5 The declining occupational basis of class? The sort of people who belong to the middle and working classes

Sort of people who belong to the . . .	**Percentage of responses**			
	1963		**2005**	
	Middle class	**Working class**	**Middle class**	**Working class**
White/blue collar	55	66	40	53
Rich/poor	20	9	29	23
Manners and morals (1963)/educated (2005)	5	6	8	8
Other response	8	8	10	5
None	12	11	13	11
N	2009	2009	2102	2102

Note: Multiple response analysis with both first and second mentions included in the numerator and respondents who said 'none' (at the first mention) included in the denominator.
Sources: BES 1963 and BSA 2005.

Meanwhile, there was a clear increase in the proportion who associated class with income differences between rich and poor. However, even in 2005, income clearly took second place behind occupation as a marker of class position in the eyes of our respondents.[8]

This evidence is then in line with the expectations of theorists who believe that change is occurring and that the occupational basis of class identity is eroding. However, the changes are modest; class is still predominantly seen in occupational terms, albeit less so than it once was. Moreover, it does not necessarily follow that because class is likely to be regarded in occupational terms, the impact of occupational position on class identity has weakened. But in any event, it appears that once again the theorists may have confused a (modest) direction of change with a wholesale transformation. It would be completely false to claim that, to paraphrase Beck, the symbiosis of occupation and class identity has been shattered. Modified, perhaps, but not shattered.

Probably the most important claim underlying the death of class thesis, however, is that class identities and subcultures no longer have the same power or influence over people's social actions that they once did. As Beck and Beck-Gernsheim asserted '[classes] lose their independent identities and the chance to become a formative political force' (Beck and Beck-Gernsheim, 2001: 39).

A simple way to explore this is to investigate whether class identity is decreasingly linked to the distinctive patterns of political partisanship traditionally associated with the different classes. Writing about the 1960s, Butler and Stokes, for example, argued that Labour was regarded as the party of the working class and that some (though by no means all) working-class voters supported Labour simply because it was the working-class party. More specifically, if class identities and class subcultures really are influential, we would expect to find that people who feel a stronger sense of community with other members of their class will be more likely to support their traditional class party. If, then, social class has lost its role as a normative reference group for its members, we expect to find not only a convergence between members of different classes in their patterns of partisanship (the so-called 'class dealignment') in general but also a specific convergence between those who feel close to their class and those who do not. After all, if people who felt close to the working class were just the same in their support for Labour as those who said they were working class but did not feel close to other working-class people, then there would be no need to invoke the concept of normative reference group: straightforward class interest alone would be a sufficient explanation.

We examine this hypothesis using the distinction between the prompted and unprompted responses to the class identity question since this question has been asked regularly over time and thus enables us to chart changes and when they occurred. However, in so far as we can, we have replicated our results using the 'closeness' questions that were only asked in 1963 and 2005.

We focus on Labour identity in Table 1.6. The variation in the overall level of Labour partisanship (shown in the penultimate row of the table) parallels the changes in the party's electoral fortunes with the party's support declining massively between 1974 and 1983 and then recovering in 1997. We can also see how in 1997 and 2005 New Labour particularly appealed to the middle class amongst whom levels of Labour partisanship reached higher levels than in any previous elections.

This rise of Labour support in the middle classes of course in turn led to a sharp decline in the overall gap between the classes and we therefore see a very clear pattern of convergence between the classes, sometimes described as class dealignment. (For detailed discussion of the class dealignment debate, see Evans, 1999.) This convergence, as illustrated by the gap between the unprompted middle and working-class identifiers (the WCU:MCU gap in the penultimate row of the table) in their support for Labour, declines albeit very unevenly from

Table 1.6 Class identity and Labour partisanship: Percentage with a Labour identity

Class identity	Cell percentages							
	1964	1970	1974	1983	1987	1992	1997	2005
Middle class unprompted	17	31	24	18	18	17	32	34
Middle class prompted	11	19	20	12	12	13	26	22
Neither	10	21	24	17	16	15	32	28
Working class prompted	47	45	42	29	29	32	43	41
Working class unprompted	66	60	63	52	51	54	61	47
All	42	41	40	31	30	32	43	37
WCU:MCU Gap	49	29	39	34	33	37	29	13
WCU:WCP Gap	19	15	21	23	22	22	18	6

WCU:MCU Gap: Percentage of working class unprompted identifying with Labour minus the percentage of middle class unprompted. Labour identifiers are those who say 'Labour' in response to the question, 'Generally speaking, do you usually consider yourself Conservative, Labour, Liberal Democrat or what?'
WCU:WPU Gap: Percentage of working class unprompted identifying with Labour minus the percentage of working class prompted.
Sources: BES 1964–1997, BSA 2005.

49 percentage points in 1964 to a meagre 13 points in 2005 – a much larger decline than any we have seen so far. However, it is also very striking that this gap does not shrink at all during the 22 years between 1970 and 1992 (a period that might be termed one of 'trendless fluctuation'), but then falls by a further 24 points in the 13 years to 2005.

Even more striking is the sharp decline in the gap between prompted and unprompted working-class identifiers (the WCU:WCP gap in the bottom row of the table). This had consistently been around 20 points from 1964 to 1997 but collapsed suddenly to six points in 2005. It is this collapse that is crucial for the normative reference group argument. What we see is that only over this most recent period, the period of New Labour when the party dropped its emphasis on its working-class roots, has class most clearly lost its force as a normative reference group. The changed politics of the Labour party looks a more plausible explanation of the weakened relationship between class identity and partisanship than theories of individualization.

Conclusions

We began this chapter by asking a series of questions. Has there been a decline in class identity in the sense that people are now less likely than they used to be to identify with a social class or are less likely to feel a deep attachment to their class? Has a sense of class identity become de-coupled either from one's social origins or from one's current occupational position – in other words, is class identity less 'given' and more 'chosen' than it used to be? Is there any sense in which class has become a less powerful 'normative reference group' than it used to be? And finally, if there are changes, does the timing of the changes give us any clues as to which of the rival theoretical interpretations is most likely to be sound?

Our research, which we believe to be the first really systematic empirical investigation of these questions, suggests the following:

- First, people still use the language of class and there has been little change in the proportions who are willing to assign themselves to a social class (either prompted or unprompted).
- But there has been a relatively small but nonetheless noticeable decline in the strength of belonging to one's class.
- People are somewhat less likely to consider class membership to be defined by occupational position, while there has been a relatively modest but noticeable de-coupling of class identity both from one's social origins (as measured by father's class) and from one's current occupation. However, this latter trend appears largely to reflect changes in the pattern of social mobility rather than greater freedom to choose one's identity.
- There has been a dramatic decline in the strength of class as a normative reference group, at least as measured by its relationship with support for the Labour Party.

All the changes we have identified are in the direction, although far from the magnitude, predicted by Beck, and we do not see a single example of a counter-trend. So in one sense Beck is right. In contrast, these changes are also predicted by Clark and Lipset, Pakulski and Waters, and by ourselves using rather different theoretical frameworks. On their own these trends do not provide strong support for Beck's claims that we are now 'forced' to choose our own identities. Indeed, the timing of many of the changes leads us to be somewhat sceptical of such claims, since there is no indication that the trends were given any marked impetus by the

Thatcherite reforms of the 1980s that liberalized the labour market and which might therefore have been expected to increase the compulsion on individuals to choose their own biographies.

However, there are signs that some of the changes we have identified were taking place from the very beginning of the period we have considered, which would fit in well with the accounts provided by Lipset and others. But in every case where change has happened what has been notable is the extent to which it accelerated in Britain during the era of New Labour, not least in the respect of the decline in the relationship between class identity and Labour partisanship. Rather than simply reflecting autonomous changes in the nature of society, it seems that the declining force of class identity as a normative reference group is best accounted for by political developments, and in particular by New Labour's move from 1994 onwards to a less class conscious centre ground. Class identities are forged in the crucible of political debate as well as the everyday experience of social life.

Notes

1. It should however be noted that Beck (2007) himself suggests that his thesis should be tested by an empirical investigation of the changing legal and institutional framework, which he sees as the driving force of individualization. While this would certainly be a key component of testing his theory, it still leaves open the question of the effects of such institutional changes and therefore leaves room for our kind of investigation in addition to his proposed approach.
2. Beck's emphasis on the degree to which individuals are forced to change distinguishes his theory from those writers, such as Inglehart, who consider increased individualism to be the result of changes in value orientations (Inglehart, 1977; 1997).
3. This was a move that itself may have been influenced by our own earlier work on social change and the future of the left which was published in *The Political Quarterly* and was, we were later told, discussed by the Shadow Cabinet at a key meeting; see Heath and McDonald, 1987).
4. In the case of the 1964–1997 BESs, the classes have been derived directly from full details of father's occupation and employment status. In 2005, father's class was assigned via a self-completion question designed to enable respondents to provide an informed statement of the class to which their father's occupation belonged. Since the necessary algorithm is not available for occupation coded according to the 2000 Standard Occupational Classification, for the 2005 survey, classes have been constructed from a recode of respondent's socio-economic group, which gives a good approximation.
5. A more formal treatment would be to use loglinear modelling to test the full set of relationships (see Heath et al., 2009).

6. In the case of the BESs, respondent's class has been derived from occupation and employment status. While this information was also available for respondents to the 2005 BSA, the necessary algorithm for deriving Goldthorpe class is not available for occupations coded, as were those on the 2005 BSA, according to the 2000 Standard Occupational Classification. Class has instead been constructed from a recode of respondent's socio-economic group, which itself is based on occupation and employment status and which can be used to construct a good approximation to Goldthorpe class.
7. Trends in social mobility are a contentious topic, with different data sources indicating rather different trends. For a review of the evidence, see Cabinet Office (2008). However, in understanding the patterns in Table 1.4, which uses the BES data, the analyses of social mobility that use the same data are the relevant ones.
8. We might note too that people were just as likely to be able to provide some kind of answer in 2005 as they were in 1963, contrary to what we might have anticipated if social class truly had become a 'zombie' term with little meaning for people.

References

Atkinson, W. (2007) Beck, Individualization and the Death of Class: A Critique. *British Journal of Sociology* 58, 349–66.

Beck, U. (1992) *Risk Society: Towards a New Modernity*. London: Sage.

Beck, U. (2007) Beyond Class and Nation: Reframing Social Inequalities in a Globalizing World. *British Journal of Sociology* 58, 679–705.

Beck, U. and Beck-Gernsheim, E. (2001) *Individualization: Institutionalized Individualism and Its Social and Political Consequences*. London: Sage.

Butler, D.E. and Stokes, D. (1974) *Political Change in Britain: The Evolution of Electoral Choice*. London: Macmillan.

Cabinet Office (2008) Getting on, Getting Ahead: A Discussion Paper Analysing the Trends and Drivers of Social Mobility. http://www.cabinetoffice.gov.uk/media/cabinetoffice/strategy/assets/socialmobility/gettingon.pdf

Clark, T.N. and Lipset, S.M. (1991) Are Social Classes Dying? *International Sociology* 6, 397–410.

Curtice, J. (2007) Elections and Public Opinion. In A. Seldon (ed.) *Blair's Britain 1997–2007*. Cambridge: Cambridge University Press.

Evans, G.A. (ed.) (1999) *The End of Class Politics? Class Voting in Comparative Context*. Oxford: Oxford University Press.

Goldthorpe, J.H. (2007) Social Class and the Differentiation of Employment Contracts. In *On Sociology*, vol. 2, pp. 101–24. Stanford: Stanford University Press.

Goldthorpe, J.H. and Mills, C. (2004) Trends in Intergenerational Class Mobility in Britain in the Late Twentieth Century. In R. Breen (ed.) *Social Mobility in Europe*. Oxford: Oxford University Press.

Halsey, A.H. and Webb, J. (eds) (2000) *Twentieth-Century British Social Trends*. Basingstoke: Macmillan.

Heath, A.F., Curtice, J. and Elgenius, G. (2009) Changing Patterns of Class Identity, 1963–2005. CREST Working Paper No. 112. http://www.crest.ox.ac.uk/papers.htm

Heath, A.F., Jowell, R.M. and Curtice, J.K. (1985) *How Britain Votes*. Oxford: Pergamon Press.

Heath, A.F. and McDonald, S.-K. (1987) Social Change and the Future of the Left. *The Political Quarterly* 58, 364–77.

Heath, A.F. and Payne, C. (2000) Social Mobility. In A.H. Halsey and J. Webb (eds) *Twentieth-Century British Social Trends*. Basingstoke: Macmillan.

Hout, M., Brooks, C. and Manza, J. (1993) The Persistence of Classes in Post-Industrial Societies. *International Sociology* 8 (3), 259–77.

Inglehart, R. (1977) *The Silent Revolution*. Princeton, NJ: Princeton University Press.

Inglehart, R. (1997) *Modernization and Post-Modernization*. Princeton, NJ: Princeton University Press.

Lee, J.L. and Turner, S.B. (eds) (1996) *Conflicts about Class: Debating Inequality in Late Industrialism*. London: Longman.

Marshall, G., Newby, H., Rose, D. and Vogler, C. (1988) *Social Class in Modern Britain*. London: Hutchinson.

Merton, R.K. (1957) *Social Theory and Social Structure*. New York: The Free Press.

Pakulski, J. and Waters, M. (1996) *The Death of Class*. London: Sage.

Reissman, L. (1960) *Class in American Society*. London: Routledge.

Savage, M. (2000) *Class Analysis and Social Transformation*. Buckingham: Open University Press.

Savage, M., Bagnall, G. and Longhurst, B. (2001) Ordinary, Ambivalent and Defensive: Class Identities in the Northwest of England. *Sociology* 35, 875–92.

Scott, J. (2002) Social Class and Stratification in Late Modernity. *Acta Sociologica* 45, 23–35.

Weakliem, D.L. and Heath, A.F. (1999) The Secret Life of Class Voting: Britain, France and the United States since the 1930s. In G.A. Evans (ed.) *The End of Class Politics? Class Voting in Comparative Context*. Oxford: Oxford University Press.

2

'I Don't Want to Be Classed, But We Are All Classed': Making Liveable Lives Across Generations

Ben Rogaly and Becky Taylor

When I was a child and a young woman I felt I knew my place. Then I moved on and got to know other people from different backgrounds. Now I feel in the middle, don't really belong either side. If I said this out loud I would be accused of being a snob.... A visitor to the house I was cleaning once said to me, 'you don't look like a cleaner'. And I said, 'What, am I supposed to have curlers in and a head scarf?'... I would have looked much as I do now. But he again had an idea in his head. About what cleaners should look like and what cleaners should sound like. And I found that a bit. That, I suppose cartoon character of cleaner. With a turban thing not a headscarf or whatever. Which I could never do. And that made me think how we are. So then I had this thing about, do I say 'I'm a cleaner'? Although I did. Sort of fundamentally honest, I suppose. But it's odd. Because if I tell people I'm a cleaner they're going to have this particular image of me, which is not necessarily the right one. It's just a very small part. And a necessity. (Lily Haley)

It's the shame factor which has gone [pauses] now. I know certainly when I grew up... it was shameful to come from the Larkman, even though most of the people around me also came from the Larkman and obviously were at Bowthorpe [comprehensive school]... I left, I went to university, so there you go... I've now qualified myself as 'survived the Larkman' (Lorna Haley)

Introduction

Lily Haley and Lorna, her daughter, are both white women who grew up on the Larkman estate in Norwich, England, a place that has been stigmatised by others in the city.[1] As we show in this chapter, superficially their backgrounds on the estate, characterised by extreme poverty and compounded by early parental death, alcoholism and domestic violence, suggest the kind of stereotypical working-class lives associated with a 'deprived' area. However, the picture revealed through the two women's telling of their life histories was much more complex, and showed the different ways in which both women had worked hard at creating liveable lives for themselves. Their stories illustrate the crucial role of self-identification and categorisation in this process and the importance of understanding how both operate relationally (see Jenkins, 1996, 2000).

In Butler's discussion of gender, she writes that 'one does not "do" one's gender alone. One is always "doing" with or for another, even if the other is only imaginary' (2004: 1). Being classed by others, or experiencing moral sentiments of class (Sayer, 2005), is similarly relational. In Butler's terms, the social norms that frame our lives are also fundamental to the 'viability of our individual personhood' (2004: 2). This is partly about recognition. Butler argues that because of 'race', sex and ethnicity some humans are understood differently by others and some are 'recognised as less than human, and that form of qualified recognition does not lead to a viable life' (2004: 2). Both 'withholding' and 'conferring' recognition can be the cause of 'undoing' a person. Thus, it may be that framing a person *within* the prevailing norms of what it is to be human is contrary to a person's desires and that one's 'sense of survival depends upon escaping the clutch of those norms by which recognition is conferred'. Consequently, there are situations in which 'estrangement is preferable to gaining a sense of intelligibility by virtue of norms that will only do me in from another direction' (2004: 3):

> There is a certain departure from the human that takes place in order to start the process of remaking the human . . . [and] to establish more inclusive conditions for sheltering and maintaining life that resists models of assimilation.
>
> (Butler, 2004: 4)

Writing specifically about class, bell hooks also spoke of resisting assimilation. For her, going to Stanford University had meant long-term and emotional absence from home, the disapproval of her parents and living among strangers. However, a liveable life meant living on her own terms:

> Throughout my graduate student years, I was told again and again that I lacked the proper decorum of a graduate student, that I did not understand my place. Slowly I began to understand fully that there was no place in academe for folks from working-class backgrounds who did not wish to leave the past behind. That was the price of the ticket. Poor students would be welcome at the best institutions of higher learning only if they were willing to surrender memory, to forget the past and claim the assimilated present as the only worthwhile and meaningful reality.
>
> (hooks, 2000: 36–37)

Like Skeggs (2009) and Sayer (2005), hooks is concerned with values as much as recognition. Skeggs has argued that the working-class women she interviewed over 11 years in the north of England were misrecognised through being seen by middle-class people as having little or no worth. Constituted as persons within this set of dominant notions of value, they actively resisted these notions through their own value talk about parenting, scorning what they saw as the questionable values of middle-class parents who went out to work and left their small children in paid care.

Both Lily and Lorna experienced extreme poverty in their childhoods, and both either witnessed or suffered domestic violence at the hands of men. These aspects of their backgrounds formed the context from which they told their stories in conversation with Ben (a white middle-class male) in interviews in 2005 and 2006. For both of them, being categorised by class and their shifting, complex and ambivalent classed self-identifications were important in the hard work of making liveable lives, and sometimes made their lives unliveable.

This chapter is organised around different sites of classed experience that Lily and Lorna talked about. In it, we do not seek to generalise about past and emerging class formations in the UK. Rather, the chapter offers a rich qualitative account of two women's lives which are deeply informative about the 'conditions of intelligibility' that have surrounded class in the UK since the 1950s. We discuss in turn Lily's and Lorna's lives as children – at home and at school; Lorna's experience of university; and both women's lives as parents. The stories were sometimes painful to tell and involved talking through material that had long remained unspoken. Woven into the telling of these stories, and highlighting the role of ourselves as researchers in the process, was Ben's tangential relationship to both these women. As with a number of encounters during the research, our contact with Lorna and Lily was made through, and reinforced, previously established social networks. Lorna was introduced to Ben through a mutual friend who had taught her at secondary school. During the life history interview, it transpired that Ben and Lorna had other friends in common, in part the result of their daughters having attended the same school. Similarly, when Ben went on to interview Lorna's mother, he found that she had friends on the same street where he had lived for seven years. Both women willingly consented to this more detailed treatment of their lives in the chapter.[2]

Childhoods

Lily was born in 1947 in a three-bedroomed council house on the Larkman estate, the fourth child of her Norfolk-born mother and her Irish father. She was later joined by four younger brothers and a younger sister. Lily remembers her mother's family disapproving of her father, about whom stories circulated, including having been discharged 'possibly dishonourably' and having been in prison when Lily was a small child. Her childhood years in the 1950s were a time of generalised poverty in the estates which stand in contrast to the more individualised experience of poverty in the 1960s and 1970s that characterised her daughter Lorna's childhood (Rogaly and Taylor, 2009). In spite of identifying her background as both working class and poor, Lily remembered being aware of classed relations *within* the extended family, and the feelings this generated in her of exclusion, of feeling out of place.

Lily's aunt owned her house in Warwick Street, which Lily remembers as making an impression on her because it was neither a council property, nor was it part of a housing estate. Aged eight, Lily had felt ambivalent about being a bridesmaid for this 'posh' aunt:

> Lily: We thought [her house] was wonderful then, because the little terrace house that you owned... Wow!
>
> BR: When might you have been conscious of a thought like that?
>
> Lily: As a very small child... this particular aunt had a son who became a teacher and [visiting] was like going to see the posh relations... but generally it was only myself and my sister I think.

The rabble – being my brothers – were not . . . allowed to visit . . . and we were bridesmaids at her only child's wedding . . .

BR: Did you feel that was a great treat?

Lily: Oh yes. Didn't much enjoy it I must say but we were quite honoured.

BR: Why didn't you enjoy it?

Lily: Feeling out of place probably. It was all a bit too, very much out of what we would have been used to . . . this posh occasion . . . and those ridiculous dresses on and a bangle that I can remember nearly cut my arm in half . . . but I don't think we had a choice . . . to refuse.

Lily remembered herself as having been an anxious child, and felt that this was connected to the absolute poverty of her immediate family as well as their relative poverty compared to the neighbours. She longed for her family to be more like everyone else:

> I think I was always aware of all the undercurrents of lack of money and the struggle . . . how my mother struggled so badly with a very feckless father . . . I can remember wanting my dad to be like other dads, you know: they had a regular job, went to work. I think as a child you want to be like other people . . . My immediate friends, my neighbours, their dads worked . . . factories, I mean all sort of manual stuff but they had a *regular* job and *regular* income and they had *fruit bowls* . . .

In contrast, the crowdedness of the house Lily's family lived in was unexceptional. 'My immediate neighbours . . . all had at least five, seven, there were lots of big families'. Lily remembered her mother working hard to keep the house and the family clean. She did not go out to earn money:

> There was a great sense of pride about your whites . . . and however poor we were I do have a memory that we were always clean children and the house, although quite Spartan I suppose . . . that's all my mother did.

In spite of performing well academically, Lily had avoided going to the grammar school because 'there would have been no encouragement [at home] and the money it would have cost would have had great influence on the school we went to'. The secondary modern was another site where Lily remembers experiencing the pain of being categorised. Making life more liveable – in this case less tense – would have entailed not having her poverty or ethnicity drawn attention to by teachers, however:

> Lily: I can remember how school always used to be about talking about religion and I hated even saying my dad was Irish and a Catholic cos I didn't want to go to the assembly with everyone else ... I don't think you single children out quite so much now ... I can just remember always being very tense because ... free school dinners were very, very public. You had to go to line up. 'All those who have free dinners' you know, and even as a small child I was very conscious of the difference. I hated it ...
> BR: Wasn't there lots of children with free dinners in the Larkman?
> Lily: Probably, but I didn't want to be one of them.

However, for Lily, it was not school that made her feel 'bitter and twisted' when she thought back. After all they were streamed, being 'the brightest pupils ... we were working toward O-level'. Rather it was home. Lily was 14 when her mother, 43 and pregnant with another child, became seriously ill. When her mother died, Lily was left to look after the house, her father and her younger brothers and take up a factory job. She had to give up school, which she had 'loved ... it [had been] such an escape for me.' Lily's father was a major problem for her and life became unliveable:

> I became mother to four younger brothers and a baby and a father [who] was just an extra large child ... It all went horribly wrong from then on. My neighbour used to look after my youngest sister, the baby, and eventually she did bring my sister up ... I don't know if the authorities were involved ... It all seems very odd and I looked after the rest of things ... We had horrible memories. I know when I was at work I'd bought a bike and you would come home and my dad would have sold it ... My mother had got us some girly bedroom furniture, we came home one day it had all gone ... He would burn anything if we didn't have any coal ... I don't mean to say he was useless in a horrible way but he *was* useless. He ... probably never made himself a cup of tea in his life.

Lily struggled on, getting married after becoming pregnant with Lorna when she was 18, and then being allocated a council house just outside the Larkman, at which point she 'very reluctantly' left her father and her brothers. 'I knew it would all go to pot... After I went my father didn't pay the rent. They were evicted... I always have this guilt about leaving my four younger brothers.'

Part of attempting to make a liveable life could mean having someone else to feel sorry for. Lorna told us that she had been in tears reading another research participant's narration of their childhood poverty in the draft manuscript of our book – emotions that she had previously kept in check in relation to her own past. For her, being able to cope had meant not feeling pity for herself. As Lily describes here, it was important to be able to feel better than someone else:

> however low you are, you like somebody else who we thought were possibly the scruffy ones... I do have memories that we were always really clean, might have been a bit shabby and patched up... there were other families you would look down on possibly. I'm sure I didn't vocalise it. I'm sure I didn't go up and call them smelly or anything

Yet Lorna knew what it felt like to be on the receiving end of this attitude, as her 1970s childhood was marked by an awareness of the negative association living in the Larkman estate had for people elsewhere in Norwich. In her view, the Larkman was a collective category for other people, including other working-class people, to look down on:

> I know myself if someone says 'the Larkman' – 'oh she lives over the Larkman, she comes from the Larkman' – that engenders a very particular response from people in Norwich, even people who, other people who are common, the people who come from what I would consider other big council estates, it doesn't matter.

For Lorna, it would be shaking off the feelings of shame and accompanying defensiveness about coming from the Larkman that would make her life liveable. For her, this shame was compounded by her home life, which included, but was not limited to, her experiences at the hands of her mother's violent partner:

> I do feel and again this is perhaps another source of my shame was that our family fulfilled absolutely every stereotype you can think of. So... my mum had a drunken Irish Catholic father who everyone

> called Paddy. In fact I thought that was his name until he died . . . he was quite abusive . . . my youngest aunt who was only a couple of years older than me was literally handed over the fence at the age of three to a neighbour who then brought her up . . . It was a mess . . . at this point, but I was obviously reasonably oblivious or it was just ordinary to me then.

Lorna's home life both caused her shame and, she reflected, may have seemed absolutely ordinary to her at the same time. Perhaps the lack of a sense of crisis was partly because she had never known things to be different and partly because

> It all seemed to be contained within that world. There wasn't . . . this sense of social workers or any kind of official authority taking a hand in any of this.

It was 18 months after Lily had given birth to her third child, the first and only one by the partner she lived with the longest, that she was allocated a council house in a nearby estate. Just as Lorna's aunt had been brought up by her neighbours, she described how

> this informal putting each other up carried on because we then moved out to the [house] . . . where my mum still lives and we then put up her brothers, her sisters, families, kids, whatever. I remember . . . we always had someone with us.

School for Lorna was a site where categorisations – by and of other children, and by teachers – were implicated in the making of classed selves. Lorna's clearest memories were of Blackdale middle school on the edge of the University of East Anglia (UEA) campus, which she described as a

> bit more mixed [than Northfields which she had attended previously] . . . I think we had perhaps . . . some UEA children . . . visiting, a bit more of a floating population . . . very middle class children but I think the majority of the school . . . was working class . . . I think children are anyway very accepting of almost anything but . . . I still have really strong memories of injustice . . . I can remember being told off and I was such a good girl but I can remember being told off for reading too much: 'you're reading too much'. But I can remember, 'look at Isabel, Isabel has finished two books this week' and sit there

> thinking that's not fair cos he's told me off for reading *too much*. And I just think that some teachers ... look at the class and they see a mass of scruffy Norfolk working class little kids and I don't suppose they invest a great deal in them.

While such incidents at school were important in the formation of Lorna's early class consciousness, she said that she had 'always [been] very conscious of class'. A similar process operated in relation to her peer group to the one described by Willis (1977) for working-class boys in the 1970s:

> although I was always in one of the top streams ... that's part of the thing of being in a working class school ... you mustn't be too brainy ... so you sort of kept your head down, you needed to belong and not have the piss taken out of you and you didn't want to be one of those ... three or four maybe in each class who did their homework.

Feeling alienated by school in spite of having stayed on beyond her O levels, Lorna said she felt that it was her 'very grim' home life that made her continue. A liveable life was not on the cards if she went out and looked for a job at that point, she reflected, so, having not shown up much in the lower sixth, she returned one more time to give school another chance. It was then that she met Susan, a very committed teacher. Susan had made an impression on Lorna when she had complicitly lied to Lily at a parents' evening, saying that Lorna had been turning up for school when she had not. At this stage, a liveable life needed an ally, someone who did not see people as permanently consigned to their current circumstances.

University

> I remember the first time Susan ... suggested the possibility of a university and this to me ... was incredible ... it had honestly never ... entered my mind that I could go to a university. It just wasn't in my realm of existence and if I'd mentioned it at home ... they would have gone 'don't be ridiculous', it just wasn't our world and in fact they weren't keen. (Lorna Haley).

While she found support from Susan, others at Lorna's school had been actively unhelpful because of their classed ideas about what it was possible for her to achieve academically. Lorna responded angrily to the constraints she felt both at school and at home:

> this careers man came along to us and I said I was thinking of possibly applying to university and he just went [sighs]. I was very defiant at this point, I was very angry... he said 'well what would you do?', and I said 'literature possibly, I don't know someone's even thought law.' And... it was amazing. He just went through a list of reasons and they were all my background basically... aim low, basically. So I, like a prat, then went and applied to do law...

Lorna explained that at the same time at home she had 'just stopped being timid' and had started having regular violent confrontations with Lily's partner: '[One day] I was down in the kitchen with things flying around and... I can remember thinking I've just got to go'. She wandered the streets for the rest of the day, eventually knocking on Susan's door. Lorna ended up living for a couple of months with Susan, her husband and her two daughters who were of a similar age to her. She observed

> such a different household. It was really very different... the culture. It was a good experience for me actually... like a little practice really... Susan did again take me in hand [and] say: 'look... if you are going to go onto university... there are certain books that most students... will have... taken for granted that you'll have read, or there are certain films they will have seen.

When Lorna went to university, as well as opening up this new world to her, it contributed to her being able to make her mother's life more liveable in practical ways:

> I sent my mum money... In those days it was... a full... maintenance grant... there were students talking about how hard they were finding it [and] what they were having to do without, whereas I was quite easily sending my mum money. It was the first time she had a phone. I paid because I couldn't contact her... she didn't have a washing machine until I was at university

Despite her many negative memories of her childhood, Lorna identified the period before going to university as one in which she still felt 'quite comfortable' about her identification as being both working class and of the Larkman. 'I knew I was working class…but I wasn't self-conscious about it'. However, as was anticipated by her narration of the injustice she had felt at middle-school, Lorna's experiences at university were distinctly less comfortable, as she found middle-class people she came into contact with difficult to relate to and (at times) patronising. She would discover simultaneous emotions of guilt, loss, shame and pride in the Larkman and in having working-class roots.

This process began even before she had left for university, as, while she much valued Susan's input, Lorna found the reaction of other middle-class people she knew – families her mother cleaned for 'on the side' at the time – to be more problematic:

> Lorna: When I got to go to university it was like they were gonna put flags up…
>
> BR: Who were going to put flags up?
>
> Lorna: A couple of the women my mum worked for, lovely women…it was like a miracle had happened…

Being at university in the 1980s was deeply painful for Lorna as, echoing hooks (2000), it made her aware of class inequalities. She described her anger as she became acquainted with middle-class culture there:

> although I'd always been very, very aware of…being working class. I hadn't lived in any other sort of world so it was all right but then suddenly…I had a hard time really adjusting and I was angry…It's also the time of the miner's strike…there were these miners' wives coming round and there's all these students collecting money for people. They only had this to live on and I was thinking, 'well I've lived my whole life on that'…I had no sympathy at that point for the miners. I did politically but…

> BR: And were these *middle class* kids coming in collecting money?
>
> Lorna: Oh yes and I remember all sorts of odd conversations. I remember the Socialist Worker students who belonged to that organisation who would say you know, 'what do you think a working class house looks like…would they have a fire place…?'…I was just thinking 'Jesus Christ!' It was awful and…of course people do make assumptions about when your mum goes to the opera or when you mum does this…it was very hard I think.
>
> BR: Did you link up with any other kids who felt they were working class in that way?

> Lorna: I couldn't find any. I found some I suppose they would have been more lower middle who felt themselves to be quite deprived but again I felt when I listened to their deprivations to me they were luxuries. 'Well we only have one holiday a year', 'well my dad's this', 'my dad only earns fifteen thousand' and I was just thinking 'God!'. It really was a vast gap.

Although she had been angry at first with the ignorance of the middle-class students at Warwick about working-class lives, her anger was combined with an attempt to engage with her new life. For life to be liveable it had to involve social agility – being able to present oneself differently to oneself and to various different others – 'I can remember learning to say to "the coast". We went to "the coast", not "we went to Hemsby"':

> It's the kind of double life that you lead... talking about the comfort... belonging to a big family... that was behind me and... [in the Larkman years] it felt very comfortable... Then life bifurcates and you start living in all sorts of different ways and... that's what happened at Warwick with all the students there talking about [their] assumptions about life and money and family and I'd had my mum at home still living with [the same man] and still living in awful poverty really and... it made me tense...

It was not only encounters with middle-class individuals who had made being at university at times deeply uncomfortable for Lorna. She felt that her extended family too had held her back, policing social norms in a way which, but for meeting Susan, might have kept her from going to university in the first place. This is what she meant by the 'bad way' in which she belonged. Her extended family

> engendered... a sense of pointlessness in trying to do anything different... I think we're very actively knocked down or told that we were getting too big for our boots or that... we were being ridiculous if we tried to do something that didn't fit into what the family expected... I know for example when I went to university one of my aunts actually didn't speak to me for several years... 'who did I think I was?' you know... it really is the crabs in the bucket thing... you don't need a lid...

For Lorna, the dislocation she experienced at university did not end when she left, but rather continued to be troubling and unresolved, profoundly affecting the ways in which she related to people within and outside her family. She contrasted the taken-for-grantedness of the sense of class belonging she had had as a child and the sense of loss she felt subsequently:

> There was a sense... we belong with our kind [laughs] which is comfortable in a way... I mean I miss that in a way now... I'm kind of a bit more unsure of where I belong... [The belonging I knew before] was very absolute... so that I think [this explains] part of the acceptance of the status quo but [I was always] very aware of class...

This ambivalence, for Lorna, has fed into the rest of her life, including as we discuss next, her own experiences of parenting.

Being parents

Life seen from below, through the relationships one has because of being someone's child, was one thing. For both Lorna and Lily, being a parent brought its own classed encounters into the work of making liveable lives, and, as we have seen, Lily felt as though she had been a parent to her younger brothers and her father as well as her own three children. Lorna has one child, a daughter in her teens, and is no longer with her daughter's father, who she described as middle class.

The school gate was an important site of class-making for both women. When Lily had moved out of the Larkman estate, she moved into an adjacent area of social housing in the catchment area of more mixed-class primary schools. This included Heigham Park School where one of us – Ben – sent his children thirty years later when he lived in College Road, in Norwich's middle-class 'golden triangle'. This was at the same time that Lorna had also sent her daughter to the same school: the two girls had been in the same year. Lily spoke openly about how she felt as parent of children at such schools:

> Lily: Because of the catchment area this way, you know, College Road, Christchurch Road, Earlham Road... it was completely different [from my previous experience of] predominately council and very ordinary people... I just think thankfully my children were all quite bright... that that got them through, that at least they weren't behind. But I did feel a bit out of my depth initially and, because... in social situations... I never really felt I had much to say because

> I never did anything or went any[where] and I also had this horrible secret [of a violent partner] in my house which prevents you from inviting people back ... so there's always this sort of sense of isolation I suppose where you never really get too friendly with people because you don't want them to find these skeletons hanging around your house ...

It was poverty too which prevented her from inviting children's friends back home. Not doing this was part of making life liveable, part of 'survival':

> Money was always an issue, obviously. And him putting forward ... reasons why things couldn't happen. I mean we did still do some normal things, I suppose. But ... it was all about survival really, rather than anything else. I mean obviously I saw mums at the school and things. But I would never invite anyone back.

Yet, Lily's ambivalence is demonstrated by her simultaneous sense that the move to this new catchment area had been for the best because it moved her children, especially her boys, away from what she saw as rougher children in the Larkman.

> Lily: I was very pleased we'd moved here and that they did go to school this way. Cos I felt it got them away from the boys ... friends I possibly didn't approve of ... We are very stigmatised by lots of people if we live on council estates ... I don't deny it. I can't. That I live here. I often find we are grouped as a type. By society in general possibly. And it's not nice. Because, you know, we don't all go burning cars and whatever they do, I don't know. You know, some of us do try to, you know, instil certain values into our children.
>
> BR: What sort of values did you want to instil in your children?
>
> Lily: Well, right from wrong. That's a really important one from the start. Respect for other people. Honesty. Not saying I've always succeeded – this was my goal. No, I have. They've all grown up into very nice people, with a few blips along the way.

Here again Lily emphasises values in a similar way to Skeggs (2009). She does this both in relation to middle classes, represented in the term 'society in general', which thinks that working-class people don't have any values, and also in relation to working-class people she sees as rougher than her own family. When she was recovering after her collapse following the departure of her violent long-term partner, Lily went to do voluntary work with a small agency active on family issues in the Larkman. A committed mother, and as someone who had suffered domestic violence, she said she found herself shocked by the parenting style she sometimes encountered:

> I did find it extremely difficult, the way the mothers I met behaved towards their children, you know, the slapping, the shouting ... but what I found most disturbing was the way even very small children knew everything ... There was no protection ... they all knew he was in prison and who done what and ... the children were always there when all these conversations were going on. I find that very disturbing, and I did stay there quite some time and I did enjoy it in a bizarre way, but I think they got me down in the end. I found ... they didn't want to change the way they felt about things and I found it rather depressing really and I didn't like the child slapping and shouting.

This sense that she was in a position to criticise residents of the Larkman estate for what she saw as their parenting practices and their values, while also maintaining how she could not abide the categorisation of people in the estate by outsiders, resonates with Skeggs' discussion of the use of the word 'common'. This, she argues is an acceptable term if it is used by people 'subject to similar judgments', otherwise it is 'shorthand for a middle-class taste judgment that says "worthless" ' (2009: 10).[3]

As with Lily, so for Lorna, the school gate was an important site for the reproduction of classed relations with other parents. She had this to say of her first experience of being a parent at Heigham Park:

> I can remember standing on the playground thinking 'god almighty this is incredible!' But there's various women that I've met there, and ... I'm quite friendly with.

While bringing her child up 'effectively ... as a middle class child', she found she would still wear her Larkman origins with pride and would not allow the people of the area to be put down by one of her middle-class fellow parents/friends:

> my daughter was going to spend the day with them. She said 'would you mind, we're doing something, can you drop her off? I'm doing

> a project thing at Larkman Middle'. 'Oh alright' I said 'Yeah I know where that is dererErer'. So I dropped [my daughter] off with her and she said 'yes' – we were in this little shed – 'but of course the children here are not like you and me'. And I was just thinking 'oh for God...!' And I said 'well actually I was brought up [here]'...I just thought the assumptions people make, it's incredible! And the way she talked about these kids and she would certainly see herself as very liberal [tuts] she would see herself as unprejudiced [pause] but incredibly patronising...

Yet, while Lorna was allowed to go and visit her friends in the Larkman unaccompanied as a child, she 'wouldn't let [her daughter] play out in the streets [there]. I'd escort her to the Larkman'. Lorna's parenting and relationship with her own daughter thus revealed and reinforced for her not only how far she had moved from her own childhood, but crucially, how far her own daughter's life was removed from her own formative experiences:

> I'm kind of floating around between working and middle and whatever I am now I don't know, but then I have a child with a middle class father who is effectively growing up as a middle class child...in some ways she feels alien to me cos you know when you have children...one of the things they give you that I wasn't expecting at all is...your own childhood back. You kind of re-experience, relive things and...but she's reliving things that I never had...It's odd when you see your own child being the sort of child that I would have been really quite intimidated by at school myself...I probably would have hated her.

Conclusion

Thinking through Lorna and Lily's life histories as stories of class-making and of struggles for liveable lives has only begun to illustrate some of the complexity of the dialectic of class identification and categorisation, and, in a context of entrenched structural inequalities, its importance in people's subjective experiences of class. Both women were simultaneously repelled by the Larkman estate and continued to feel part of it. For Lorna, who was no longer a council tenant and was bringing up her daughter middle class, thinking about her connections to the estate brought about mixed emotions of guilt, loss and shame. Lily, whose own schooling had been constrained by poverty and was ended by the early death of her mother, had seen advantage in sending her children to schools with mixed-class intakes, while simultaneously experiencing isolation at the school gate.

In continuing to champion the Larkman, both women needed (in Butler's terms) to take a path of estrangement from dominant classed perspectives, which looked down on residents of that estate, in order not to be done in by accepting them, and assimilating themselves into a position of inferiority. This was made explicit in Lily's statement used in the title of this paper: 'I don't want to be classed, but we are all classed'. Such struggles over meaning cannot be separated from the material struggles that both women experienced at different times in their lives. As Sayer has put it in relation to recent studies of the history of discourses of class by authors such as Bev Skeggs,

> [t]hese contributions are important not only for understanding the subjective experience of class: the ascriptions of value or lack of value to self and other produce real effects on people in terms of how they are treated, and hence on their life-chances.
>
> (Sayer, 2005: 76)

After Lily's long-term partner left in the mid-1990s, she was required to take a set of NVQ (National Vocational Qualifications) courses in computing and became an NVQ assessor. Although she met her current partner via that route, it did not lead to long-term employment. It was, rather, when she became a shop worker in a larger retail outlet that, as Lily explained, while 'it wouldn't have been my intended career I'm so proud just to get a normal job and be like other people and pay my taxes. And, bit late, but I've finally done it... Finally sort of feel part of the fairly crappy human race'.

Notes

1. The names of research participants referred to in this chapter have been changed. The chapter draws on a larger study of three estates in Norwich, which included the North Earlham and Marlpit estates as well as the Larkman. We are grateful to Kirat Randhawa for comments on an earlier draft. The wider findings of the research project can be found in Rogaly and Taylor (2009).
2. We felt this was required although both women had given written consent to taped interviews, to the use of the anonymised life history transcripts in our forthcoming book, and to the deposit of the same transcripts in the UK Data Archive.
3. Page number refers to pre-publication version. Thanks to Bev Skeggs for permission to quote it here.

References

Butler, J. (2004) *Undoing Gender*. London and New York: Routledge.
hooks, b. (2000) *Where We Stand: Class Matters*. London and New York: Routledge.
Jenkins, R. (1996) Categorization: Identity, Social Process and Epistemology. *Current Sociology* 48 (3), 7–25.
Jenkins, R. (2000) *Social Identity*. London: Routledge.
Rogaly, B. and Taylor, B. (2009) *Moving Histories of Class and Community: Identity, Place and Belonging in Contemporary England*. Basingstoke: Palgrave Macmillan.
Sayer, A. (2005) *The Moral Significance of Class*. Cambridge: Cambridge University Press.
Skeggs, B. (2009) Class, Culture and Morality: Legacies and Logics in the Space for Identification. In M. Wetherell and C. Talpede Mohanty (eds) *The Sage Handbook of Identities*. London: Sage.
Willis, P. (1977) *Learning to Labour: How Working Class Kids get Working Class Jobs*. Farnborough: Saxon House.

3
Steel, Identity, Community: Regenerating Identities in a South Wales Town

Valerie Walkerdine[1]

Introduction

This chapter sets out to explore relation of work identity to community by thinking about the role of trauma and affect in the production of forced identity change. It builds upon research carried out in a town in the South Wales valleys, which we will call Steeltown, the site of long-term steel production, which closed permanently in 2002. The South Wales valleys were a major site of coal mining and iron and steel but the area has become very depressed as most mines have now closed and steel production has been relocated outside the valleys. The valleys have poor transport links as most people who worked there lived in the settlements attached to the mine or steel foundry. The area has high unemployment, with the local authority in which Steeltown is located suffering 33% youth unemployment. Given the poor transport links, finding other work is difficult.

Steeltown has been producing iron and then steel since the 18th century. It was originally populated by migrants who came mostly from England and Ireland, but has had a very settled population since then. We can compare Steeltown with the various international studies of rust-belt towns, with which it shares considerable characteristics. In this sense, the study we will discuss allows us to think about how de-industrialisation affects close-knit communities built around workplaces. While many studies do point to a specific number of effects (rise in poverty and crime, loss of social fabric of the community, rise in stress-related illnesses, sense of failure, loss and helplessness, see, for example, Linkon and Russo, 2002), most research does not explore in depth the relationship between affective relations and regeneration.

Our research used a psychosocial approach to understand this issue. This means that we interviewed redundant steel workers and others in the community (women and young people) using a method of open-ended narrative interviewing which is psychodynamic in orientation, as it aims less to ask specific questions and more to explore feelings and experience in response to redundancy.

Communities of affect

The argument of the chapter is that, although neo-liberal discourses and practices do produce a shift in worker identity towards entrepreneurialism, if we follow a standard governmentality thesis (Rose, 1999), we miss the central local specificity, which needs to be understood in relation to the history of the area. The argument about identity is therefore made more complex, because I argue that specific ways of being are produced through the affective relations of community, formed in specific cultural and historical circumstances. It is then in relation to these that responses to the closure of the steel works and the changing organisation of work should be understood. In this section of the chapter, I will begin by outlining the claim that the historically forged affective relations and practices of community form the basis, through time and space, of the containment of anxieties which provide a basic sense of the continuity of being.

Susan, a woman in her 30s, tells me about her childhood growing up in Steeltown. In particular, she recalls the disposition of the houses and the temporal/spatial relation to them:

> ...then they were all at home but they all then got to know each other. With the street where I grew up you had your houses in a row, then you had a back road, I called it and then you had your garden. A back road which was about two cars wide. And obviously then your coal-bunkers were round the back. So the back road was like where everyone congregated. You'd go up the garden to peg your washing out and what have you, you'd see next door or two doors down. 'Oh hi ya' and then you'd have a natter with them. They don't sit out the back in the summer, we don't have a game of cricket out the back in the summer, um everyone would get, you know, we'd draw hop scotch out the back in the summer, but today most houses then their gardens are attached to their house and then they're fenced off. So, unless you're sort of six feet tall you don't see anyone from next door.

What is noteworthy about this for me is the careful description of the arrangement of the houses with their back roads, gardens and low fences and the ways in which these spatial arrangements were part and parcel of the affective community. In Deleuze and Guattari's (2004) sense, I think we can say that the affect passes through the houses, back road, gardens just as it passes through people. We could equally understand this in psychoanalytic terms through Bollas's (1992) work on the relation between external and internal objects and the Tavistock Institute's work on collective projections (Trist and Murray, 1990). In addition, as Susan makes clear, this spatiality and organisation of objects is temporally organised. Now, with the steel works closed, she has a higher fence and so cannot talk to people as part of her day-to-day activities. This is further exemplified in the next extract from Susan, in which she tells us that in addition to the issue of the height of the fences, there is also the performance of femininity. As a girl she was able to join in the affective practices of the women in which they used the space to talk to each other and offer emotional support. Now, again, the absence of the space signals for her is a loss of this kind of affective communication:

> Yeah, that's right. Yeah, yeah people did share more with you whether it was personal problems, you know, I can remember my mother and my next door neighbour and her mother. Because she lived next door to her because it was like all little clusters of family, you know, they'd come in, in the evening, or if it was a nice night they'd sit out the front with their little chairs and what have you and you'd talk about really personal, and I used to sit there as a little girl, and listen to it all. And they used to find it really amusing, that, that I wanted to sit there with all the older ladies. I mean I was only 8 or 9 and I'd be sat there listening to them thinking oh and now and again I'd chip in you know. Um, but some of the things they talked about I would never dream of talking about with my neighbours today.
>
> Interviewer (Valerie): Like what?
>
> Financial worries, relationship problems. Even, even maybe if they were having sexual problems with their husband or what have you, you know. It wouldn't be anything rude or anything like that, But it would be like oh God there's something wrong with him lately you know he won't leave me alone and but I don't... I wouldn't be able to speak to my neighbours like that because It's just 'Hello, how are you' you know and that's about as far as the conversation goes. I don't really say a lot else to them. I mean I get in from work, get

> out the car, go in the house, OK, a lot of them do take parcels and things for me. And I mean the street was 30 houses long but everyone knew each other. I always felt that everyone liked each other as well because like I say their husbands worked hard, they were out all day.

Many inhabitants told us of the difficulty in thinking about moving out of the community in order to find work. Even younger people found it difficult to find a valid reason that justified for them the need to move out and be separated from the network of affective relations that they knew and valued. Philip, the 17-year-old son of an ex-steel worker, describes what would count as a valid reason and motive for him to relocate outside his community:

> No, I couldn't move. I'm a local boy like, I got to stay here. I couldn't go anywhere else, no way unless it was a different country where the sun is like, I couldn't move like, no way, 'cos here I know everyone here, I feel comfortable like, but I couldn't move anyway, not knowing anyone unless the weather's there its like very good and different isn't it, but I couldn't do that, I just couldn't.

As Philip says, a key reason for him not to move out is his realisation that he would not know people from other towns and that he wouldn't feel comfortable with people he doesn't know.

This reveals the very strongly communitarian sense of doing things, which is present in memories of some steel workers, who, for example, found work at the steel works because their fathers had worked there and so mates 'looked after' the younger men. However, this nostalgia can be set against the talk of the danger and dirt of the steel works. This is a community founded upon a collective organisation to engage with the exploitative and dangerous conditions, something which has endured for generations.

> It was hairy enough in the works when I first started, obviously, because I was er, um, serving my apprenticeship, when I came out of my time, I worked in the heavy end which, I mean, you have to have your wits about you, it's er, it was a place of, when you've got sort of er, 30, 40, 50 tonnes of molten metal going above your head in a weak ladle, it's, you've got to have your wits about you like.

It could be argued that this collective organisation has been developed to allow the community to exist in a hostile environment. Coal and steel production have been in the area for a long time, and the community has had to endure generation after generation of exploitation and hardship, with periods of relative calm and stability alternating with hardship. It would not be surprising, then, that the workers and their families developed, over generations, ways of coping with and surviving these conditions. I am arguing that the affective organisation of the community and the practices which ensued were to some extent a way of creating safety within danger.

I want to explore this in some detail. That is, it is the rhythms and patterns of everyday life, both materially and emotionally, which held the community in place and provided what is looked back on as a place of safety and security – the terraced houses, the patterns of work organisation, the rhythms of the gendered organisation of work and domestic life, provided a sense of space which allowed the community to feel emotionally contained – what the psychoanalyst Didier Anzieu (1989) calls a psychic envelope and which other schools of psychoanalysis understand as the affective containment of anxieties (Bion, 1994; Mitrani, 1996, for example).

Object relations and relational schools of psychoanalysis argue that the most basic and primary anxieties relate to a baby and child's sense of literal and later emotional holding or containment by the adult caregiver. Those analysts working with children (e.g. Bick, 1968; Mitrani, 1996; Tustin, 1981) set out the difficulties that can occur when a child's sense of containment is not developed. Described as un-integration, this sense is experienced as the absence of a firm boundary of the skin, as though the body is spilling and is uncontained. This can produce terrifying anxiety. In addition, difficult later experiences (usually referred to as trauma) can produce a sense of disintegration or falling apart.

Extending this to groups, Earl Hopper (Gantt and Hopper, 2008) argues that 'trauma activates and provokes the fear of annihilation and its vicissitudes' (p. 106). This can be, he says, expressed phenomenologically as psychic paralysis and the death of psychic vitality. This can be characterised either as clinging together or breaking apart/fragmenting. How does a community which has faced a difficult history provide a sense of containment for its inhabitants? In other words, how can feelings of un- and disintegration be prevented? What affective practices are mobilised to bolster the sense of community and does the community either cling together or fragment in the face of the catastrophe? Could we understand this whole process of providing practices of containment as the manner in which the community survives the constant fear of annihilation which characterises its history? I want to extrapolate from this work, and work with children which usually gets limited to a rather ahistorical notion of a family, to think about the community as a family-like organisation. In fact, so many research participants likened Steeltown to a family that at first I thought they were using the term as a metaphor, but on closer reading, I realised that the everyday practices they were describing (a neighbour feeding and clothing children on a routine basis when the mother couldn't do it, for example, plus a whole sense of the community acting as a quasi-familial support network) were experienced as those of a family.

As Susan says

> As with me yeah, you know, when my Mum was in and out of hospital a lot, you know, and my father was still trying to work shifts in the steel works. To keep the money coming in, my next-door neighbour she was like a mother to me. You know, I'd just go straight in her house, there would be tea on the table for me and my brother, you know, she'd give us clean clothes, she'd go... She'd go in our house... Yeah. I mean, I always said she was like a second mother to me. But that's the way we were. Um, you'd just walk in, in each other's houses, you'd leave your door open, you know, if times were hard you'd help each other out, you'd give someone a lift, you'd take em to the shops, you'd help em if they were sick, you'd cook em some dinner or, you know. But today, I don't feel like you've got that, you can walk down the street now and maybe you won't bump into anyone you know.

Martha echoes this sentiment:

> So the the attitude of people in (Steeltown) is fantastic we're like one big family, it's sort of we're all belonging to one another.

My interest here then is to understand how historically a community such as this has developed affective practices which are familial in character, in the sense that these practices provide basic containment and have developed to deal with the specific circumstances of the steel works and its demands, as well as being a unit through which mutual support could be obtained. I want to argue that the community's practices provide a form of basic containment of anxieties, which both helps to support integration and which also provides a buffer against un- and disintegration (a strike, a tragedy at the works or the closure of the works, for example). Just as psychoanalytic work with children demonstrates the central importance of parenting practices which stress a rhythmical quality – rocking, singing, playing and later, patterns of going and coming, so the affective practices of the community provide a basic sense of being and continuity – that one is and one goes on being in time. This concept of affective containment is produced in what I have called affective practices in which the historically developed ways of coping become sedimented as ways of being and doing things.

Affective practices

I have demonstrated how this emerges in talk about the arrangement of houses, the daily practices of community, the impossibility of moving away and so forth, but we can also find it, I think, in practices of speaking and silence. There are, as people told us, things you can say and things you never talk about. As one man says, there were rules at work about what you could say – you could malign your fellow male workers but never the family – this was considered out of bounds.

Similarly, tacit agreements between workers stated that certain topics were out of bounds, particularly talking about families with workmates. Over the years, communication practices have also evolved within the community to contain difficulties which might damage community cohesion. In particular, these are practices such as not speaking about problems such as depression outside of the family because people have their own problems.

As the wife of a man diagnosed with depression, says

> That was a very difficult time for me, I could cry now urm because I still had to go to work and urm keep the family together urm because at one time he was so poorly that I used to go to work and I didn't know whether he'd be here when I come home, because he was really ill and urm I used to go to work and when you're in work people don't always want to know what's going on at home, you know you go to work you've got to be pleasant you know I've still got to do my job so I didn't tell anybody in work. Oh I told you know my closest workmate that we were having problems and it went on for months and months, didn't let it affect my working life because I still had to go to work and I still had to keep things ticking over, urm didn't miss no time, turned up every day even though I didn't want to go I had to go back to work crying you know and being really upset and it was just awful, it was the worst time that I can remember. All the things

> that have happened to us through the years possibly the worse, it was a very difficult time and urm I never told, like I say I didn't tell many people in work urm and then the one day I just went into work and somebody just asked me a simple question you know and I can't remember what it was now I just broke down. So they sent me home (laugh) they said you can't work like this you know, so they sent me home, I took a couple of days off sorted myself out and just went back. I told my friend in work but (sniff) you know there's only so much you want to say isn't there to a friend I mean you know she's a good friend and but I tried to keep it, I suppose wrongly in a way I tried to keep it private, I didn't even tell my husband's family for instance, they're a really close family and urm even they don't know half of what he was like when he was poorly because we haven't told them. I don't know he just, I suppose you don't want to worry them you know and my husband's sister she's not really been very well so I suppose you didn't want to worry them and you know just try to work through it.

We could perhaps speculate that such practices of speaking and silence, the said and the unsayable, could be said to be part of a necessary defensive organisation that allowed the possibility of social cohesion, the ability to cope without burdening others and the maintenance of feelings of support and solidarity which were necessary for survival. We might also think about the strong chapel tradition with its own injunctions. All of these might be said to bind the community in patterns of affective organisation which allowed it to survive and which defended against anxieties which might threaten the breakdown of the community.

In this sense, the catastrophic closure of the steel works has to be set against the affective practices which make the community work. The loss then is set against these and the loss is experienced not only of the closure and loss of work but the affective practices and rhythms of being and life which have been lost.

Neo-liberalism and globalisation

So what happens when this community faces its own dissolution? If the hypothesis of communities of affect has any validity, we need to understand the closure of the steel works and the production of changed work identities in relation not simply to patterns of global governance, but to what happens locally.

I propose that we need to understand this in at least two ways:

(1) How does a community cope with annihilation of a way of life? What practices are used to stop fragmentation? Are there attempts at 'clinging together' which aim to stop 'falling apart' or vice versa?
(2) How do workers in this kind of community respond to the changed globalised and neo-liberal labour market?

Coping with annihilation

Clearly, this is a topic deserving of a chapter in its own right, but I want to give one small example of an attempt to stop fragmentation which can be understood as defences against the threat of annihilation. It is reported by Sheila, a resident in her 60s, whose late husband was a steel worker, while she owned a market stall and had lived in Steeltown all her life. This is a second interview, in which I am checking out my reading of things she has told me in the first interview. I ask her how she thinks a sense of community might come back. She describes a chain with the miners and steel workers as the links in the chain, which have been broken. We could understand this chain metaphor as implying a chain of continuity of being.

> Well the first link to go was the mines. But that was ok after a while, it was devastating for the miners that was ok really because then some of em could get work here, in the steelworks. Some people moved away but a lot of em came back as well. A lot of the miners came back and the second chain, the second link in the chain was British Steel. When it was announced it was closing. And to me that was a death knell in the town. And everybody stood still, oh my god. And it was like, if that chain was broken and it was flung away and everybody just, they just didn't know what to do none of us really.

For her, it is regeneration which has promised new life for the town. So the break in the chain of being, which the closure of the steel works represents, signals death for the town.

Two issues strike me here. The first is that the mines and steel works are about life and their loss is death. Historically, the mines and steel works are what gave the possibility of life to the valley's communities. It is not overstating the case, to link their loss to death. But taking this further, Sheila goes on to say that the town is like an extended family.

> We're like one big family. The the the families that are here are families that have been here generations. Now let's stand together, shoulder to shoulder. They've put us down we might be down but we're not out. And like the phoenix we will rise from the ashes.

The beginning of the interview confronts us with life and death and rebirth – the chain of being, the death of the town and the phoenix rising through regeneration.

> I I think about 8 9 months and then people started right let's got on with it. We've gotta live our lives. We got children, we've got grandchildren we've gotta keep them here in Steeltown.

The two metaphors of boxing – down but not out and the phoenix present us very powerfully with the community as a family which has been struck by tragedy – there has been a death in the family and the family has to come out of that death and re-establish life for the children and grandchildren still to come. I am struck here by the fact that I am confronted both by an anxiety about death and a libidinal force which tries to get up, move on and revive. How far might we say that the anxiety about death is defended against by the practices of regeneration and the insistence on being down but not out and like a phoenix? Or how far does the stress on those anxieties and their working through prohibit and forestall the creativity immanent in the desire to bring the community back to life?

What I want to dwell on is the way in which Sheila shows a determination to reconnect the links in the chain, to bring the Steeltown family back together. To do this, she draws on affective practices and ways of coping which she says have been handed down for generations, that is, you just get on with it.

> Yes yes it is I I think it is umm when when when you see you see a man lose his job it's err it's terrible, you feel sorry for him you feel sorry for his wife his children. But I I dunno what it is about women they they down for a while and then they just sort of shrug their shoulders and think right, someone gotta do something. And they sort of they have to lift the family. And it's amazing to see it's amazing to see these people who have lost their jobs and I know women that hadn't worked for 15–20 years say right well I'll go and I'll find a job. You stay home and you do the housework and I'll go and I'll find.

So, she states clearly some of the historically developed affective practices through which she and others have learnt to cope with adversity and uncertainty. These practices demand that one carries on; one keeps trouble and grief within the family and just gets on with things. It is this which forms the bedrock of her determination for Steeltown to be a phoenix rising from the ashes. This is how Sheila tells the story of a plan to bring Christmas lights to the town.

> Really I mean erh the council hadn't put any Christmas lights up here for 7 years. And we were the only town without lights and two of the girls that worked here put a piece in the paper and asked people to go to a meeting to raise funds for the lights. So we went along. And my husband said I hope you are going because you have moaned enough about it. I said yes I'm always on to the councilors. I said I they stopped dodging me now when they see me coming so we went along to the meeting out of the whole of Steeltown we had 13 people there. That included the Mayor and the Mayor's driver. Anyhow we formed a committee out of that and the first year we raised £27,000 and had the electrics put through the town. Cos the electrics was no good, and we bought the strings of lights and we bought a stainless steel Christmas tree which cost us over £6,000 and we had umm we had to purchase a lamp post to put it on we had to pay the council money for planning permission to dig a hole. Yeah to put the lamp post. Then down the bottom end, down at Peacocks and that there was nothing for us to attach the lights to so we bought six posts and put those in. And we got lights right from down the bottom end of town right up to here to the market, we got the Christmas tree outside the library. Which we were we're only the second people in Great Britain to have, and we've just added on year to year. We've got over 100 Christmas trees over the shops . . . and we got 3 men that go round every year and put over 100 Christmas trees up we now purchased a welsh dragon and we put that down at the end of the town there. So as you're coming in from the bottom end you can see the dragon, we've purchased the greetings from. Yeah Seasons greetings from Steeltown. And we put that over Weatherspoons. So this year last year we put a lot of electrics in again but this year the money isn't so forthcoming up to now whether we can speed things up and get enough money I don't know but over the last three years we've raised about £50,000.
>
> Oh it is and when we switched the lights on. From Woolworths right the way through the town, right to the bottom you couldn't move.

> It was literally jammed packed. Right the full length from into the town all the way down. So so we had umm I can never think of the man's name he he's broadcaster he is Welsh and I can't remember, never remember the man's name he came and switched the lights on. Erh we had entertainment right through the day. So I was out on the town actually from half past seven in the morning and I finished eight o'clock on the night. I was absolutely shattered but it was wonderful to see that. To see the people's faces when they actually switched on those lights, because what we done, all the town lights were switched off and we put the tree on first cos nobody had ever seen the tree. So we put the tree on first and that was fabulous and then once the people had got used to that then we switched the lights on right through the town. And it it was absolutely wonderful it was the children they were wonderful. Just to watch their faces just children 2, 3, 4, 5 had never seen lights in Steeltown. They had to go elsewhere to see lights. And it was absolutely marvelous. Yeah it it is it is it it people said how lovely it was to come down town shopping at Christmas cos because the lights are on from we always switch them on the last Saturday in November.

She tells me that they also ran car boot sales and bingo to raise more money because it was impossible to get money out of the council. In addition to this, they have since run other activities, also by raising money.

The affective practices that Shelia presents to me suggest that there are established ways for coping with loss and grief and that these must be countered by aiming to bring life back, to mend the link in the chain of being, to allow generational continuity to happen and thus to counter feelings of annihilation. Light in the darkness of the Christmas lights is deeply symbolic of new life and therefore triumph over the death of the town and it is through the creativity immanent in the loss that allows the community to be brought back to life and therefore for the chain to be mended and life to go on.

Adjusting to globalisation and neo-liberalism

If fantasies of bringing the community back to life are demonstrations of the effects of the traumatic and catastrophic closure of the steel works, how might actual redundant workers cope with the loss of old forms of work and work identity and engage with new forms of work? Again, this is a topic deserving of a paper in its own right, but for the purposes of this chapter, I want to divide the responses of workers into two categories: those who do manage to move on and those who are stuck and unable to give up their attachment to the old ways of being, though there are many shades in between and our current research demonstrates how much the shock of the closure circulates amongst all the residents, old and young, men and women. I am not going to review those two kinds of response here, but simply to point to the complex ways of coping and changing which were produced.

The sociological work we took as our baseline at the beginning of the research was the work of Nikolas Rose on governmentality and advanced liberalism (Rose, 1999). This work assumes that advanced liberalism operates through the production of discourses and practices which promote self-management techniques. A rational subject who has choice, freedom and flexibility. And who must continue to develop their work on themselves throughout their lives as lifelong learning in the place of jobs for life (Walkerdine and Bansel, in press). This approach suggests workers alone and cast adrift from others, from communality and collective organisation towards a Robinson Crusoe type of existence which promises freedom at the price of continual working on the self.

Such promises are very powerful and there is no doubt that they are attractive and do have some effectivity in Steeltown. However, what this approach neglects is that experience does not just consist of working on the self, but inheres in the cultural practices and modes of being which have been handed down from the affective practices associated with the steel works. In this sense then, the new modes of governance meet the ways of being and belonging formed by the history of the steel works as I have outlined above. This meeting is a site of creative tension in which new ways of being and managing are created. Within this space, we should not simply expect the steel workers and others in the community simply to drop their previous practices and embrace neo-liberalism. Rather, what we can see are sets of hybrid practices through which members of the community work out ways that things can change in order to preserve most of what existed before. Of course, this applies to older workers. For the young people, the dynamics are more complex as they play out anxieties about loss from the previous generation.

The examples I will give in this section relate to one worker, Colin, in his 40s, who took up suggestions by the trade union that redundant steel workers think of building new work upon their interests and aptitudes. This alone, of course, was a new idea to the workers and we can see it in itself as a neo-liberal move. So, in that sense, a realm of choice and freedom appears before Colin as he moves into work in an entrepreneurial way, becoming a youth and community worker. This requires attendance at university which is challenging for a man who left school with one GCE in Art. This shift is made successfully, however, and it brings huge differences to the daily lives of himself and his family.

Colin thus moved from leaving school with no qualifications to pursing a university degree, while working to support the young people of his town. As he says eloquently, 'I didn't realise there were jobs like this'. The phrase 'I didn't realise there were jobs like this' signals the opening up of a world of work previously unknown, rather than any sense of wanting or needing to work towards a new or better form of work, or for upward class mobility. This shift happened because he mentioned the fact that he enjoyed coaching children at rugby and from this and a first interest in social work, youth and community work was suggested to him.

> Urm, there was I think up three thousand pound per employee, urm, to go in and use the training, basically anything you wanted to do ... but people from Careers Wales came in, urm, other agencies came in to try and find out exactly what your skills were, were there transferable skills you could use from inside sewers you could use outside, urm, obviously what you wanted to do, urm, through coaching rugby and things like that, urm I sort of knew I had a bit of talent with working with kids and that, so my first choice was either, was teacher or social worker ... But the woman said to me, which is another girl that works here, she said have you ever thought of youth work, and I said what does that entail, and she's wrote down a lady's number, she said phone her and make an appointment to go and see her. Found out then that she was the head of the youth service in (the local authority), so I went to see her, started doing a bit of the training, urm, after completing the initial first two sections of the training I enrolled for university, because I knew the money was there and it was only one day a week, so I enrolled for that, started doing a bit of voluntary work in the youth club, urm, two, I think it was, I got accepted for university in the October and started, I managed to get a job with the Prince's Trust, urm, in January, the start of January, urm, and I haven't looked back since then ... if somebody had told me like four and a half years ago that I'd be doing this now, managing people, I'd have told them they was bonkers, complete change but, urm, I'm lucky everything has worked out for me. I didn't realise, when I was still at the steel works, I didn't realise there were jobs like this,

> do you know what I mean? So I'm, I'm fortunate like that, that I've fallen into something that I really enjoy. Compared to the steel works this isn't like a job.

The phrase 'compared to the steel works, this isn't like a job' tells us how he understands the new world of work, not as aspiration but as a revelation in which the rigid boundaries between work and pleasure have been broken down. But what we see is that he had never sought these out. The history of steel work in the area, often done by father and son for generations, produced class-based modes of relationality in which aspiration may have been frowned upon or distanced from. We can glimpse it in phrases like 'class traitor', 'pencil pusher' – a term commonly used by working-class men to describe non-manual workers. These serve to create sets of relations in which difference is 'othered', keeping the community solid. In this instance, however, 'othering' has been forced onto the ex-steel worker and he is able to enter a world about which he knew nothing and which does not feel like work.

Other examples involve workers working from home, for example, where the organisation of time and space is so different from that experienced in the steel works. If we simply look to governmentality, we miss this complexity and the ways that concepts, practices and discourses travel. We miss the complex relationalities in which neo-liberal shifts are received and taken on board.

Conclusion

The shifts described by and undertaken by Colin are enormous and he has found considerable pleasure in the changes, pleasure that could not even have been known about in a community in which son followed father into a steel works which kept the community together and ticking. Clearly, some workers can and do move on and in moving on they engage with neo-liberalism, with enormous consequences for themselves and their families. It is significant that Colin is working with youth in the community to help them build a new future. This too could be understood as an attempt to introduce new ways of fending off fragmentation or 'falling apart' and the fear of annihilation.

Change in worker identity in this analysis cannot be separated from the affective and relational practices of community through which it is produced. Any engagement with forced identity change in rust-belt communities needs to look at the production, disintegration and rebuilding of affective practices and relational ties as a central part of understanding community regeneration and identity change. The affective ties and practices have to be understood as having been produced at specific historical moments and in specific locations. In this case, the history of struggles around the development of iron and steel production from the 18th to the end of the 20th centuries, which brought with it modes of being and belonging, coping and getting by. This period itself contained, no doubt, many moments of trauma: threatened closures, lay-offs, strikes, depressions, hunger, pit disasters in nearby communities and so on. But that history, which brings its own pattern of affective relating, defensively as Hopper suggests, is threatened by the final closure of the works. Here the shared history and shared affective practices no longer work and death stalks the community. It is this death, the threat of annihilation, which produces specific affective responses, from the attempt to bring light into the darkness with the Christmas lights, to a refusal to let go of the past, to the development of new ways of being and coping. Overall, then, I have argued for the need to develop and extend approaches to identity theories so that communities can be understood as communities of affect, placing subjectivities, biographies and identity trajectories in much broader webs of affective relations situated within global economic contexts.

Note

1. This research was conducted with Professor Peter Fairbrother and Dr Luis Jimenez, to whom I am extremely grateful. Although this particular write-up is my responsibility, the research was conducted by us all.

References

Anzieu, D. (1989) *The Skin Ego*. New Haven: Yale University Press.

Bick, E. (1968) The Experience of the Skin in Early Object Relations. *International Journal of Psychoanalysis* 45, 448–466.

Bion, W. (1994) *Clinical Seminars and Other Works*. London: Karnac.

Bollas, C. (1992) *Being a Character: Psychoanalysis and Self Experience*. New York: Hill and Wang.

Deleuze, G. and Guattari, F. (2004) *A Thousand Plateaus*. London: Continuum.

Gantt, S.P. and Hopper, E. (2008) Two Perspectives on a Trauma in Training Group: the Systems-Centred Approach and the Theory of Incohesion. *Group Analysis*, 41(1), 98–112.

Linkon, S.L. and Russo, J. (2002) *Steeltown, USA*. Lawrence, Kansas: University of Kansas Press.

Mitrani, J. (1996) *A Framework for the Imaginary: Clinical Explorations of Primitive States of Being*. New York: Jason Aronson.

Rose, N. (1999) *Powers of Freedom*. Cambridge: Cambridge University Press.

Trist, E. and Murray, H. (eds) (1990) *The Social Engagement of Social Science, Vol 1: The Socio-Psychological Perspective*. London: Free Associations.
Tustin, F. (1981) *Autistic States in Children*. London: Routledge and Kegan Paul.
Walkerdine, V. and Bansel, P. (in press) Neoliberalism, Work and Subjectivity in Two Locations. In M. Wetherell and C. Talpede Mohanty (eds) *The Sage Handbook of Identities*. London: Sage.

4
White Middle-Class Identity Work Through 'Against the Grain' School Choices

David James, Diane Reay, Gill Crozier, Fiona Jamieson, Phoebe Beedell, Sumi Hollingworth and Katya Williams

Introduction

Charles Taylor underlined the inescapably social nature of identity when he wrote '...we are only selves insofar as we move in a certain space of questions' (1990: 34). In this chapter, we examine a particular 'space of questions', namely that of families making and living with choices about secondary schooling. Our research project *Identity, Educational Choice and the White Urban Middle Classes* sought to understand

- Why some white middle-class parents chose urban socially diverse comprehensive schools with average or below average examination results for their children, and how this choice sat with their identities;
- The psychological and social implications of these choices that went against the white middle-class norm;
- The impact on children's identities;
- The effect on social cohesion and the common good.

We were thus concerned with school choice practices and processes in terms of orientations and motivations, and ethnicity and class, and we aimed to investigate how such practices were related to identity and identification in the light of contemporary conceptions of the middle-class self.

The study began in mid-2005 and covered a 30-month period. We interviewed 180 parents and 68 children, from 125 white middle-class households in London and two provincial cities in England, 'Riverton' in the South-West and 'Norton' in the North-East.[1] In each case, families had made a positive choice in favour of a state secondary school that was performing at or below the England average according to conventional examination league-tables. These compare the percentage of pupils gaining five or more high-grade passes in the General Certificate of Secondary Education[2] qualifications. The chosen schools were more ethnically mixed in London than in Riverton or Norton. Interviews took place in the homes of the families. For parents, these covered their own biography and educational background, the process of choosing a secondary school and their experiences of primary and secondary schools. For children, interviews included looking at the part they had played in choices of school, current and past experiences of schooling and their attitudes to social and ethnic diversity.

The study offers insight with regard to some processes in contemporary identity work. In this chapter, we offer a snapshot of three key areas of our analysis: processes which maintain or disrupt the white middle-class habitus; issues of social justice, instrumentality and their relation to civic involvement; and social change and the positioning of the 'other' in white middle-class identity. The chapter concludes with a consideration of identity in relation to the concepts of habitus and field, arguing for the dynamic and relational understanding that these concepts offer.

Maintaining and disrupting white middle-class habitus

The measurement and comparison of secondary school examination results is intended by policy-makers to provide the information needed in a market in which people will make informed choices, thereby rewarding the 'best' schools and bringing to bear a pressure for improvement on lower-performing schools. In this situation, middle-class parents appear to be the ideal consumers because they are likely to be in a position to make choices that will place their children in the best situation for academic achievement.[3] Many fight hard for places in specific, high-performing schools, and this may involve house purchase and moving home, renting an extra address, paying for private schooling, renewing religious allegiances and so forth. Some are prepared to engage in fraud or deception, such as using a false address so that they appear to live closer to a desired school (BBC, 2008; Harvey, 2008).

In contrast, for most of the parents in our sample, crude league-table position had not been regarded a valid indicator of the quality of education on offer in any particular school. Some parents were motivated by a commitment to the welfare state, to state-funded education and to egalitarian ideals, and many were dismissive of privileged educational routes on the grounds that they were socially divisive. Most described themselves as 'left-wing' or 'soft left' or 'liberal', though only a very few were currently politically active in any formal sense. It is worth noting that they were themselves very highly qualified: 83% to degree level, with over a quarter holding some form of postgraduate qualification as well. A high proportion (69% overall) were 'incomers' to the area in which they now lived, and in 70% of families, one or both parents worked in the public sector.

Family history, and especially parental experiences of schooling, appeared to function as a key point of reference for contemporary and recent choices of school. A majority (59%) of the parents had themselves attended either selective state or private schools (32% and 27%, respectively), with many of the latter having been highly focused on academic achievement. A number of the parents spoke in detail about a wish to avoid aspects of their own schooling being repeated in that of their children, essentially on 'identity' grounds. Negative experiences of private schooling were frequently cited. John Levy, a London parent, offered one of the more forthright rejections of private schooling and its role in identity making. He had himself been to a well-known major boys' independent school. His parents were established upper middle class:

> My own experience of education has had an enormous effect on me not just in terms of my views about my children's education but I'd say just about everything, my outlook on life, how I view the world. I think I could trace it all back to what happened or rather started to happen to me at 7. At 7 I got sent away to a prep boarding school... that was bad enough, the sense of being exiled. I missed my family, my mother in particular, terribly. But you know that was what families like ours did and it was bruising.

We gain a sense, in what he went on to say, of the ways in which earlier experiences are internalised, becoming layers of dispositions onto which later layers are melded:

> I think I took on the ethos, absorbed it to the extent I began to think it was normal and I suppose that isn't unsurprising because alongside the brutality there was friendship, support, you know, a whole lot of nurture. You bought into the package and to an extent just got on with it. But in retrospect a lot of it was horrific, as I said brutal and

> brutalising. But there was another aspect I found deeply troubling when I looked back that we all just took for granted at the time, that it was incredibly limited socially, a sort of complacent sameness.

John's view of private schooling also appeared to be shaped by two other facets. The first was seeing his brother become very ill whilst at (the same) school. He told us '(elite, private) school was supposed to make upper middle class men of us but it crushed my brother'. The second was the narrowness of the education as a preparation for life, and he spoke at length about having to confront this later in life in order to become equipped to work successfully in his profession as a criminal lawyer. Such experiences gave him reason to turn his back on generations of family tradition when it came to his own children. He talked of a pivotal moment when he read somewhere

> ...that Daniel Day Lewis had been to an urban comprehensive. I remember thinking that's alright then. I don't know how many qualms his father had but he's come out creative and fairly sussed so you can choose that for your kids and they can survive. And I do remember thinking when I read it, and the children were very young at the time, this is good.

In other cases, more convoluted processes of school choice were nevertheless equally telling as regards the importance of family habitus. Annie Denton in Riverton reflected on her own schooling and spoke about how she went to her 'mother's old school, which was a boarding school in Ballywater, as a day girl, and absolutely hated it'. She objected to the great stress placed on academic achievement, but also to the isolation of her situation:

> Well I had no awareness of the outside world at all. Talk about an ivory tower – in an all girls school, you're completely...well I was completely cocooned...and I think worse so than the Riverton schools, because I think the Riverton schools, even then, had a sort of social overlap you know...I was in Ballywater, by the sea – you might as well have been on a planet, on the moon really.

This experience was a key one in the decision by Annie and her husband to reject what she called the 'natural' choice of private education being made by many of their current friends for children now reaching secondary school age. The Dentons' first preference was that their children should go to nearby high-performing state schools, but this became more complex when it transpired that Ralph, one of their three children, had special educational needs. Annie told us that this fact had 'taken her slightly outside the general soup of what parents . . . our social group, look at'. It had 'made us rethink a lot of our own attitudes to things . . . it liberates you from that whole middle class thing actually'. She was advised by a teacher within Mountstevens (a nearby high-performing state secondary school, formerly a Grammar school) not to send Ralph there because the school's focus on maintaining its high league-table position detracted from the quality of support that would be available. This brought Redwood School, the local comprehensive, into contention:

> I was beginning to think . . . and I said 'Redwood School's our next option, (but) no child of mine is ever going to go to Redwood, you know, dreadful place'. And all my middle class prejudices came back and we went to see a solicitor . . . and she said 'If you want to put him into Waterford, you're going to have to prove . . . that Riverton can't meet your needs, so you're going to have to go and have a look at Redwood'. So I thought – it was a complete, you know, dragging myself through the gates with my nose in the air, I'll be brutally honest. But went in, met the special needs lady and thought 'She's really nice'. Really nice room, nice feel to it, nice atmosphere, you know, gut instinct really. And I just thought wherever he goes, he's not going to find it easy, but I think the support mechanism is here. So I came out and thought well for better or worse, we haven't got a lot of choice, we'll send him here . . . I spent all the summer holidays trying not to worry about it. He's gone there, I'm not sure academically he's doing great things, but he's incredibly happy for the first time ever.

Annie was particularly keen that her son should not become 'cocooned'. She called Redwood a 'full-on city comprehensive' where he would either 'sink or swim'. However, her other two children attended Mountstevens and Hammerton (an above-average performing, out-of-town school), respectively. Emma, the one at Hammerton, went to the induction day at Redwood, and the experience speaks strongly of the family habitus and how, if it is sufficiently adrift of field, the habitus finds itself as a 'fish out of water':

> (We had decided) she was going to go to Redwood . . . we'd been lulled I think, by Ralph's experience. It's not a popular school, it's not the

school of choice for parents around here, Redwood just isn't. So we didn't even look at another school for her, she was going to go to Redwood and she was fine about it, but no girl was going from her school. She went to the induction day, I just dropped her off – fine, but how wrong I was. And I think also because of the other two, because sometimes I can take my eye off the ball with her a bit, like my parents did with me, just think 'Emma's probably the age where she's going to get on with it'. And I picked her up and she was practically hysterical, which is unlike her, she's very straightforward, and she just looked at me in that way that you think I can't actually ignore this... She said 'Please don't send me there'... So she went down for a day, absolutely, absolutely hated it.

Interviewer: What did she dislike most or did you not get to the bottom of it?

No, I absolutely got to the bottom of it and I knew the minute she said 'Please don't send me there'. I knew she's too middle class... she didn't see anybody there that... she didn't know anybody which I think is a disadvantage for any child. And I think it does come down to identity really. (I said) 'well you can't tell me that everybody in your tutor group was horrible'. She said 'they weren't horrible, but nearly everybody came up to me and said, you're really posh aren't you?'

Interviewer: And her friends had gone elsewhere?

All gone elsewhere. There were a lot going to the private sector.

This episode resulted in Emma going instead to Hammerton with her best friend, as Annie described it 'my sanity and her happiness had to come above all other worthy principles... at the end you have to go against your principles because actually I thought by sticking to them, I'm actually not doing what's right for her as an individual'.

In other interviews with parents who had been to private schools, the focus was not so much on the narrowness of the curriculum or experiences of discomfort or distress, but on their distaste for the kind of social reproduction that they felt such schools fostered. In Norton, Ella Rosen and her husband both came from families where everyone went to private school, yet she spoke of the worrying tendency for those in power in government and civil service to have been to such schools, in turn making them detached from the lives of everyone else. This was a view we heard frequently. In another Norton family, Libby Greensit did not express any specific or personal disappointment with her own private education, but nevertheless expressed a strong commitment to locality and state education. Libby Greensit was a GP, and she argued that both schools and the health service needed to work for everyone. In these and other examples, personal experiences of private education underpinned a point of principle, and contemporary professional experience had sharpened an awareness of the effects of privileged schooling. Even so, in many families, parents talked as Libby did about 'going private' remaining as a last resort if things went wrong with the choices that had been made.

Social justice, instrumentality and civic involvement

Contemporary political concerns about social cohesion often focus on segregation between schools and communities. We were interested to see whether counter-intuitive school choice made a positive contribution to social mixing, and therefore, potentially, to social cohesion. Our research found segregation *within* schools with white middle-class children clustered in top sets. They were often benefiting from 'Gifted and Talented' schemes, which channel extra resources into schools for

> ...those who have one or more abilities developed to a level significantly ahead of their year group (or with the potential to develop those abilities). *Gifted* describes learners who have the ability to excel academically in one or more subjects such as English, drama, technology; *Talented* describes learners who have the ability to excel in practical skills such as sport, leadership, artistic performance, or in an applied skill.
>
> (Department for Children, Schools and Families, 2008)

The scheme is controversial, and a significant proportion of primary and secondary schools were avoiding participation in it at the time of our study. The Government's own figures showed that black students were seriously under-represented on the scheme, and this led one observer to a diagnosis of institutional racism (Gillborn, 2005) and may have prompted a recent revision of the web-based description of the scheme, which now stresses 'the expectation that there are gifted and talented learners in every year group in every school', and that because 'ability is evenly distributed throughout the population, a school's gifted and talented pupils should be broadly representative of its whole school population' (ibid).

Despite the often declared hopes of parents that their children would make friends across ethnic groups, on the whole, friends were other white middle-class children. The children in our study rarely had working-class friends and their few minority ethnic friends were predominantly from middle-class backgrounds and were high achieving. There was much evidence of *social mix* but far less evidence of *social mixing*. Both parents' and children's attitudes towards classed and ethnic others sometimes displayed a perception of cultural and intellectual superiority that would work against social cohesion and the development of common ground and common understandings. Even in this group of pro-welfare, left-leaning parents there was little declared support for measures to tackle inequalities; few made any protest at the schools' intent upon further advantaging their own children by allocating them to the 'Gifted and Talented' Scheme, even though they were openly critical of it in a more abstract sense. Furthermore, whilst many of the children also appeared to have an understanding of wider social inequalities, this did not transfer to understanding the consequences of material disadvantage for educational attainment. Rather, achievement and social mobility were usually seen to be matters that reflected the inherent qualities of different individuals.

A surprisingly high proportion of families contained at least one parent who was currently serving or had served as a school governor (57% in London, 43% in Riverton and 22% in Norton families). Across the sample there were 11 chairs of governors. Becoming a school governor appeared rooted in a desire to make a civic contribution, but as with the many other explicit connections with schools (friendships with teachers or the Head, or professional links with education), it also appeared to be a way of managing the risks in sending children to inner city state schooling. In turn, schools seemed especially responsive to the wishes and concerns of white middle-class parents and their children.

Beyond governorship there was little civic and other local engagement that might indicate explicit contributions to social cohesion. Amongst participants, the most politically active parents were in the London sample (22%), where there were three Labour party activists, a chair of the local neighbourhood society, a couple who were campaigning against a local Academy (a new school to be built in partnership with private capital and control) and two members of a pressure group, the Campaign for State Education. However, for the most part, political activism and civic engagement lay in our parents' past histories, and many talked about their disillusionment with politics, and in particular, New Labour, following the Iraq invasion. Almost all talked about their commitment to the welfare state. The communitarian ideals that were once actively pursued by many of the parents had mostly given way to pragmatism and pessimism about the possibilities of political action and community involvement. However, this is not to posit some kind of loss of moral bearings. Most of the parents worked as public sector professionals, and they sometimes cited beliefs about their work in a general support for public sector institutions. But rather than expressing recognisably political positions in relation to public sector provision, support for state education tended to be voiced in terms of individual morality and what was ethically desirable, and in terms of what sorts of people their children would become (see Crozier et al., 2008: 265). As Audrey (a GP, in Norton) put it:

> I don't want my children to think you know, that everybody's got a holiday house in Sardinia, and everyone's daddy drives a four by four and you know and everyone you know can go to tennis club and squash club and blah, blah, blah, have holidays skiing and this that and the other. You know, they've got to realise that you know not everyone does that, we're not all the same... and I just think, God, if everybody would just go to state schools it would be so much better, but a lot of people don't.

Social change and the positioning of the 'Other'

Parental accounts of these school choices often made reference to broad ideas about 'how the world has changed', and how such changes had to be prepared for when it came to their children. There were strong perceptions that society had fundamentally shifted in nature since these parents themselves went to school. Though often expressed in vague terms, we can sum up these perceptions by saying that for these parents, society had become more cosmopolitan and multicultural, more globally connected and more uncertain in terms of the routes and trajectories it appeared to offer their children. It is worth noting that these perceptions have considerable overlap with analyses offered by some influential sociologists (e.g. Elias, 1991; Giddens, 1991, and see De Jong, 2001). There is a specific resonance with Giddens, and with the connection between his notion of the reflexive, self-mastering person and the ideology of liberal individualism (see Elliott, 2001).

Echoing the views of independent schools mentioned earlier, some State schools that were characterised by high examination pass-rates were regarded by the parents as too narrow in their social composition and focus – as not providing the sort of socialisation that would best equip a young person for the way the world had become. In contrast, the social and ethnic diversity of many of the chosen comprehensive schools was seen as inclusive and as providing conditions for generating multicultural harmony. It produced children who were 'socially fluent and adaptable', more 'worldly' and 'more resilient'. Some parents explicitly referred to their children's exposure to instances of racist abuse and language, or to certain social problems they associated with race or ethnicity, as important opportunities to learn. Many appeared to regard social and ethnic diversity as a cultural resource for the 'production of the ethical self' (see Skeggs, 2005: 973) and as the basis for an education that would leave their children able to deal with a more complicated and globalised world (see Crozier et al., 2008). Comprehensive schooling was thus explicitly valued as an opportunity to put democratic, civic values into practice as well as for the related identity work it could perform. Avril Smart, a journalist in the London sample put it like this

> There is definitely something about producing a different kind of middle-class child. This is a speculation but I think there is definitely something about not being arrogant or not appearing arrogant. There is some kind of modesty that some people might see as them not being confident. You are not being educated to be a woman of the world; you are being educated to take your part, a place. And I think there is an understanding of others you can only have if you are sort of with them all the time. It is something to learn of other cultures, but to actually learn with other cultures, of other cultures, it is a completely different thing.

Our data also led us to look closely at 'whiteness', and our analysis suggested that some of the white middle-class parents saw themselves as 'a darker shade of pale', that is, as occupying a white ethnic identity that was distinguished by its cosmopolitan acceptance and tolerance of ethnic diversity and even its anti-racism. However, this notion of whiteness was also constructed in opposition to that of both the white working classes and those white middle classes who made more conventional middle-class school choices (see Reay et al., 2007). There were many negative references to white working-class young people, some of which suggested fear or contempt. Terms like 'white trash', 'chav' or 'charver' were quite common. In these and other ways, counter-intuitive school choice exposes rifts and tensions that are normally held apart by more conventional patterns of school choice (see Crozier et al., 2008).

Identity and habitus

We were struck by the frequency with which some parents expressed anxieties about their choice of school, and the associated close monitoring of progress and experience which we have elsewhere termed 'parental managerialism' (James and Beedell, 2009). To the extent that we can generalise, there was considerable concern about these children doing well, and slightly more anxiety amongst 'first generation' middle-class parents than those from more established middle-class backgrounds. The asset of social diversity also brought dangers, because young people might come to identify with 'the other'. At the same time, the parents in our study seemed more certain in their choices than the middle-class parents making more conventional middle-class choices in Ball's study (Ball, 2003).

We suggest that whilst the difficulties and anxieties expressed were genuine, they need to be understood against the backdrop of resources that appeared to generate confidence. Firstly, there was the acknowledged capacity, in many families, to change tack and change schools – sometimes to 'go private' – should the need arise. Secondly, there seemed to be a general 'sociological' appreciation that, other things being equal, white middle-class children can be expected to do well in education. We have evidence that this last point is an important source of cultural capital, because there were instances where both parents and schools acted in explicit acknowledgement of it. Parents spoke a great deal in terms of their children being 'bright', 'floating to the top', 'rising to their natural place' or being able to stand out in a way that would be more difficult in a higher-achieving school. Schools, for their part, went to great lengths to attract, and then hold on to, middle-class students.[4] This suggests that there is more at stake than the serving of mutual interests: There is also a process akin to Giddens' *double hermeneutic* (Elliott, 2001) where both parents and schools operate in the light of well-established knowledge derived from the social sciences, particularly explanations about the relationship between social class and education. In other words, this knowledge has become part and parcel of the actions it was derived to explain (see James et al., in press).

The following quote, from a Riverton family, is telling in this respect. We had been talking about whether, in retrospect, the choice of school was a good one:

Father: ... I feel vindicated...
Mother: Yes, I do (too).

> Father: ... in that because our feeling is that we're not interested in results, we're not interested in percentages of A–Cs, what we're interested in is what our own children are going to achieve. So it could be that a year group do appallingly, but if the teachers have given our children *the opportunity to rise to their natural place* and get the qualifications that they're capable of, a good teacher will work with children and if they have *one bright child* in that class they should be able to take them *where they need to go.*
>
> (Tom Foster & Trudy Henderson) (emphases added)

The Hendersons here expressed a recurring theme in our data, where many parents seemed to recognise, without articulating it directly, that the social background of their own children offered forms of capital that were readily converted into academic success. In Bourdieusian terms, this is a form of *misrecognition,* and is fundamental to the role of education in structures of social inequality.

There are many different definitions and ways of understanding 'identity'. Our data highlighted for us the utility of Bourdieu's concepts of *habitus* and *field* in making sense of some of the identity work that is attempted and achieved through school choice and schooling. There are several useful commentaries on the strengths, promise and limitations of these concepts (see for example Grenfell and James, 1998; 2004; Nash, 1999; Reay, 2004; Sayer, 2005). Here we will confine ourselves to one well-used example of Bourdieu's own attempts to describe the purpose and reach of the terms:

> The notion of habitus ... is relational in that it designates a mediation between objective structures and practices. First and foremost, habitus has the function of overcoming the alternative between conscious and unconscious ... Social reality exists, so to speak, twice, in things and in minds, in fields and in habitus, outside and inside agents. And when habitus encounters a social world of which it is the product, it finds itself 'as a fish in water', it does not feel the weight of the water and it takes the world about itself for granted.
>
> (Bourdieu in interview with Wacquant, in Bourdieu, 1989: 43)

Educational processes have a particularly important place in the development of habitus:

> The habitus acquired in the family underlines the structuring of school experiences ... and the habitus transformed by schooling,

> itself diversified, in turn underlies the structuring of all subsequent experiences (e.g. the reception and assimilation of the message of the culture industry or work experiences) and so on, from restructuring to restructuring.
>
> (Bourdieu, 1977: 87)

Here, Bourdieu helps us see the high stakes of school choice in the formation of identities. Schooling is 'itself diversified', and choosing a school may appear as the *only* significant opportunity that parents have to influence, beyond the home setting, the further development of the established *habitus* of their child. It is important to underline that habitus does not only refer to a process of cognitive acquisition, and that it is a much less individualised notion than 'personality' (see Burkitt, 1991; Grenfell and James, 1998). It refers to the embodiment of social relationships and positions, so that they become dispositions. These add up to a sense of reality, of limits and possibilities, and are mostly about difference and diversity and knowledge of where one sits in a particular *field*. Habitus sets a frame for what individuals do, without narrowly determining their agency.

Conclusion

> Relational aspects of schooling choice reverberate within and down the generations; and whether family hierarchies and traditions are followed, broken or adjusted; they comprise measures against which current choice is made, shaping the way schooling is consumed and identity formed.
>
> (Allatt, 1996: 170)

We were able to say with some confidence that a general outcome of 'against the grain' school choice was a confirmation of the white middle-class identities of the young people, though these identities were forged quite differently to those of most parents. The spread across a range of ages enabled us to see that all those who were old enough to have completed GCSEs did well, and that the vast majority of those who were old enough to go to University did so (with a very high proportion [15%] of these going to England's two most prestigious universities). However, for present purposes, we concentrate on how the study offers insights into processes of identity formation, and how the concept of *habitus*, together with *field*, helps us capture something of the inherently relational and dynamic nature of this identity work. The parents and children in our study were, as far as we could tell, acting in good faith and doing their best to cope with a rapidly changing, marketised system. They were coping with anxiety producing situations which, at many junctures, challenged or compromised their values. At the same time, they acted in ways that would advantage their children and which could, possibly, disadvantage other children. As a research team, we felt much empathy: the participants were 'people like us' (most members of the research team were white and middle class and some had children who attended ordinary state comprehensive schools – see Reay et al., 2007).

The general point we wish to underline here may seem an obvious one to those who have followed the history and location of changing conceptions and practices of the self (what Rose called the 'genealogy of subjectification' [1998: 23]). At its simplest, it is that a focus on 'the individual', whilst important, is only one, rather narrow perspective, on questions of identity. What our analysis shows is that whatever else it is, identity is always necessarily a product and enactment of social relations. There are two senses in which this appears to happen. Firstly, for all their uniqueness and creativity in making lives that are 'liveable', most people cannot realistically avoid the 'steer' that their habitus gives them (Bourdieu, in describing the problematic social location of the petite bourgeoisie, described a particularly impotent view of the world as 'a dream of social flying, a desperate attempt to defy the gravity of the social field' – 1984: 370). The conditions for identity formation via education are of course shifted by the aggressive promulgation of policies to put in place a more diverse and marketised system of school choices and the accompanying inherent concept of the individualised, enterprising self-as-consumer (Rose, 1998). Yet these shifts do not magically or completely recast all the players in a new image or erase other long-standing modes of engagement between individuals and institutions. Habitus remains key, and what our study suggests is that a relative abundance of capital in white middle-class families does not just yield advantages to those making 'good', conventional choices in the educational market: it also favours those making what some would term 'bad' choices (James et al., in press).

Secondly, when people engage in social spaces such as opportunities for educational choice and in schools themselves, they are not mere recipients of a set of services of a particular 'quality': They develop, confirm or disconfirm aspects of their own social identities *and at the same time*, those of other people (see Brantlinger, 2003). In considering identity, then, concepts like *habitus* and *field* offer us a shift in insight parallel to the one that Einstein's physics represents over its Newtonian forerunner. This is a shift away from the illusion that identities in a social world are to be understood *primarily* via individuals who happen to interact, towards seeing that people's positioning in current and previous fields and the relationships between them are just as important.

Notes

1. 'Riverton' and 'Norton' are pseudonyms. We also used pseudonyms for all individuals and schools in the study.
2. General Certificate in Secondary Education (GCSE) examinations are normally taken by 14–16 year olds, and constitute the main qualifications at the end of compulsory secondary schooling. The proportion of students gaining five passes at higher grades is widely used as a performance indicator, especially at school and local authority level. See for example http://www.direct.gov.uk/en/EducationAndLearning/QualificationsExplained/DG_10039024 (accessed June 2008).
3. The system in England combines both choice and entitlement. Every child is offered a place in a state secondary school by their Local Authority, but parents may seek a place in any other school, and many do this – often taking into account the percentage of high examination passes. If a school has more applications than places, it will use a combination of factors set out in a formula by the Local Authority (factors like distance of home from school or whether there are already older siblings in the school). There is also a system of Appeals for parents who are not happy with any place they have been offered. Any parent can opt out of the State system, if they have the money, and pay for private secondary schooling. For a summary of the current situation, see for example http://www.parentscentre.gov.uk/educationandlearning/choosingaschool/schoolchoiceyourrights/ (accessed June 2008).
4. 'Critical mass' was a regular theme in interviews with parents (i.e. so that the white middle-class child would not be alone, or not completely alone). In one of our discussions with a head teacher, he spoke of trying to forestall this fear by meeting middle-class parents whilst their children were still in Primary school to 'persuade them all to jump at once' (and to his disappointment, on the particular occasion, only one or two of them actually 'jumped' in his direction).

References

Allatt, P. (1996) Consuming Schooling: Choice, Commodity, Gift and Systems of Exchange. In S. Edgell, K. Hetherington and A. Warde (eds) *Consumption Matters: The Production and Experience of Consumption*. Oxford: Blackwell.

BBC (2008) 'More Parents Lie to Get Schools' BBC News online, 19 March 2008, Available at http://news.bbc.co.uk/1/hi/education/7304588.stm (accessed 7 June 2009).

Ball, S. J. (2003) *Class Strategies and the Educational Market: The Middle Classes and Social Advantage*. London: Routledge.

Bourdieu, P. (1977) *Outline of a Theory of Practice* (R. Nice, trans.). Cambridge: Cambridge University Press.

Bourdieu, P. (1984) *Distinction: A Social Critique of the Judgement of Taste.* London: Routledge.

Bourdieu, P. (1989) in L.Wacquant, Towards a Reflexive Sociology: A Workshop with Pierre Bourdieu. *Sociological Theory* 7, 26–63.

Brantlinger, E. (2003) *Dividing Classes. How the Middle Class Negotiates and Rationalises School Advantage.* London: Routledge.

Burkitt, I. (1991) *Social Selves: Theories of the Social Formation of Personality.* London: Sage.

Crozier, G., Reay, D., James, D., Jamieson, F., Beedell, P., Hollingworth, S. and Williams, K. (2008) White Middle-Class Parents, Identities, Educational Choice and the Urban Comprehensive School: Dilemmas, Ambivalence and Moral Ambiguity. *British Journal of Sociology of Education* 29(3), 261–272.

De Jong, M. J. (2001) Elias and Bourdieu: The Cultural Sociology of Two Structuralists in Denial. *International Journal of Contemporary Sociology* 38(1), 64–86.

Department for Children, Schools and Families (2008) *Standards Site*, Available at http://www.standards.dfes.gov.uk/giftedandtalented/who/ (accessed October 2008).

Elias, N. (1991) *The Society of Individuals.* Oxford: Blackwell.

Elliott, A. (2001) *Concepts of the Self.* Cambridge: Polity Press.

Giddens, A. (1991) *Modernity and Self-Identity.* Cambridge: Polity.

Gillborn, D. (2005) Written Evidence on the Education White Paper (2005): Race Inequality, 'Gifted & Talented' Students and the Increased Use of 'Setting by Ability'. Available at http://www.ioe.ac.uk/schools/efps/GillbornRaceEqualityandTheWhitePaper.doc (accessed October 2008).

Grenfell, M. and James, D. (1998) *Bourdieu and Education: Acts of Practical Theory.* London: Falmer.

Grenfell, M. and James, D. (2004) Change in the Field – Changing the Field: Bourdieu and the Methodological Practice of Educational Research. *British Journal of Sociology of Education* 25(4), 507–523.

Harvey, M. (2008) 'Parents who cheat at school' *The Times*, 29th April 2008. Available at: http://women.timesonline.co.uk/tol/life_and_style/women/families/article3840412.ece (accessed 10 June 2008).

James, D. and Beedell, P. (2009) Transgression for Transition? White Urban Middle Class Families Making and Managing 'Against the Grain' School Choices. In K. Ecclestone, G. J. J. Biesta and M. Hughes (eds) *Transitions and Learning Through the Lifecourse.* London and New York: Routledge.

James, D., Crozier, G., Reay, D., Jamieson, F., Beedell, P., Hollingworth, S., and Williams, K. (in press) Neoliberal Policy and the Meaning of Counter-Intuitive Middle Class School Choices. *Current Sociology* 58(4) (Special Issue on Education in a Globalising World).

Nash, R. (1999) Bourdieu, 'Habitus', and Educational Research: Is it all Worth the Candle? *British Journal of Sociology of Education* 20, 175–187.

Reay, D. (2004) It's all Becoming a Habitus: Beyond the Habitual use of Habitus in Educational Research. *British Journal of Sociology of Education* 25 (4), 431–444.

Reay, D., Crozier, G., James, D., Hollingworth, S., Williams, K., Jamieson, F. and Beedell, P. (2007) A Darker Shade of Pale? Whiteness, the Middle Classes and Multi-Ethnic Inner City Schooling. *Sociology* 41 (6), 1041–1060.

Rose, N. (1998) *Inventing Ourselves: Psychology, Power and Personhood*. Cambridge: Cambridge University Press.
Sayer, A. (2005) *The Moral Significance of Class*. Cambridge: Cambridge University Press.
Skeggs, B. (2005) The Making of Class and Gender through Visualizing Moral Subject Formation. *Sociology* 39(5), 965–982.
Taylor, C. (1990) *Sources of the Self*. Cambridge, Mass: Harvard University Press.

Part II
Ethnicities and Encounters

5
Ethnicities Without Guarantees: An Empirical Approach

Roxy Harris and Ben Rampton[1]

Introduction

What can the close study of everyday interactional life in a multi-ethnic urban setting reveal to us about contemporary ethnicity? Both in public debate and social science research over the last 50 years or so in the UK, the discussion of race and ethnicity has centred on conflict, discrimination, racism/anti-racism, equal opportunities policies and so on, placing ongoing struggle between clearly demarcated dominant and subordinated racial and ethnic groups in the foreground. In the process, overwhelming attention has been given to explicit (and often sincere) propositions and statements, whether these are the utterances or labels produced by social actors in the public arena (e.g. the 2006 Jade Goody/Shilpa Shetty controversy on British TV's 'Big Brother'), the views expressed by research subjects in qualitative interviews, or the conclusions drawn by quantitative survey research about race/ethnicity and differential outcomes in, for example, educational achievement.

There have been very good reasons for the dominance of this idiom, and this chapter in no way seeks to underplay the continuing prevalence and pernicious effects of racism. But the dominant perspective rarely looks beyond explicit statements to *non-propositional* expression and the many ways in which race and ethnicity are *indirectly* evoked, performed or noted in the ordinary encounters of everyday life. This chapter starts to repair this neglect, pursuing an interest in the emergence and negotiation of 'liveable lives' and identities within the fleeting contingencies of interaction. Focusing on the spontaneous activity of a group of 14-year-old girls at a multiethnic, multilingual London comprehensive school in 2005–2006, it uses linguistic ethnography to go beyond the surface meaning of words to dimensions of race and ethnic relations that are often overlooked.

We begin by outlining the forces that have shaped the dominant race/ethnicity idiom in Britain, and then move to the reconceptualisations of ethnicity provided by Hall and Gilroy. There are grounds, though, for questioning the success of empirical social science in coming to terms with Hall and Gilroy's 'new' and 'convivial' ethnicities. So in the rest of the chapter, the second section provides a glimpse of the kinds of everyday interaction in which such ethnicities emerge; the third takes a closer look, drawing on the resources of linguistic ethnography; and the last concludes by pointing (a) to the kinds of account that linguistic ethnography helps us circumvent and (b) to reasons for preferring it to research based primarily on interviews (or questionnaires).

Old and new thinking about race/ethnicity

What we are calling the dominant idiom on race/ethnicity has been influential throughout the period from 1945 to the present day, and with a little arbitrary license, we can divide this into three phases: 1945–1975, 1975–1997 and 1997–2008.

The phase 1945–1975 began with the dominance of social, economic and political systems which were explicitly committed to racial hierarchy, sustained by direct colonial rule in the European Empires (British, French, Dutch, Belgian, Portuguese, etc.), by segregation (USA), and by apartheid (South Africa). The challenge to these systems increased throughout the period, and culminated in their overthrow or serious weakening. There was an important catalyst to this process of change in the rhetorical claim that the allies were fighting World War II to preserve freedom and democracy – in 1941, Churchill and Roosevelt had initiated The Atlantic Charter, a ringing declaration that democracy and human rights for all were essential international requirements. In London, in 1944, black and brown colonial subjects responded with a Charter for Coloured Peoples which they circulated worldwide, demanding that the British state make good its Atlantic Charter commitments (Ramdin, 1987). The following year, the historic 5th Pan-African Congress was held in Manchester to articulate a demand for colonial freedom (Adi and Sherwood, 1995), and after World War II, challenges to explicit systems of racism took a variety of forms. There were (i) *Independence struggles*, movements for independence from colonial rule taking the form of mainly mass movements of civil protest (e.g. the

Caribbean, West Africa, India); (ii) *Liberation movements*, armed struggles for independence from colonial rule (e.g. Kenya, Malaya, Mozambique, Angola, Guinea Bissau); and (iii) *Civil Rights movements*, particularly in the US (e.g. Martin Luther King, the Black Power Movement [Black Panthers + Malcolm X]).

Changing gear away from attempts to suppress these challenges, in the phase 1975–1997 a settlement emerged in the US and UK acknowledging that racial discrimination existed, was wrong, and should be countered (as a minimum) by state interventions in support of (nominal) racial equality and against discriminatory practices (c.f. the UK Race Relations Acts 1965, 1968, and the comprehensive 1976 Race Relations Act). The definition of *institutional racism* provided by Stokely Carmichael and Charles V. Hamilton in the US played a key part in precipitating this change:

> Racism is both overt and covert. It takes two, closely related forms: individual whites acting against individual blacks, and acts by the total white community against the black community. We call these individual racism and institutional racism. The first consist of overt acts by individuals, which cause death, injury or the violent destruction of property. This type can be recorded by television cameras; it can frequently be observed in the process of commission. The second type is less overt, far more subtle, less identifiable in terms of *specific* individuals committing the acts. But it is no less destructive of human life. The second type originates in the operation of established and respected forces in the society, and thus receives far less public condemnation than the first type.
>
> (1967, 20, original emphasis)

This stimulated the idea that state institutions could counter racism with systems of ethnic monitoring for all official bodies. Monitoring would provide a ready and practical way of disclosing racially inspired discrimination and disadvantage, leading in turn to remedial action, at least by implication. Critics would argue that state interventions of this kind were only ever symbolic, tokenistic and deliberately designed to leave racially constructed power structures and relations intact. Nevertheless, these schemes typically involved special funding allocations, building on the racial/ethnic classifications and labels through which the obligatory ethnic monitoring procedures were conducted. Since 1997 in the UK, the 'New Labour' Government has consolidated legally backed actions against institutional racism, as in, for example, the relatively comprehensive Race Relations Amendment Act (2000). This has been supported by moves to strengthen the visibility of black and brown people in Parliament and at the highest levels of the governmental apparatus, and more generally, their appearance in wider spheres of public life has become more normal.

Throughout the post-World War II period, group classifications have been highly problematic. The British Empire was deft at using both *racial* and *ethnic* categories. On the one hand, notions of race reinforced a commonsense in which 'white European' was superior, 'black' was inferior and 'brown' was in between (as in the North American rhyme 'if you're white you're all right, if you're brown stick aroun', if you're black get back'), while on the other, ethnicity was deployed as a subtle tool to divide and rule subordinate colonised populations (e.g. within Africa, Asia or the Caribbean). With ethnic monitoring in the period from 1975 onwards, 'ethnicity' started to displace race as the pre-eminent discursive construct, but there was still a tension between a residual concentration on relations of dominance (race) and the emerging focus on relations of difference (ethnicity). Monitoring itself tended towards a tripartite conceptualisation of *'white'* (the majority of the British population), *'black'* (people of Caribbean and/or African descent) and *'Asian'* (Indian, Pakistani, Bangladeshi), and there was often a confusion between *colour* (with implied notions of biological race – 'White', 'Black'), *nationality* ('Pakistani', 'Bangladeshi') and *ethnicity* ('Asian'). Even policy-makers acknowledged the practical problems involved in ethnic monitoring, with 'other' and 'unclassified' becoming an increasingly significant category in survey returns (more than a third in e.g. the monitoring of schools – DfE, 1995; Harris, 1997: 16–18).

More fundamentally and whatever the labelling used, there was an essentialist tenor to all of these discourses, and for different reasons this was widely accepted by both the dominant majority and subordinate minorities (c.f. Bauman, 1996). The crucial *break* with these modes of thought and action came with Stuart Hall's (1992) seminal formulation of a 'new ethnicities' perspective and with Paul Gilroy's critique of ethnic absolutism (1987), extended more recently in his conceptualisation of urban 'conviviality'.

Insisting that race and ethnicity have 'no guarantees in Nature', Hall challenges the dominant idioms of classification and sees the search for 'goodies' and 'baddies' as limiting. He argues for:

> the 'end of innocence', or the end of the innocent notion of the essential black subject [...]. What is at issue here is the recognition of the extraordinary diversity of subjective positions, social experiences, and cultural identities which compose the category 'black'; that is, the recognition that 'black' is essentially a politically and culturally *constructed* category, which cannot be grounded in a set of fixed transcultural or transcendental racial categories and which therefore has no guarantees in Nature. What this brings into play is the recognition of the immense diversity and differentiation of the historical and cultural experiences of black subjects [...]
>
> Once you enter the politics of the end of the essential black subject you are plunged headlong into the maelstrom of a continuously contingent, unguaranteed, political argument and debate: a critical politics, a politics of criticism. You can no longer conduct black politics through the strategy of a simple set of reversals, putting in the place of the bad old essential white subject the new essentially good black subject.
>
> (1992: 254–255)

In the perspective that Hall develops, discourse plays a crucial role (1992: 253–254), and picking up this view of ethnicity as discursively constituted and situationally contingent, Gilroy considers the implications for everyday life in British cities:

> Largely undetected by either government or media, Britain's immigrants and their descendants have generated more positive possibilities. Other varieties of interaction have developed alongside the usual tales of crime and racial conflict. These patterns emerge, not from a mosaic pluralism along US lines, in which each self-sustaining and carefully segregated element is located so as to enhance a larger picture, but with an unruly, convivial mode of interaction in which differences have to be negotiated in real time [...]
>
> Recognising conviviality should not signify the absence of racism. Instead, it can convey the idea that alongside its institutional and interpersonal dynamics, the means of racism's overcoming have also evolved [...] In this convivial culture, racial and ethnic differences have been rendered unremarkable, [...]. they have been able to become 'ordinary'. Instead of adding to the premium of race as political ontology and economic fate, people discover that the things

> which really divide them are much more profound: taste, life-style, leisure preferences.
>
> (2006: 39–40)

At the same time, it is very difficult for social science to describe in any detail how convivial culture actually works (Gilroy, 2006: 28), and indeed Hall (2006) also admits 'that "new ethnicities" (like almost everything I have ever written) was not very empirically based'.

This is where our work seeks to make a contribution, and in what follows later, we outline linguistic ethnography and the analysis of ordinary interaction as productive ways of describing the kinds of ethnicity identified by Gilroy and Hall. But first, here is some data.

An interaction involving text messages, mobile phones and racial statements

The data in this section come from the project 'Urban Classroom Culture and Interaction'. This followed nine adolescents (5F, 4M) over two years in a London secondary school, and data collection involved participant observation, interviews, radio-microphone recording (180 hours) and playback interviews focusing on the radio-mic data. To set the scene for the interactional episode which follows, two points are in order.

First, the episode is not particularly unusual in the attention that the girls give to popular and new media culture (PNMC) in general, and to text messages in particular. In an observational survey of kids' involvement with PNMC at school, we listened to 80 hours of radio-mic recordings of five pupils over two years (3F,2M), identifying over 530 episodes in which they audibly used, referred to, or performed: music, TV, mobiles, mp3s, PSPs, PCs, internet, electronic games, magazines, newspapers, fashion, body-care, 'recreational food' and sport (c.f. Dover, 2007; Rampton, 2006: Ch. 3). There was considerable variation between individuals – 237 episodes with one girl, 24 with another – and there were also striking differences in how (and with what degrees of success) young people drew PNMC into the negotiation of their school and peer group relationships. Even so, these five youngsters' involvement with non-curricular, popular and digital culture at school averaged about seven episodes an hour, and for Habibah, one of the main protagonists in the transcript below, there were 122 episodes in 16 hours of radio-mic recording.

Second, although we were on the alert for any evidence corroborating the dominant idiom on race and ethnicity (and had four minority ethnic researchers in our team of six), we found very little in our 100+ days of observation and radio-mic recording to justify the emphasis on racial/ethnic trouble. Adolescents certainly recognised ethnic differences – in Nadia's friendship group, for example, whiteness had lesser value in popular culture contexts, and in looks, mixed race and light brown rated highest. But this wasn't a crisis. References and allusions to ethnic difference featured as subsidiary issues in conversations addressed to far more insistent concerns – friendship responsibilities, male–female relations, popular media culture, etc. – and indeed there is evidence of this in the episode that follows.

In this interaction, some 14-year-old girls of South Asian and Anglo descent are talking about boys, text messages and phoning, and in the course of their conversation, one of them says:

> 'I don't mix with [kɑɭe:]((= *'black boys' in Punjabi))* I don't like [kɑɭe:], cos they... cos you know what they're like... that's why I don't like them'
>
> (lines 92–95 below)

What significance can we attach to this? Within the dominant discourse, the temptation would be to jump in and accuse the girls of making a 'racist' statement, but the ethnographic discourse analysis we are proposing cautions against taking words too literally, insisting instead on paying serious attention to the discursive and social contingencies involved. To start building an understanding of these contingencies, here is quite an extensive transcript of the episode in which this statement was made.

An episode in which ethnicity becomes salient

Participants (all pseudonyms)*:* Habibah (Indian descent), Lily (White British), Masouda (Pakistani descent) (and Mena, who makes a brief appearance around line 97).

Background: Wednesday 18 May 2005 – Habibah is wearing a lapel radio-microphone. A drama lesson, in which as a 'treat', the class is watching a video because quite a lot of pupils are absent at a residential week. But Habibah and Lily aren't interested, and have instead been chatting near the door, singing duets for the last

10 minutes or so. At the start of the episode, they are joined by Masouda, who has left the video viewing, motivated, it seems, by a text message she's just received on her mobile from a boy. So far this morning, Habibah and Lily's relations with Masouda have been strained, following a falling out over recent weeks, and later on, Habibah & Lily say it's been about a week or two since they've spoken with her.

Transcription conventions:

[text [text	overlapping turns
text= =text	two utterances closely connected without a noticeable overlap, or different parts of a single speaker's turn
( )	speech that can't be deciphered
(text)	analyst's guess at speech that's hard to decipher
((*italics*))	stage directions
(2)	approximate length of a pause in seconds
te::xt	the colons indicate that the word is stretched out
>text<	words spoken more rapidly
TEXT	capitals indicate words spoken more loudly
[kaɭe:]	phonetic transcription of Punjabi
text	text message read out loud
text	singing
text	speech in an Indian English accent

1 Habibah: ((*referring to trainers which they've found in a boy's bag by the*
2 *door:*)) he's got some big feet boy (.)
3 ((*Masouda comes up with her mobile*))
4 Habibah: [fuck you scared me
5 Masouda: [(   ) pick it up and say "Um she left my phone with you"
6 I was so fuckin scar[ed
7 Habibah: [>woa::h< ((*sounds excited*))
8 who is it (.) who is it
9 Masouda: I just got this text (.)
10 Habibah: sha' I answer it (.)
11 ((*proposing a response:*))
12 "well can you fuckin fuckin stop callin' my fuckin phone
13 what the fuck is your problem bitch="
14 Lily: = >no no< I'll do it I'll do it
15 Masouda: I'm gonna missed call the person

16 I don' wanna look
17 I'm so scared now (.)
18 Habibah: *((reading the text message slowly and in monotone:))*
19 "do you (want) me
20 I [want you
21 Masouda: [I don't like this black boy
22 Habibah: "(it's) me *((Lily joins in the reading:))* (the black boy)
23 [come to (my house) my name is
24 Masouda: [I don't know who the FUCK he is he knows who I am
25 Habibah: "ANDREW"
26 Lily: ["black boy come to=
27 Habibah: ["call me [or
28 Lily: ["see me I
29 Habibah: "me and you can do something today
30 so call me
31 you've seen me
32 and I want you to be [( )"
33 Masouda: [give me it
34 Habibah: what
35 I know what number it is
36 Lily: missed call him then init=
37 Masouda: =yeah
38 Lily: and then if he-
39 when he ring[s I'll answer
40 Masouda: [Lily I want you to do it
41 I'm so scared
42 I ain't jokin I'm so scared
43 Lily: I'll do it
44 I'm a gangster
45 I'll do it
46 (.) [gangsta
47 Habibah: [what shall I say
48 can I do it
49 [I know I know
50 Masouda: [any of you two
51 as long as one of you two do it
52 Lily: [let me do it let me do it
53 Habibah: [yeh go on
54 what you gonna say
55 Lily: I'm gonna say ( )-=
56 Habibah: =shall I fuck him off
57 (.)
58 *boy* him off
59 Lily: no I'll [(fucking)
60 Habibah: [*((rehearsing reply:))* "cn can you stop *fucking* fucking
61 calling my phone yeh
62 [don't fucking call my phone" 01.08
63 [*((some conversation in the background too))*
64 Masouda: I missed called him ([and it's gonna)
65 Lily: [when it ring yeah
66 I'll go like this yeah
67 I'll go "hello (West) yeah
68 Masouda left her phone"
69 can [I-

70 Masouda: [NO no
71 he doesn't know my name
72 Lily: [alright
73 Masouda: [my name he thinks my name is Aisha
74 yeh
75 Lily: alright=
76 Masouda: =Aisha
77 Alright I'll say 'hi' >yeah yeah yeah<
78 Habibah: *(directing her attention to Masouda in particular:))*
79 see! [kaɭe:] *(('kale:' = 'black boys'))*
80 [that's it you're gone
81 Lily: [why d-you why d-you keep ringin' me
82 Masouda: *((responding to Habibah:))*
83 NO I didn't
84 no::
85 I I know one of his friends
86 that's why
87 (.)
88 Lily: that's a [lie
89 Masouda: [I know one of his friends
90 I don't- I d-
91 Ha- Ha- Habibah
92 I don't mix with[kaɭe:]
93 I don't like [kaɭe:]
94 cos they're cos you know what they're like
95 that's why [I don't like them
96 [*((A banging of the door opening and closing))*
97 Lily: *((addressing Mena, the girl causing the banging?:))*
98 stop stop stop
99 (Miss) gonna come (.)
100 I'll say why-
101 Masouda: >Mena stop it<
102 Habibah: Mena stop
103 Masouda: [cos they're tryin to-
104 Lily: [( )plea:se
105 (.)
106 Masouda: I've got credit *((for the phone))*
107 Habibah: *((singing to herself:))* "*when you're not here*
108 *I sleep in your T-shirt*"
109 Masouda: don't understand (why)
110 Habibah: (eh) eh speak speak *((is Habibah referring to the radio-mic?))*
111 Lily: "ello Moto"
112 Habibah: Masouda say something (.) *((into the radiomicrophone))*
113 Masouda: oh
114 Lily: "ello Mo[to"
115 Habibah: [*((laughs))*
116 >no no don't take it off< *(('it' = the radio-mic?))*
117 (.)
118 *((sings:))* "*when you're not here*
119 *I sleep in your T-shirt*"
120 (.)
121 Masouda: [that's why I don't like [kaɭe:] man
122 Habibah: [*wish you were here*[*to sleep in your T-shirt*"
123 Masouda: [oh [

```
124 Lily:                      [there's some buff black boys man
125           seriously
126 Habibah:  half-caste (I go)
127 Masouda:  [>half-caste<
128 Lily:     [na na
129 Masouda:  [yeah but this guy is blick
130           this er- bu- [not
131 Lily:                  [na blood
132           I'm not fucking about (.)
133           [(d-you know that    ) buff man   that boy
134 Masouda:  [he's burnt toast
135 Lily:     that tall black boy is
136           (.)
137           buff
138           don't fuck about
139 Masouda:  ((with a hint of laughter in her voice)) he's bu::rnt toast man
140           ((in a constricted voice:)) he's burnt toast
141 Lily:     ((exhaling:)) na::
142 Habibah:  fucking why's it not ringing
143 Lily:     ((quieter, with the argument dying down:)) he's bu:::ff
144           ((very quietly:)) (buff)
145           (.)
146 Habibah:  how the fuck did he get your number
147 Masouda:  I don't know
148           (.)
149           cos I don't- [
150 Habibah:               [((singing:)) "I wish you were here
151           to sleep in your T Shirt
152           (.)
153           then we make lo::ve
154           (.)
155           I sleep in your T-shirt"
156 Masouda:  (he picked up (('he' = Andrew, returning the missed-call))
157           ((half-laughing:)) (jus as you were singing)
158 Lily?:    did he pick it up
159 Masouda:  yeh he picked it up (.)
160           just (killed it)
161           (4.0)  ((teacher talking in the background))
162 Lily:     mad cow
163 Habibah:  does he go to this school
164 Masouda:  no
165           (2.0)
166           somewhere in (Shepherd's Bush)
167           (5.0)
168 ?Masouda: is it ringing
169 Habibah:  how the fuck do you get
170           yeh- pass-
171           (.)
172 Masouda:  yeah (  just) flash (('flash' = let the phone ring once and hang up))
173           [(cz my minutes          )
174 Lily:     [(that's what I thought)
175           and then I go
176           "eh eh (.) (ex-blood)"
177           (.)
```

178 Habibah: Say ((*in Indian English*)) "**hell:o who this calling me**
179 **don't call me next time**"
180 Lily: I'll go like this
181 ((*carrying on in Indian English*)) "**eh hello please**
182 **who you ringing**
183 **this my phone (not)**
184 **gil**[**this ol lady**"
185 Masouda: [and (wants) to
186 come to ((St Mary's)) on Friday
187 Habibah: ((*laughs*))
188 Lily: ((*continuing in IE*)) "**this is ol' lady**"
189 Habibah: ((*deeper voice, with an Elvis impersonation?*)) 'hello hello'
190 Lily: I'll be like [hello
191 Habibah: shall I do that
192 do you dare me to
193 ((*deeper voice, Elvis impersonation?*))'hello'
194 Lily: [( )
195 Masouda: [([ )
196 Habibah: [((*continuing the rehearsal in IE:*)) "**this is her dad**
197 **leave her alone**"
198 Girls: [((*loud laughs*))
199 Habibah: [((*not in IE:*)) "I'm gonna kill [you"
200 Lily: [let do
201 do you dare me to do that-
202 do you dare me to do that
203 Habibah: yeh go on
204 if you can but don't laugh
205 Lily: ((*more rehearsing Indian English for the phone-call:*)) "**hello hello**
206 **this her dad**
207 **how can I help you**
208 Girls: ((*laughter*))
209 Lily: **okay bye bye**"
210 Girls: ((*laughs & giggles*))
211 Habibah: no let's talk normal
212 Lily: yeh >I'll be like<
213 hi (.)
214 yeah (.) yeah I-
215 Habibah: >>oh he's (ringing)<<
216 Masouda: pick it up
217 Lily: (J) (it's flashed) again
218 Masouda: oh you fucking shit
219 is that the number though that he (gave) me?
220 ?: (I bet-)
221 Masouda: Yeah this is what Asif sent to me (.)
222 ((*discussion turns to the text-message sent by another boy*))

Presented in a fuller context like this, it isn't so straightforward reading racism into Masouda's original statement about not liking 'kale'. But are the prospective gains made in moving past a simplistic interpretation immediately cancelled out by the rather daunting task of trying to get to grips with everything else that seems to be going on in this episode?

This is where linguistic ethnography and interactional discourse analysis can help, providing relatively systematic frameworks and procedures for working one's way through the complicated organisation of an episode like this *without* losing sight of all the situated and emergent particularities, which, if we follow Hall and Gilroy, are actually crucial to the meanings of ethnicity.

Linguistic ethnography and an initial analysis of the girls' interaction

Contemporary linguistic and interactional ethnography generally takes a 'practice' view of identity, concentrating on how identities affect and get configured in people's social activity together (c.f. Rampton, 2007; Rampton et al., 2007, for fuller discussion of linguistic ethnography). In studying the embedding of *ethnicities* in everyday life, the aim is to understand their significance without either exaggerating this or ignoring the flexible agency with which people process ethnicities in everyday encounters. Analysis starts with careful description of real-time interactional discourse, but from there it looks to the relationship between communicative practices, social actors and the institutional processes in which they are participating. So race and ethnicity can be conceptualised and empirically explored in three closely interlocking 'sites':

- If the analyst's main interest is in *social actors*, then ethnicity is construed as those aspects of a person's (semiotically manifest) resources, knowledge, capacities, dispositions and embodiment that have been shaped over time in networks regarded as distinctively different from others in the locality.
- When *institutional processes* are the central concern, race and ethnicity are treated as elements in well-established ideologies which frame the situations in which social actors find themselves, inclining them to particular kinds of action and interpretation before, during and/or after an encounter.
- Where the interest is in *communication* itself, race and ethnicity are located in the semiotic activity – in the signs, actions and practices that reflect, invoke or produce the resources, capacities and ideologies associated with actors, networks and institutions.

At the same time, however, even in highly racialised and ethnically marked situations, racial and ethnic identifications exist alongside a myriad of other role and category enactments, and it is in their dynamic interaction with these other identity articulations that much of the meaning of ethnicity and race takes shape. Zimmerman (1998) usefully suggests at least three kinds of identity at play in any social encounter:

- *discourse (or interactional) identities,* such as 'story teller', 'story recipient', 'questioner', 'answerer', 'inviter', 'invitee', etc., which people are continuously taking on and leaving as talk progresses;
- *situated (or institutional) identities,* such as 'teacher', 'student', 'doctor', 'patient', which come into play in particular kinds of institutional situation;
- *'transportable' identities* which are latent, travel with individuals across situations, and are potentially relevant at any time (e.g. 'middle-aged white man', 'working-class woman', 'adolescent black boy', etc.)

These identities can either be 'oriented to', actively influencing the way that people try to shape both their own actions and the subsequent actions of others, or they may be merely 'apprehended' – tacitly noticed but not treated as immediately relevant to the interaction on hand. And the interactional and institutional identities that a person projects at any moment may be ratified, reformulated or resisted in the immediately following actions of their interlocutors.

To see how different kinds of identity get activated, displayed and processed in situated interaction, the analysis of interactional discourse focuses on the ways in which participants handle a wide range of linguistic/semiotic materials in their exchanges together – pronunciations, accents, words, utterances, gestures, postures, ways of speaking, modes of address, texts, genres and so on. But – and here we return again to the contingency emphasised by Hall and Gilroy – the meaning and interpretation of a linguistic or semiotic form is always influenced by the way in which people read its *context,* with context minimally understood as:

(i) the *institutional and social network relations* among the participants and their *histories of interaction* both together and apart (here institutional and 'transportable' are most immediately relevant);
(ii) the *type of activity* in which participants are currently engaged, the stage they've reached in the activity, and their different interactional roles and positionings within it (c.f. institutional and interactional identities);

(iii) their position and manoeuvring in and around institutional *discourses* and circumambient *ideologies* (institutional and transportable identities);
(iv) what's just been said and done, and the options for doing something right now *(the moment-by-moment unfolding of activity)* (interactional identities).

Of course it is often hard knowing exactly *which* aspect of context is relevant to an utterance (and how), and it only takes a small shift in how you conceive of the context to change your understanding of what an utterance means. But this is an issue that participants themselves have to address throughout their interaction together, and so to prevent the analysis becoming an interpretive free-for-all, researchers can try to track the way in which participants develop, monitor and repair an intersubjective understanding together from one moment to the next.

Putting all of this together, we can see that in the interactional negotiation of meaning, things move very fast, and people are extraordinarily adept at using very small pieces of linguistic/semiotic form to guide or challenge the understandings of the world emerging in the talk – the choice of one word rather than another can introduce a different issue, a particular pronunciation can reframe the significance of what's going on, a shift in facial expression can convey a specific stance or attitude. And so as well as looking closely at semiotic forms and slowing things down to capture the processes of adaptive improvisation from one moment to the next, analysts also need a lot of background knowledge of the local contexts if they are to have any chance of picking up and understanding what it is that these crucial nuances and intimations are pointing to. People generally do manage to communicate fairly well together, but they don't just go around expressing themselves in explicit, well-formed and readily quoted sentences.

This perspective is consonant with Gilroy's interest in 'mode[s] of interaction in which differences have to be negotiated in real-time', 'largely undetected by government and media' (see above), and our contention is that for a fuller – or indeed maybe for even only an *adequate* – understanding of what people mean when they speak, the combination of linguistics, interaction analysis and ethnography provides valuable support. To illustrate this, it is worth now returning to the episode presented in the previous section.

Analysts interested in race and ethnicity could, of course, draw attention to a number of different aspects of this episode, and there are many ways in which the girls are living the historical and institutional effects of large-scale racial/ethnic processes well beyond what they are either consciously aware of or actually discuss. Nevertheless, to illustrate our larger point about the importance of meanings that are not explicitly stated, it is worth focusing on two fairly conspicuous sequences in the interaction when the girls themselves orient actively to ethnicity:

- *Focal sequence* 1: lines 78–95 and 121–140, from Habibah's 'see! *kale*' to Masouda's 'he's burnt toast'
- *Focal sequence* 2: lines 178–211, when the girls switch into Indian accented English ('IE') in their rehearsals of speaking to Andrew over the phone.

Following Hall and Gilroy's injunctions, as well as the methodological tenets of linguistic ethnography, these moments of racialisation/ethnification need to be situated in their contexts, taking context as:

(i) the institutional and social network relations among the girls, and their (recent) histories of interaction together,
(ii) the types of activity they are involved in,
(iii) the broader discourses, ideologies and moralities they live amidst, and
(iv) the acts and utterances immediately leading up to and following ethnifying utterances.

The tables 5.1, 5.2 and 5.3 below take the first three of these as the point of entry into analysis of '*kale*', the Indian English voicing and of the episode as a whole. They explicate in a little more detail both how and where these contexts are relevant to the interaction, and try to show how one might start to navigate the structuring of this episode while also beginning to reckon with some of its vital particularities.

Table 5.1 Institutional and social network relations, histories of interaction, etc.

Institutional identities	Schoolgirls in year 9 (aged 13–14)
Family networks	Family links with different countries: Habibah (India); Masouda (Pakistan); Lily (white, England)
Peer relations & recent interactional history	Habibah and Lily are good friends, and they spend a lot of time together talking about boys. Masouda has recently fallen out with them, but is keen to re-establish friendship (later during break, she gets a friend to tell Habibah that she wants to say sorry for anything she's done, but Habibah tells the friend not to interfere and to get lost)

Table 5.2 Types of activity

THE MAIN ACTIVITY IN THIS SEQUENCE	
RESPONDING TOGETHER TO A TEXT MESSAGE FROM A MEMBER OF THE OPPOSITE SEX – Masouda, Habibah & Lily. The girls are active protecting this from potential interruption/disruption by the teacher or others.	Lines 5–219
SUBSIDIARY ACTIVITIES	
(These are either abbreviated or ignored as the girls' attention shifts back to texting/phoning, the main activity)	
AVOIDING INTERRUPTION FROM THE TEACHER	96–102
RESUMING A DISPUTE – Habibah & Masouda. Prompted by the discovery that Masouda has actually played an active part in soliciting the text message (telling the boy she was called Aisha), Habibah puts an accusation to Masouda ('See! [*kale*] That's it, you're gone') which Masouda denies. (See Table 5.3 below for further discussion.)	78–95, 109, 121–140, 146–149, 169
SOLO-HUMMING & SINGING – Habibah. Habibah sings snatches of a song by Destiny's Child to herself ('T shirt')	107–108, 118–119, 122, 150–155
BEING RESEARCHED – Habibah, Lily, Masouda	110–116

Table 5.3 Ideologies and institutional and moral codes variously in play in the episode

THE PROPRIETIES & POSSIBILITIES OF CONDUCT & CONVERSATION DURING LESSONS: These are largely **suspended** (though there is a risk of their being reasserted at any time)	
THE CONVENTIONS AND EXPECTATIONS OF FRIENDSHIP: For the most part, these are **enacted** – they are implied, negotiated or indeed questioned in the way these girls initiate, reciprocate or refuse actions and activity together.	5–222
But drawing on our ethnographic knowledge of Habibah's friendship with Masouda, as well as on what she says later, there is a good case for saying that issues of friendship and loyalty are central to Habibah's 'See! [*kale*] That's it, you're gone' in lines 78–80. Later in the recording (not in this extract), Habibah says: 'that was funny, boy… see, see, how the fuck did	

Table 5.3 (Continued)

she get in contact with those boys, and then she calling me a whore'. So it looks as though her 'See! – *kale*' alludes to the defamatory claims that Habibah thinks Masouda has made about Habibah's contact with black boys in particular. 'See!', in other words, seems to be implying that Masouda is a hypocrite. In the event, of course, Masouda's response in lines 82–95 fails to address these rather inexplicit accusations of defamation & hypocrisy, and instead she responds by denying an interest in black boys. But Habibah never explicitly accepts this, and she never lets her off with for example an 'okay'. Instead she carries on with questions about the contact ('how the fuck did he get your number' [146, 169]), and then she blanks Masouda's answer in lines 147–149 by singing to herself (150–155)

THE PROPRIETIES & POSSIBILITIES OF CONTACT BETWEEN GIRLS & BOYS/ WOMEN & MEN.
These are **explicitly debated in talk, written in text-messages, and sung** – they constitute topics that all the girls are interested in, and that serve as a source of laughter, excitement, stories, and argument (both more & less light-hearted) etc. Within this broad field of interest, ethnically marked moral codes also become salient...

PUNJABI PROHIBITIONS ON GIRLS ASSOCIATING WITH (BLACK) BOYS are **evoked** by the introduction of elements from the Punjabi language (vocabulary and pronunciation).

But the girls shift their stance on the (relatively stable) view that Asian girls shouldn't associate with black boys. In the 'kale' sequence, Masouda appears to accept the prohibition, and denies that she has transgressed, but in the phone voicings, the prohibition is subject to comic impersonation and implicit ridicule. These shifts are an effect and articulation of fluctuations in the spirit of Habibah's relationship with Masouda.

Focal sequence 1: Habibah: 'See! *Kale*' (*'kale' = 'black boys' in Punjabi*).

Habibah's switch to Punjabi introduces a co-ethnic angle on her 'See! That's it – you're gone'. This seems to be forceful. Rather than responding to Habibah's 'See!' with 'So what?', or to 'you're gone' with 'why?' or 'how', Masouda dwells on the issue of black boys in her rebuttal, first appealing to a shared ethnic understanding ('I don't like *'kale'* cos you know what they're like') and then claiming that Andrew is 'burnt toast' (134, 139, 140).	78ff

But there is a strong case for saying that Habibah is more concerned with Masouda's hypocrisy about Masouda's own contacts with black boys and with her gossiping, than she is with the notion of contact with boys of the wrong race and colour *per se* (see above). Indeed, in a subsequent playback interview, Habibah made it clear that she likes black boys ('I think they're buff, innit'), Masouda confirmed this, and talking to the researcher (who is a black woman), both of them were embarrassed about having used the word *'kale'*.

Focal sequence 2: Rehearsing for the phone conversation with Andrew with Indian English accents – Habibah & Lily.

Indian English is widely used as a stereotypic voice, even by Lily who's white British – as Masouda comments in a playback interview, 'Lily uses it A LOT. I've got this video clip in my phone – oh my gosh – she done this Indian accent, it was so funny'.

More than that, Habibah had previously been seen being severely reprimanded by her father for being alone with some boys from school, and his reproachful injunction 'don't look at 'em' has temporarily become a jocular Indian English catch-phrase directed at Habibah by her peers. 178ff

So Habibah's dad doesn't like her hanging around with boys – indeed, he doesn't allow her a mobile and he has cut back on her MSN contact list. *But* he doesn't actually speak English with an Indian accent – 'my dad don't speak like that, my dad speaks proper English' (playback interview). In addition, Habibah also says subsequently that she partly understands his views – 'it looked wrong [being alone with the boys], but still... I wasn't doing anything wrong'. Overall, she considers her parents 'not strict, they have – we have limits like', and her mum 'understands everything... she knows I won't do anything wrong'

This description is very preliminary and says hardly anything about the turn-by-turn sequencing in the interaction ('context [iv]' above). But it already opens several potentially productive lines into the investigation of contemporary ethnicities, and we might dwell, for example, on the resonance of African American popular culture (Habibah's humming and singing), processes of ethnic boundary crossing (the acceptability of Lily's Indian English impersonations), or new technologies and the renegotiation of sexuality, gender and generational relations. But rather than elaborating on these here (c.f. Harris, 2006; Rampton, 2005), the argument in this chapter dictates that we turn instead to the types of interpretation *eliminated* by data and analyses like ours.

Understanding better

If we allowed our interest in ethnicity to take us straight to '*kale*' and the Indian English voicing, hurrying past the contexts of activity, interactional history, network relations and circumambient discourse sketched out in Tables 5.1–5.3, we might find it hard to resist several stock interpretations from a rather well-rehearsed repertoire of racial/ethnic analyses.

- In lines 78–80, Habibah's '`See` *`kale!`* `That's it, you're gone`' might be treated as the expression of ethno-moral purism, upholding traditional values in the face of Masouda's alleged deviation. Linguistic ethnographic description, though, makes it clear that instead of reflecting the irrepressible dictates of a compelling ethno-moral conscience, '*kale*' points to the fragility of the girls' on-and-off friendship, and constitutes a moment of retaliation to the moral character-assassination that Habibah thinks Masouda's been engaged in.
- In lines 92 and 93, Masouda's '`I don't mix with "`*`kale`*`", I don't like "`*`kale`*`"`' might be read as straight racial hostility. But even a cursory reading of the transcript shows that this is a defensive protestation, and our wider ethnographic knowledge repositions this in the very active interest in black boys that Masouda, Habibah and Lily all share.
- The shift in tone between our focal sequences – the switch between the rather serious argument about '*kale*' and the very light-hearted Indian English voicings – might be viewed as a contradiction or confusion in the girls' ethnic ideologies and perspectives on Punjabi/South Asian sexual codes, tempting us into a 'caught-between-cultures' formulation. But if we reckon with the interactional purposes driving these invocations of ethno-morality at the particular moments when they're produced, then the girls' utterances seemed perfectly coherent, very effective (in terms of their impact on the recipients), and actually rather assured. If there is trouble and contradiction, it has far less to do with East vs West than with (a) Habibah and Masouda's friendship and (b) the general business of male–female relations among adolescents.

In saying all this, we are certainly not denying that the episode reveals ethnically linked differences in sexual morality, as well as ethnically inflected conflict between the peer group and home-based proprieties. If it were not for these tensions, then as rhetorical actions, the switches into Punjabi and Indian English would have been entirely inert. *However*, it cannot be claimed that conflict around race and ethnicity was the girls' principal preoccupation in this episode, or that it somehow incapacitated them. Instead, they were obviously much more concerned with the tensions and excitement of prospective boy–girl relations and the vicissitudes of adolescent female friendship, and rather than being disempowering, ethno-moral conflict featured as a resource that the girls exploited quite skilfully in pursuit of their really pressing interests.

In fact, even though there were lots of allusions and evocations of the kind shown here, it was very rare in our dataset of 180 hours of radio-microphone recordings to see race or ethnicity pushed into the foreground as the central issue in an interaction. Contrary to the claims of what we have characterised as the dominant idiom, race and ethnicity featured for the most part as subsidiary and incidental issues, very much in the 'unruly convivial mode of interaction' identified by Gilroy and illustrated in the episode above. And indeed all this points to one of the most general ways in which our data and analysis can contribute to wider discussions of ethnicity and race. Holding closely to the contexts of everyday life, linguistic ethnography helps get ethnicity and race *into perspective*, as significant but by no means all-encompassing processes, intricate but much more ordinary and liveable than anything one might infer from the high octane, headline representations of the political and media arena.

As the work of Hall and Gilroy amply demonstrates, linguistic ethnographies of routine practice certainly aren't the only path to this kind of perspective – participant observation in non-linguistic ethnography is another route, as is first-hand experience of everyday urban life. But our account does raise quite serious questions about the adequacy of the standard social science interview as a means of assessing the significance of race and ethnicity amidst all the other social relations that people live (see also Savage, 2007: 893–894). In the transcript we have presented, (i) the talk is jostling, allusive, multi-voiced, partisan and interwoven with physical movement and action; (ii) ethnic issues are introduced amidst a range of other concerns, contested and collaboratively reformulated over time (and across settings); and it is obvious (iii) that you need a lot of contextual knowledge to understand what's going on. In contrast, research interviews typically privilege: (a) orderly progression, explicitness, relatively detached (and detachable) commentary, illustrative narrative, and speech separated from movement and action; (b) they seldom serve as sites for the contestation of identity claims against a background of shared knowledge; and (c) researchers often lack the local understanding to pick up on allusions, looking for quotably literal encapsulations instead (see also Georgakopoulou, 2008).[2] All this favours the dominant idiom in the representation of ethnicity and race. If researchers don't grasp (i), (ii) and (iii) – if they lack access to local activities and to the ongoing co-construction/renegotiation of racial or ethnic meanings among everyday associates amidst a host of other concerns – then the accounts of context produced in interview research are not only likely to be limited. There is also a risk that in trying to identify a context for what interview informants say, researchers draw on (and position their informants 'inter-textually' within) only the most obvious discourses at large. Unfortunately, these tend to be essentialist and crisis-oriented, and if these are used as the main framing for the utterances of interviewees, then research cedes the terms of engagement to dominant formulations. This makes it much harder to pick up on the articulation of alternative/different agendas, and more likely for research to find itself confined to 'the strategy of a simple set of reversals' (Hall, cited above).

When we presented our perspective at a seminar on ethnicity organised by the Identities Programme, Hall agreed that it represented an empirical advance.[3] But he also wondered 'how you ever get back to the larger field' from all the contingent detail. As both of us are committed to using fine-grained data to address much bigger questions (about e.g. ethnicity, race, class, education and contemporary culture), we see this as a vital question, and elsewhere, we have made extended attempts to address it (Harris, 2006; Harris and Rampton, 2002; Rampton, 2005, 2006, 2007). Nor, as we said at the start, do we want to underplay the significance of contemporary racism, and we know that in order to address it, sometimes it certainly is necessary to go straight to the big concepts, in acts of strategic essentialism. So we are not advocating a retreat from larger generalisations about ethnicity and race in contemporary society, either in analysis or politics. We do hold, though, that in the process of abstracting and simplifying, it is vital to refer back continuously to what's 'lived' in the everyday, and that ultimately both academic and political generalisations must be made accountable to the kinds of activity represented in our transcript. Without that anchoring – without a sense of how in one way or another, most people *do* manage in the generally rather low-key practices of the day-to-day – it is impossible to identify changes in the terms of everyday ethnic/racial encounters, and discussion is left vulnerable to the dramatisations of the dominant idiom, panicked and unable to imagine how anyone copes. And we're also not convinced that on its own, talk of 'multiple, fluid, intersecting and ambiguous identities' provides recovery from this, assuming as it often does (a) that the identities that get mentioned all count, and (b) that it's really hard working out how they link together. In our view, it is essential to look searchingly at how in their everyday practices, people do make sense of things, work them through, and bring quite a high degree of intelligible order to their circumstances. This sometimes reveals that people aren't as preoccupied, fractured or troubled by particular identifications as we initially supposed, and that they are actually rather adept at negotiating 'ethnicities without guarantees', inflecting them in ways that are extremely hard to anticipate in the absence of close empirical observation. And then this in turn prompts some crucial critical reflection on the relationship between political, academic and everyday constructs and practices. Of course there are no pure truths or easy readings in/of the everyday – no 'guarantees' – and its empirical study and representation require a host of historically located interpretive frameworks and procedures, as we've tried to illustrate. Still, we see ordinary activity as a vital resource and reference point for discussion about identities in general, quite often cutting the ground from dominant accounts, pointing in new or different directions.

Notes

1. The ethnographic fieldwork and data collection for this chapter was carried out by Lauren Small, and as well as drawing on Lauren's work, we are highly indebted to other members and associates of the Urban Classroom Culture and Interaction project team – Alexandra Georgakopoulou, Constant Leung, Caroline Dover and Adam Lefstein.
2. We recognise, of course, that interviews take many shapes, are often embedded in ethnography, and can themselves be productively analysed as culturally situated interactional events. Indeed, when we interviewed senior teachers in this school and conducted focus groups with others, ethnicity didn't emerge as more of a pressing issue than in our recordings of youngsters' spontaneous interaction, and in this regard, the interview and radio-mic data are complementary. Still, though our characterisation may be a little too stark, we don't think it completely misses the mark, and it actually also extends to survey questionnaires.
3. '[W]hat I have heard is a very substantial deepening of the [new ethnicities] paradigm .... I think the move to ethnography, the move to discursive

analysis, discourse analysis of interviews, is a way of methodologically exemplifying the conceptual complexity that the paradigm talked about.... I hope you learn very much more exactly what it means to say the end of the essential social subject – how to look at this question when we don't have fixed, essentialised subjects who are the endless bearers of these positionalities whether they are race identity, ethnic identity, etc. What that actually means methodologically and conceptually – very important work' (Hall in an unpublished ESRC ISA Programme transcript of the Ethnicities Workshop held at the London School of Economics, 21 June 2006; Rampton et al., 2006).

References

Adi, H. and Sherwood, M. (1995) *The 1945 Manchester Pan-African Congress Revisited.* London: New Beacon Books.

Bauman, G. (1996) *Contesting Culture: Discourses of Identity in Multi-Ethnic London.* Cambridge: Cambridge University Press.

Carmichael, S. and Hamilton, C. V. (1967) *Black Power.* Harmondsworth: Penguin.

Department for Education (DfE) (1995) *Ethnic Monitoring of School Pupils: A Consultation Paper.* London: DfE.

Dover, C. (2007) Everyday Talk: Investigating Media Consumption and Identity Amongst Schoolchildren. *Participations* 4 (1). http://www.participations.org/ (accessed 8 December 2008).

Georgakopoulou, A. (2008) 'On MSN with Buff Boys': Self- and Other-Identity Claims in the Context of Small Stories. *Journal of Sociolinguistics* 12(5), 597–626.

Gilroy, P. (1987) *There Ain't No Black in the Union Jack.* London: Hutchinson.

Gilroy, P. (2006) Multiculture in Times of War: An Inaugural Lecture given at the London School of Economics. *Critical Quarterly* 48(4), 27–45.

Hall, S. (1992) New Ethnicities. In J. Donald and A. Rattansi (eds) *'Race', Culture & Difference.* London: Sage.

Hall, S. (2006) Comments. Unpublished ESRC Identities and Social Action Programme transcript of the Ethnicities Workshop held at the London School of Economics, 21 June 2006.

Harris, R. (1997) Romantic Bilingualism?: Time for a Change. In C. Leung and C. Cable (eds) *English as an Additional Language: Changing Perspectives.* Watford: NALDIC.

Harris, R. (2006) *New Ethnicities and Language Use.* Basingstoke: Palgrave Macmillan.

Harris, R. and Rampton, B. (2002) Creole Metaphors in Cultural Analysis: On the Limits and Possibilities of (Socio-)Linguistics. *Critique of Anthropology* 22(1), 31–51.

Ramdin, R. (1987) *The Making of the Black Working Class in Britain.* Aldershot: Gower.

Rampton, B. (2005) *Crossing: Language and Ethnicity among Adolescents.* 2nd edn. Manchester: St Jerome Press.

Rampton, B. (2006) *Language in Late Modernity: Interaction in an Urban School.* Cambridge: Cambridge University Press.

Rampton, B. (2007) Linguistic Ethnography and the Study of Identities. *Working Papers in Urban Language & Literacies* 43. http://www.kcl.ac.uk/ldc (accessed 20 May 2009).

Rampton, B., Harris, R. and Small, L. (2006) The Meanings of Ethnicity in Discursive Interaction: Some Data and Interpretations from Ethnographic Sociolinguistics. http://www.ling-ethnog.org.uk/publications/html

Rampton, B., Maybin, J. and Tusting, K. (eds) (2007) Linguistic Ethnography: Links, Problems and Possibilities. *Journal of Sociolinguistics* 11(5), 575–695.

Savage, M. (2007) The Coming Crisis of Empirical Sociology. *Sociology* 41(5), 885–899.

Zimmerman, D. (1998) Identity, Context, Interaction. In C. Antaki and S. Widdicombe (eds) *Identities in Talk*. London: Sage.

6
'Con-viviality' and Beyond: Identity Dynamics in a Young Men's Prison

Rod Earle and Coretta Phillips

Introduction

This chapter explores the configuration of identity, social relations and ethnicity within the confines of a young men's prison. The site of intense deprivations, referred to by Sykes (1958) as the 'pains of imprisonment', prisons gather together many of those people also bearing the pains of structural disenfranchisement and marginalisation which characterise deprived neighbourhoods (Wacquant, 2007).

England and Wales have the highest per capita incarceration rate of Northern Europe after the Baltic states (Walmsley, 2007). Twelve per cent of this prison population comprises young men aged 18–21 years held in Young Offender Institutions (YOIs). Like adult prisons, YOIs are characterised by ethnic, national and religious diversity (Ministry of Justice, 2007), which is partially fuelled by the long-standing over-representation of black people in the prison population compared to the general population (see Phillips and Bowling, 2007). Within the exceptional conditions of prison life an institutional prisoner identity is sometimes assumed to take precedence (Sykes, 1958), delivering what Foucault (1979: 236) describes as 'a recoding of existence'. Other perspectives see prisoners maintaining racialised identities imported from wider society (Jacobs, 1979).

The work we present here considers how young men's identities are shaped through the encounter with the austere routines of prison life and each other's ethnicity. Despite the multiplicity of ethnic identities among prisoners of England and Wales – in 2006, for example, 27 per cent of male prisoners were of minority ethnic origin and 15 per cent were foreign nationals (Ministry of Justice, 2007) – prison ethnographies in England and Wales have tended to neglect issues of ethnicity and race relations (Phillips, 2008). As a result relatively little is known about the way prisoners' ethnicities influence their social relations.

The site of our study, HMYOI Rochester in Kent, was selected for having an ethnically mixed population of young male prisoners from both urban and semi-rural settings. Young men arrive at HMYOI Rochester from London, where Black and minority ethnic youth are over-represented in the criminal justice system, and from courts, or other prisons, in the neighbouring counties of Kent, Essex and Sussex where white ethnicities predominate. The prison accommodates up to 400 convicted young men, of which approximately 56 per cent were White British, White European or White Other. Black/Black Caribbean/Black African young men comprised 30 per cent of the population, while 7 per cent were of Mixed Heritage and 6 per cent Asian.

The authors attended the prison for up to 3–4 days each week over a period of eight months in 2006/2007 and conducted 60 in-depth interviews. A relatively long-term period of access allowed us to encounter something of the rhythms and routines of prison life. Prisoners spend anything from 15 to 22 hours a day locked in their cells, depending on the availability of workshops and other activities. We spent as much time as we could engaging with prisoners through conversation, presence and interaction during their out-of-cell time; before and after meals, on the wings, in workshops and during times of evening 'association'.

Affirmation and disavowal of ethnic identities

Many of the prisoners who contributed to the study demonstrated an understanding of ethnicity that equated it with culture. Their narratives revealed a Barthian (1969) sense of an ethnic and bounded self, historically embedded in a shared culture, but not grounded in essentialist characteristics, thus allowing permeation from, or penetration into, the cultures of other ethnic groups.

In the main it was minority ethnic prisoners who described investing in dynamic cultural practices and symbols which united them with others similarly ascribed. Various kinds of plaited or twisted hairstyles (corn row, chiney bumps, two strand twists), as well as longer afros, loxed hair and shaved styles offered black prisoners some expression of individuality and collective presentation. Most white prisoners lavished considerably less attention on their hair and distinctive stylings were less in evidence. However, other emulations of black prisoner's urban expressions, tone and dress style were not uncommon among white prisoners. Rochester prisoners, both black and white, often went 'backsy' with their emerald green prison-issue trousers or grey jogging bottoms worn well below their hips showing their undershorts. Talking 'slangs' on the wing, 'rude boy' or 'street' talk was also a source of connection and a means of performing identity for many black prisoners of British nationality.

For some white prisoners familiarity with the vernacular associated with urban black youth not only established a prisoner's provenance but also helped to transcend the boundaries of sub-cultural affiliation. The cultural currency of black stylistic forms has long been observed in studies of urban youth cultures (Back, 1996; Frosh et al., 2002; Nayak, 2003; Sharma et al., 1996) and the current study indicated their prevalence in the social world of the prison too.

Though these emulations continue to have a contested viability among the young men, largely based on a register of their supposed authenticity, they appear to have escaped, at least in part, some of the essentialised loading in which the use of language, and specifically patois, reifies racialised difference. Fanon referred to the ways in which the assumption by white people of a black vernacular signified an attack on the black person in an effort to 'attach him to his image, to lime him, to imprison him, to make him the eternal victim of an essence, of an appearance for which he is not responsible' (Fanon, 1975: 27). As Fanon pointed out, however, there is more than one level of agency at work in this relationship for while '[I]t is the white man who creates the 'negre'... it is the black man who created negritude' (Fanon, 1968: 29). The implied and offensive essentialism of race has been thoroughly diffused through the common experiences many of the young men from London talked about: of growing up on the same estates, attending the same schools, living on the same streets and, in some cases, the same households. One bi-lingual young white man from West London described himself as White Asian and talked proudly of a mixed heritage derived from his Asian step-father:

> My boys call me ['Switch'[1]] cos I'm half white, half Asian so they say it was a [switch] of personality, so they call me ['Switch'], so I got that name... everyone that knows me will say that I'm the only white Asian who knows more about the Asian culture than Asians themselves.
>
> (White, British National, Christian – R41)

Racial logic has been unpicked by these young men as a result of the durable insistence of black presence that Fanon identified as a consequence of diaspora: 'You come to terms with me, I'm not coming to terms with anyone' (Fanon, 1975: 106). As Paul Gilroy (2004) has explored recently there is emerging evidence of a new urban postcolonial conviviality that generates possibilities hitherto only imagined at the utopian fringe of progressive politics; the collapse of racial categorisation.

Although some of the fundamental problematics of racialisation remain far from absent in the prison we also discerned evidence of new forms of convivial living whose viability was contested and constructed on a regular basis in the 'thrown together' (Serge, 1967/1937) collections of young men in the prison. Nothing exemplified this better than when the (young, white, female) writer-in-residence at Rochester organised a small in-house Performance Poetry event. In a prison workshop over a dozen contestants performed their prepared lyrics to a small audience of their peers. With musical backing tracks the styles ranged from fast-chat rhymes to slower paced reflections on prison, life, romance, crime and cops. Some were awkward and inept, though the crowd was, somewhat 'officially', supportive. There were two white contestants and a few more in the audience. One of them won the contest by a country mile and by popular acclaim. His ultra-fast-chat stylings drew from his itinerant immersion in a criminal life-world that extended from the ports of Kent to the suburbs of London and beyond. The stumbling efforts of one black foreign national prisoner to achieve the required speed and expressive virtuosity were received with the same mixture of gentle ridicule, good-humoured disdain and harsh encouragement as the efforts of another, equally faltering and unsuccessful, white contestant.

In another part of the spectrum was a multitude of prisoners for whom ethnicity had a dormant or undeveloped sense lacking personal, social or political meaning. Regarded as something suspiciously prescriptive, ethnicity was actively disavowed and considered irrelevant to the young men's sense of self both inside and outside prison. This was particularly true in many of the accounts of White British prisoners. This is consistent with much of the empirical and theoretical work on the perceived normative character of whiteness where white ethnicities are invisible, denied or regarded as devoid of ethnic content (Garner, 2007; Nayak, 2003). White British ethnicities had an evacuated, vacant quality as if emptied of the imperial glory that once stood for a whiteness they might claim. They stand in stark contrast to 'culture-rich' black and

Asian ethnicities (see Gilroy, 2005; Ray et al., 2004). Many responses from White British National prisoners to questions about ethnicity in this study were consistent with this and chimed with Nayak's (2003: 173) view of whiteness as '*the ethnicity that is not one*'.

Several of the white young men found our enquiries about ethnic identity, and the existence of standard ethnic categories, perplexing: 'It's just what you say isn't it when you tick an application form and that, that's what it means to me... I've never really thought about it to tell the truth' (R47 White, British). As Macey (1999) notes it is quite possible, and probably not uncommon, to grow up in a largely white community in England without knowing in any real sense that you are white – there is simply no need to know, just as a fish would have no sense of wetness. By contrast national categorisations appeared far more intelligible with prisoners offering varied national or ethnic family lineages subsumed within the British national category. For others, though, this hybridity was emerging as problematically inclusive. According to this young white respondent (R4):

> The reason why I say that [White English] is because, like, British, you don't know what British is. You know what I mean, there's just so many ethnic minorities, not even minorities now, majorities should I say, do you know what I mean. They're everywhere and to me, and I mean they never say, the African minorities never say they're English, they say they're British, so I'd like to be separated from that. I don't wish to be too close to that. I know it's a bit controversial, but that's what I believe, you know what I mean.

As this account suggests although 'Whiteness' may appear vacant it is not undefended and the axis of defence often turns on notions of exclusive national belonging as a cipher for race.

Ethnicity had a latent quality for many minority ethnic prisoners too, portrayed simply as a formal descriptor rather than being at the forefront of lived experience. Here a black prisoner resists the cultural boundedness of his own official and social ethnic ascription:

> I don't really see the point of that [HMPS ethnic monitoring codes]... I say it's where I'm from but I don't really talk about it as much as if it's something special... The most thing that I've seen is like Irish men, they're proper proud of being Irish. But... [CP: Can you understand that?] No, not one bit.
>
> (Black, British National, Christian – R48)

Prisoners' reluctance to engage with ethnicity seemed to mask a lack of willingness to actively engage with difference, perhaps because race and ethnicity occupy particularly difficult terrain in the late modern prison (Phillips, 2008). Prisons are, at several levels, an attempt to shape and categorise 'the self' of the convicted young men. They are inherently authoritarian regimes that in both popular and practical consciousness involve the erasure of a personal identity, symbolised by the substitution of a prison number for the individual's name (Sykes, 1958). Though the practice of referring to prisoners exclusively by their number is now officially discouraged the legacy remains vivid. This prison context intensifies the ways in which talk of ethnicity conveys a sense of oneself as constructed by others, of being objectified and being seen as 'something' rather than 'someone'. More and more, as the explicit parameters of whiteness enter the structured domain of ethnicity, white people are beginning to encounter this exteriority (Macey, 1999). Resisting the implicit invitation to occupy a pre-prepared template of the self was expressed, with some vigour and frustration, by this young White British national (R41):

> What do you mean? I'm not an ethnic group, I'm just [Dimitri], I don't class myself as any ethnic group. If someone want to ask me where do I come from, I come from Cyprus and I don't class myself as any ethnic group. I'm just [Dimitri] and I don't feel this little communities with ethnic groups and whatnot, I don't care, I'm not interested. I don't get involved in that.

The sentiments expressed by many white and some minority ethnic prisoners reflected a desire to see themselves and others simply as human beings, not defined by their race or ethnicity. An Asian Muslim prisoner (R51) remarked, for example: 'Ethnicity is not really a big thing. Obviously it is a big thing but nobody takes it as a main mark. It's more on the lines of who you are personally. Not your race as an individual, exactly'. A white prisoner (R6) put it like this:

> No, I don't feel white, I don't feel white, you know. I know I'm white and all that, but the thing is, though, I'm still the same person as a Black and Asian, Chinese people, you know, I'm still, they're still the same person as me. You know, we all growed up from the apes and everything you know.

In these accounts from the young men in prison there might be something of the 'wise passivity' associated with Keats' notion of 'negative capabilities'.[2] This refers to a kind of intuitive awareness of powerful affective forces in the face of which it is wise to be passive. Prisoners' responses to our enquiries about ethnicity and identity suggest varying degrees of recognition, or fit with something of which they have a lived knowledge, but also a wariness that it also 'lives' as something else, such as racism, coercive categorisation or even anti-racism, which is not entirely coterminous with their own experience or readily intelligible to them. Negative capability is a frame of mind to let things be in whatever state of uncertainty they might be in, an incapacity or unwillingness to impose a schema of knowing on a phenomena, such as 'their identity'.

Living diversity under constraint – conviviality

Prisoners' narratives acknowledged the reality of diversity, and racial and ethnic difference was, on the surface, rendered banal and unremarkable, something that prisoners were at ease with, as this extract indicates:

> Yeah like servery, I mean back in the day there were like me, there was all different, there was a white person, there was a Caribbean person, there was like a Jamaican person, and there was a Mediterranean person and there was me, mixed race persons, so it was always different, yeah... When you're in jail it's all mixed you know what I'm saying, it doesn't matter.
>
> (Mixed Race, British National, Muslim – R15)

At play in the struggle for hegemony in the prison, it seemed, was the 'harmony discourse' detected by Back (1996) in South London, and promising, perhaps, what Gilroy (2004) has described as the possibilities of 'anti-racist solidarity' brought through a 'liberating ordinariness' which dispenses with a focus on racial differences, division and conflict.

This impression was reinforced by an unexpected but consistent feature of our fieldwork in which there were repeated references to the relative absence of racism between prisoners. Here an Asian Muslim prisoner (R51) remarks:

> my present experience, I've never found anyone to be racist or just 'I'm a Christian so I'm staying with my Christians', or 'I'm a Muslim and I'm staying with my Muslims'. For me, and for everyone on this wing that I know, it's not like that at all.

In fact, explicit racism was so highly stigmatised that a self declared racist, a swastika-tattoo bearing member of the National Front from the West Country, had frequently to be segregated for his own protection in the prison. Incidents were revealed to us in which groups of black prisoners responded violently to expressions of racism by other prisoners, with news of their response rapidly spreading around the wing and across the prison. Such retaliatory actions were rare but viewed as entirely legitimate by prisoners and as morally appropriate.

For some white prisoners the difficulties of navigating everyday contact with black prisoners led to a resigned withdrawal in which they opted to nurse their bewilderment and resentment behind closed doors and closed minds. With the risks of being labelled racist having such serious consequences, and their difficulty in finding any compensatory refuge in 'whiteness' some white prisoners attempted to avoid contact with black people altogether. We found evidence in some of our interviews of the way in which expressions of racism had become thoroughly privatised as conventional affirmations of racial superiority could only be safely shared in exclusive white company, which the crowded, enclosed and structured prison environment tended to frustrate. These prisoners described how an active effort of separation was required, and the resentment expending this effort fostered. As this young man (R13) indicates this could sometimes also be an extension of earlier habits of 'white flight', social withdrawal and avoidance:

> I don't really talk to Black people . . . It's like I say, I don't really interact with Black, Black community in here, or Asian community. It just, it's about the same on road,[3] I don't really mix with them on road either.

As Phillips (2008) notes the fragmented terrain occupied by ideas about race and ethnicity in Late Modernity generate confusion, anxiety and ambiguity for white prisoners. Familiar and reassuring privileges of racial hierarchy are manifestly not what they were, or where they were; the comforting fantasies of racialised power appear withered by the persistence of lived contradiction, they are less stable and heavily, openly and constantly contested. The interpretive framework for the signification of race has none of the clarity or simplicity it formerly rested on. It is certainly feasible that the difficult and potent mix of social isolation, continual surveillance and enforced proximal living in the prison promoted a desire among many prisoners to simply make life more bearable for each other and themselves. Making prison life liveable meant 'learning to live together' (see Goffman, 1961) in semi-permanent, semi-public space even if this meant suspending or suppressing privately held prejudices. It is also consistent, however, with the social psychological insight of Allport's (1954) 'contact hypothesis' where exchanges with different racial and ethnic groups is assumed to reduce prejudice and increase tolerance. One white prisoner (R6) from a rural area remarked on such a process by referring to his, outsider, impression of a racially segregated and dangerous London that contrasted with his, insider, prison experience of multicultural conviviality:

> In here it seems to be going quite well. But if you live round London or something, white lad walks down the black country, mate, Bang! You're dead. You know, if a black lad's walking down the white country in London, Bang! You're dead, you know. You get that out on the up but in here it's different, you know. Blacks are mixing with White, the Whites are mixing with Asians, Blacks, the lot.

At the same time, however, our fieldwork suggested that friendship groups and other informal groupings were frequently same-ethnicity, based on shared cultural understandings rather than racial or ethnic exclusion. Fieldwork notes pointed to the relatively relaxed inter-ethnic interactions between prisoners during leisure activities in 'soash' (evening association) and during freeflow.[4] Thus, while friendship groups and informal gathering indicated a strong ethnic component, this was low-key and did not appear to reflect rigid or harshly conflicted boundaries between prisoners of different ethnicities, faiths and nationalities.

Prisoners remarked frequently that the opportunities for informal and elective mixing were seriously constrained by the regime timetable. The removal of choice in movement, location and co-presence was identified as central to the ensuing social relations:

> And like, yeah, people like, see when you live in one place together, yeah, you get along, you're forced to live together in one place . . . On the outside you have choice; if you don't want to get along with someone then you won't see them the next day if you don't want to.
>
> (Black, British National, Muslim – R3)

> You have to [mix] in here though don't you because there's no choice about it is there? Because on road you can avoid that mixing with people but in here like you're all here, aint you.
>
> (White, British National, Christian – R39)

Racialised antagonism between prisoners were not entirely absent but appeared to be mostly suppressed in everyday social relations in the prison. They were liable to surface in specific instances as tensions rose or relations became more stressed. For white prisoners, racism had become a resource to be drawn upon more privately than publicly, as an affirmation of self in company where it was unlikely to be ill-regarded. Its open expression was contingent on some element of collective power being present to maintain its assertion in the face of such widespread hostility, and these opportunities were few. The result was a convict-conviviality (i.e. prison specific) composed of slightly wary social relations in which racism was present but manifestly unstable, inconsistent and contradictory. This conviviality was conditioned by the specific, structural, modalities of prison life; the enforced proximity of 'lightly engaged strangers', its impermanence and the imminence of moving onward elsewhere in the prison system on reaching 21 years of age or out of it altogether on release.

Religious identities, practices and collectivities

Just as the assertion of Muslim identities in the wider world has thrown into sharp relief some of the unseen assumptions and prejudices of the 'The West' their presence in the prison system has prompted new lines of enquiry into the dynamics of prison regimes and prison life (Beckford et al., 2005). There is a tendency in the resurgent interest in Islam and the forms of identification that accompany it, to neglect questions concerning the hegemonic position of Christianity, the prevailing religious faith on which the foundations of the prison as a social institution were built. During fieldwork prisoners and prison staff frequently commented on the Muslim presence in the prison. Both saw Islam as a point of connection, an identity marker, and, to varying degrees, a source of tension. Neither prisoners nor officers identified any corresponding function for, or effect of, Christianity. The two major faiths occupy very different positions in the lives of prisoners and their social relations with each other, with Christianity assuming for the most part 'an invisible habit of mind' (Webster, 1990).

Despite lower overall numbers in the prison, attendance at Friday Muslim prayers attracted a similar quantity of prisoners as the main Christian service (40–70), with the fewer white members of the congregation drawn largely from the prison's foreign national population. There was far less evidence of the mischief, expectancy of disorder and subversive humour than characterised attendance at Anglican services.

Several Muslim prisoners identified the routines of devout observance as assuming greater consequence in prison:

> Obviously I'm more focused ain't it. I try to pray five times a day when I can. Read the Qur'an more, I read the Qur'an now and again. I practice my faith more now than I did on road, innit, because well, mostly all, I've got is, got more time innit, so you know, it's something constructive innit.
>
> (Black, British National, Muslim – R50)

The routines of Islamic observance provided Muslim prisoners with a countervailing timetable to that of the routines of the prison regime. The disciplines of Islam co-exist alongside the notionally secular disciplinary regime of the prison. They are actively taken up as an ontological resource by Muslim prisoners in ways that sometimes ironically recall Foucault's citation of the idealised Christian 'penitent' in 17th century France (Foucault, 1979: 283). They stem from the recognition that Islam is institutionally exterior to the prison and Islam may thus have an additional appeal to prisoners which draws from this autonomy. Because it can represent the possibility of social solidarity, and hence some degree of resistance to the monad order of the prison, it is regarded with considerable ambivalence by other, non-Muslim, prisoners. The concerns of some prisoners, like that of some officers, focused on the sense of a delimited collective presence in prison, potentially operating with hidden agendas and unknown boundaries.

The seductive legend of a unitary, cohesive Muslim Brotherhood was widespread among non-Muslim prisoners but did not correspond with the diverse accounts of our representative sample of Muslim respondents who indicated a variety of forms of identification and observance. Despite this, the idea that many weak or vulnerable prisoners converted to Islam to avail themselves of protection, or were coerced into the faith, had considerable currency. Comments from non-Muslim prisoners such as 'if I turn Muslim half the population of the jail can't touch me because I've got half of the jail which are Muslim on my side' (White, British – R30) were common. Some Muslim respondents were quick to express scepticism and disdain at Islam's notoriety and prominence. One remarked: 'They just do it because they think it's cool and it's the new phase that's going round London. It's a fast fame religion.' (Mixed race, British, Muslim – R15)

The accounts provided to us by prisoners, supplemented by our observational fieldwork, suggest that religious practice and identity in HMYOI Rochester are animated by the emergence of an Islamic presence. Islam in prison, as elsewhere, creates a conceptual space and experience of encounter in which different cultures may find different political vocabularies to address the constraints they face (Sayyid, 1997). White prisoners' relative absence from Christian congregations in the prison indicates the limited capacity of conventional Anglican practice to provide such vocabularies for them. Those 'invisible habits of mind' that continue to structure a great deal of prison thinking are rendered more visible by Islam's presence, and in many respects, found wanting.

'Area zones': local identifications beyond and within the prison

Among the most striking features of the fieldwork in HMYOI Rochester was the apparent unanimity among the young men of the importance of a sense of local belonging. A sense of local rootedness and attachment was frequently and powerfully expressed. In their interview accounts and interactions with us they conveyed their primary identification was with the localised spaces in which their lives had been lived before prison – the streets, shops, parks, schools, colleges and clubs. These zones operated at the level of particular estates, streets or neighbourhoods, and at town level (particularly the latter for prisoners from Kent and Essex). They established for prisoners an ontological anchor to a known and owned space.

Among the young men there was much talk of who belonged to a particular area, and how they were known by their locality. Powerful sentiments of territorialism or 'postcode pride'[5] were commonly expressed and referred to in our interviews. Below a prisoner from London E8 (Hackney) describes the strictly delineated streets in a part of East London where area boundaries were actively policed. Some of the gendered dynamics of these territorial claims (see JRF, 2008: 26) are suggested by his account:

> Like me, I got rushed on Valentines Day in E9 by some people that I was just hating because I went out with some girl from their area that

> they all wanted, but she didn't go out with them because they were low lifes and they were broke. So I was going out with her so they rushed me on Valentines Day just so I couldn't go out with her.
>
> (Black, British National, Christian – R48)

Other prisoners' narratives echoed what Robins and Cohen (1978) claimed is integral to masculine working-class cultures – participation in the symbolic process of 'owning' a material locality. For young people, mainly but not exclusively young men, this is typically managed through 'gangs' or 'fighting crews' which are pitted against rivals who engage in ritualistic displays of aggression. In this account a prisoner from Kent describes a fervent estate-based territorialism:

> ...there's Quinten Estate where I live, then you've Kemsley, Middleton and Murston and like, probably they're the four main estates known in [the town of] Sittingbourne. And like we're at more at war with them sort of thing, we don't get on with them if you know what I mean...we all go out on a weekend tooled up or whatever because we know we're going to bump into them...
>
> (White, British National, Christian – R28)

Prisoners' local affiliations sometimes resulted in local disputes, or 'area beefs', crossing over into the prison. Rival groupings from 'on road' were imported and sustained in the prison. Quite commonly, however, it seemed that these disputes were 'squashed' or mediated by the inevitability of individual interactions that the proximities of prison life imposed. One black prisoner (R12) from Brixton described long-standing disputes with the nearby 'Peckham boys' being put to one side in prison.

These spatialised identities were of central significance in the young men's lives both inside and outside prison with area-based solidarities often usurping or overlaying identities organised through race or ethnicity. This is from one prisoner, for example:

> ...on my estate we don't care who you are, what colour you are, if you don't double cross, don't cause trouble then you're okay, you can do stuff then you're basically good with us. And then if like if you can fight, you'll back us then we'll get your back.
>
> (White, British National, Christian – R45)

Implicit in such commentaries is a masculine working-class experience which resonates strongly with Robins and Cohen's (1978) earlier work. It was similarly reported by Back (1996) in his South London study of urban youth cultures, where 'neighbourhood nationalism' prevailed amidst notions of inclusion and racial harmony, at least between white and black people. Most recently territoriality has been identified as central to the lives of the young in many British cities (JRF, 2008). It may be that these local identifications link with the convergence among the accounts of many white *and* minority ethnic prisoners in describing the emptiness and latent quality of ethnicity for their self-identities As Gilroy (2004: 132) has suggested, 'factors of identity and solidarity that derive from class, gender, sexuality and *region* [authors' emphasis] have made a strong sense of racial difference unthinkable to the point of absurdity.' Whilst prisoners' accounts at Rochester support such a contention, albeit centred around locality rather than regional identity, it is worth remembering that the residential clustering of ethnic groups within the UK (Simpson, 2007) mean that a local or neighbourhood identification is often synonymous with an ethnic one. One prisoner describes this overlap in how a small group of Asian prisoners collected together on the wing:

> ... and surprise, surpise, these seven Asian lads, they're all from – what is it called – in East London, not Brick Lane, the other one, Bethnal Green, an Asian community there, majority Asian community. And if they're all from Bethnal Green they're all going to be bound to be hanging around together. If you got a bunch of lads all from Chatham [dock area of north Kent, implicitly white] they're all going to be together.
>
> (Black, Foreign National, Muslim – R47)

Significantly, however, even when this overlap has been the case for the young men their identification is primarily articulated through a sense of locality rather than ethnicity, the mechanisms of shared local knowledge appear to take precedence over shared experiences of ethnicity, as if the former is considered more viable than the latter.

Bauman's (2004) work on insecurity and uncertainty also sheds light on the young men's postcode pride. Bauman sees fervent territorialism as a means for individuals to claim safety and ontological security by defining and policing boundaries of belonging and exclusion. Symbolic 'ownership' of these 'area zones' enables these young men to demonstrate status and dominion among their contemporaries: the young people whose lives are lived on and among the streets of London, Essex or Kent. This largely masculine, unruly, working-class claim over public but local spaces stands in contradistinction to more orderly middle-class claims to a life lived 'quietly', in well-resourced, spacious private properties, funded by jobs that ensure a greater degree of comfort, security and global mobility.

Postcode pride's narrower, inverted, local ambition appears to act as an antidote to the stigma and blame which dogs the socially, politically and economically marginalised men of late modern society. Young men's localised, martial masculinities recall medieval, seemingly pre-modern, models of manhood (see Rose, 1993) and are quickly demonised. They do not conform to the features demanded of workers in the low-wage service economy that have replaced traditional working class male manufacturing job prospects. As Kenway and Kraak (2004) argue the key features of the desirable 'First World' worker now include mobility, i.e. they should not be rooted in place, and flexibility, i.e. they must be prepared to work in any mode, at any time, for any pay. Similar observations on a masculine working-class disenfranchisement from traditional labour process are noted in McDowell's (2003) account of marginalised white young men. Her respondents struggle to fit in with the docility, deference and neat embodied performance demanded by the low-wage service economy that hails them as their formal education ends. For many working-class men conventional masculine possibilities have become largely disconnected from such forms of labour. However, contrary to Bauman's vision of a new underclass lacking in identity and position within mainstream society, young prisoners' local identifications are firmly agentic and defiant, asserting male working-class claims to an identity through claiming space as property and value otherwise denied to them (see JRF, 2008).

The young men's accounts of postcode pride operate as a 'transcript of resistance' (Scott, 1998). Their claim to be of their area is an assertion about how they want to know themselves as opposed to how they might be known by others in authority. The accounts of the young men in HMYOI Rochester that reveal the primacy of their identification with their immediate locality, the pride they take in their knowledge of its contours, flavours and opportunities, are consistent with Scott's account of *metis*. *Metis* is localised knowledge, a kind of folk knowledge that is not particularly useful to processes of distant government. The young men's accounts of local identification can be read as a resistance to other forms of knowing them and their lives, particularly a knowledge that seeks to rule them. In their references and claims to a postcode and local area the young men generate a short-hand for potent social networks. In de Certeau's (1984) terms they deploy the tactics of the weak in the face of strategies of the powerful.

Conclusion

The prison environment is in many ways institutionally antithetical to most of what we might associate with that which makes life liveable. Prisons are places for lives to be reduced. They are places which expend enormous effort to suppress spontaneity, extinguish vitality, condition individuality and deny collectivity. They are intensely 'masculine' but institutionally, officially, purged of sexuality. Prisons are deliberately austere environments burdened with restraints that consciously seek to exclude 'the plasticity of space, its modelling and appropriation by groups and individuals of the conditions of their existence' (Lefebvre, 1968: 79). They are quasi-urban places where the struggle against monotony and boredom, the effort to *inhabit*, as Lefebvre suggests, becomes elevated. This tends to foster among the young men in prison, we suggest here, a kind of resistant but constrained and deliberately instrumental conviviality as an assertion of their humanity in an institution infamous for diminishing it.

Contemporary prisons, such as HMYOI Rochester, are readily identifiable as institutions exemplifying those dimensions of post-colonial melancholia that so concern Gilroy. Prison's after all are deeply implicated in the colonial project, quintessential objects of the colonial imagination. Post colonial melancholia, suggests Gilroy, neurotically diverts the vitality of multi-culture into the 'pleasures of a morbid militaria'. There is considerable tension in reconciling the modern prison's founding obsession with order, hierarchy and discipline with the emancipatory promise of an egalitarian multi-culture. Beneath the superficial equanimity of conviviality in HMYOI Rochester we found familiar anxieties about race lingered obstinately and obscurely in the social relations of prisoners and the regime itself.

Paul Gilroy's (2004) work is challenging in this penal context for framing European possibilities specifically against all too real American neo-liberal legacies and penal nightmares. He seeks a counter-history of cultural relations and influences from which new understandings of multicultural Europe can emerge. He talks of the liberating possibilities in recognising the proliferating hybrids that convivial culture can produce – those that celebrate ordinary, spontaneous anti-racism, that generate the little triumphs that bring real pleasure (p. 161), that foster the small arts and crafts of living-with-others that can make a life viable. In our study of prisoner's social relations inside HMYOI Rochester we were surprised by the extent of such habits and they give us hope that even in the bleak and unforgiving landscape of prison a convivial imagination is actively fostered by prisoners and refuses to be extinguished by the enormous morbid and melancholic force of imprisonment.

Acknowledgements

The authors gratefully acknowledge the kind support and assistance of the Governor and staff of HMYOI Rochester. We are equally grateful to all the young men serving sentences there who made us welcome and generously shared their experiences and thoughts with us.

Notes

1. The name has been adjusted to preserve anonymity but hopefully retains some of the original nominative qualities.
2. Although the term is conventionally associated with 'the artist/poet' struggling to achieve creative empathy and is controversial for lack analytical specificity or rigour it is, nonetheless helpful here.
3. 'On Road' is prisoner's evocative term for life outside prison.
4. Where prisoners are unescorted by officers between the wings and place of work, education, gym, etc. It is a time of informal congregation in the rigid schedule of the prison day, allowing prisoners from different wings to chat, organise trade or engage in illegitimate activities.
5. This term was first used by Rod Earle in a co-presented conference paper (Earle and Phillips, 2007).

References

Allport, G. W. (1954) *The Nature of Prejudice*. Reading, MA: Addison-Wesley.

Back, L. (1996) *New Ethnicities and Urban Culture: Racisms and Multiculture in Young Lives*. London: UCL Press.

Barth, F. (1969) *Ethnic Groups and Boundaries: The Social Organisation of Culture Difference*. Long Grove, IL: Waveland Press.

Bauman, Z. (2004) *Identity*. Cambridge: Polity.

Beckford, A., Joly, D. and Khosrokhavar, F. (2005) *Muslims in Prison – Challenge and Change in Britain and France*. Basingstoke: Palgrave Macmillan.

de Certeau, M. (1984) *The Practice of Everyday Life*. London: University of California Press.

Earle, R. and Phillips, C. (2007) 'Of "Govs" and "Bruvs"? Young Men's Prison Lives: Ethnographic Glimpses' British Society of Criminology Annual Meeting, London School of Economics.

Fanon, F. (1968) *Sociologie d'une Revolution*. Paris: Maspero.

Fanon, F. (1975) *Peau Noire, Masques Blancs*. Paris: Collection Points, Seuil.

Foucault, M. (1979) *Discipline and Punish: The Birth of the Prison*. Harmondsworth: Penguin.

Frosh, S., Phoenix, A. and Pattman, R. (2002) *Young Masculinities*. Basingstoke: Palgrave Macmillan.

Garner, S. (2007) *Whiteness – An Introduction*. London: Routledge.

Gilroy, P. (2004) *After Empire: Melancholia or Convivial Culture?* London: Routledge.

Gilroy, P. (2005) Multiculture, Double Consciousness and the 'War on Terror'. *Patterns of Prejudice* 39(4), 431–443.

Goffman, E. (1961) On the Characteristics of Total Institutions: The Inmate World. In: D. Cressey (ed.) *The Prison: Studies in Institutional Organization and Change*. New York: Holt, Rinehart and Winston.

Jacobs, J. B. (1979) Race Relations and the Prisoner Subculture. In: N. Morris and M. Tonry (eds) *Crime and Justice*. Chicago, IL: University of Chicago Press.

Joseph Rowntree Foundation (JRF) (2008) *Young People and Territoriality in British Cities*. York: Joseph Rowntree Foundation.

Ministry of Justice (2007) *Offender Management Caseload Statistics 2006*. London: Ministry of Justice.

Kenway, J. and Kraak, A. (2004) Reordering Work and Destabilising Masculinity. In: N. Dolby, G. Dimitriadis and P. Willis (eds) *Learning to Labor in New Times*. London: Routledge.

Lefebvre, H. (1968) *Le Droit a la Ville*. Paris: Anthropos.

Macey, D. (1999) Fanon, Phenomonology, Race. *Radical Philosophy* 95, 8–14.

McDowell, L. (2003) *Redundant Masculinities: Employment, Change and White Working Class Youth*. Oxford: Blackwell.

Nayak, A. (2003) *Race, Place and Globalization: Youth Cultures in a Changing World*. Oxford: Berg.

Phillips, C. (2008) Negotiating Identities: Ethnicity and Social Relations in a Young Offenders' Institution. *Theoretical Criminology* 12(3), 313–331.

Phillips, C. and Bowling, B. (2007) Ethnicities, Racism, Crime and Criminal Justice. In: M. Maguire, R. Morgan and R. Renner (eds) *The Oxford Handbook of Criminology*, 4th edn. Oxford: Oxford University Press.

Ray, L., Smith, D. A. and Wastell, L. (2004) Shame, Rage and Racist Violence. *British Journal of Criminology* 44(3), 350–368.

Robins, D. and Cohen, P. (1978) *Knuckle Sandwich: Growing up in the Working-Class City*. Harmondsworth: Penguin.

Rose, G. (1993) in Jeffrey Jerome Cohen 'Medieval Masculinities: Heroism, Sanctity, and Gender'. Available at: http://www8.georgetown.edu/departments/medieval/labyrinth/e-center/interscripta/mm.html (accessed 08 June 2009).

Sayyid, B. (1997) *A Fundamental Fear: Eurocentrism and the Emergence of Islamism*. London: Zed Books.

Scott, J. (1998) *Seeing Like a State: How Certain Schemes to Improve the Human Condition Have Failed*. New Haven, CT: Yale University Press.

Serge, V. (1967/1937) *Men in Prison*. London: Writers & Readers.

Sharma, S., Hutnyk, J. and Sharma, A. (eds) (1996) *Dis-Orienting Rhythms: The Politics of the New Asian Dance Music*. London: Zed Books.

Simpson, L. (2007) Ghettos of the Mind: The Empirical Behaviour of Indices of Segregation and Diversity. *Journal of the Royal Statistical Society* 170(2), 405–424.

Sykes, G. (1958) *The Society of Captives: A Study of a Maximum Security Prison.* Princeton, NJ: Princeton University Press.

Wacquant, L. (2007) *Urban Outcasts: A Comparative Sociology of Advanced Marginality*. Cambridge: Polity.

Walmsley, R. (2007). *World Prison List*, 7th edn. London: International Centre for Prison Studies.

Webster, R. (1990) *A Brief History of Blasphemy – Liberalism, Censorship and* 'The Satanic Verses'. Southwold: The Orwell Press.

7

Imagining the 'Other'/Figuring Encounter: White English Middle-Class and Working-Class Identifications

Simon Clarke, Steve Garner and Rosie Gilmour

Introduction

Although there is a vast corpus on 'race' in the British context, a relatively small proportion of this is devoted to the ethnic majority, i.e. white Britons. While there is no direct parallel with the investigation of white identities that has occurred in the USA with the multidisciplinary field of 'whiteness studies' (Garner, 2007), this chapter provides a contribution to the analysis of how people discursively make 'white' identities in contemporary Britain, in both working and middle-class milieux in places where there are fewer BME people than average.

In recent years, a series of opinion polls and qualitative surveys have demonstrated a more hostile turn in British public responses to immigration and asylum (CRE, 2007; Lewis, 2005; YouGov, 2004, 2007). Our project was aimed partly at exploring the why and the how in this equation. Why are attitudes to minorities becoming more hostile, and how are they articulated outside the confines of opinion polling, which produces particular types of response to usually very direct questions?

Between January 2005 and May 2006, we conducted 128 interviews with 64 people in four areas (two in Plymouth and two in Bristol). We selected a large estate and a middle-class residential area (chosen according to a variety of socio-economic indicators from the 2001 Census) in each city. We also chose places with below average proportions of BME residents because the geographical work (Dorling and Thomas, 2004; Simpson, 2004) shows that the vast majority of UK nationals live in electoral wards with fewer than 5 per cent BME residents. As the bulk of the work on ethnicity and 'race' in post-war England has been conducted in large multicultural cities, ours was an attempt to problematise white majority identity.

The two rounds of interviews served different functions: the first was a life story centring on how the interviewees defined themselves and thought about 'home' and 'community', while the second asked broad questions about Britishness, immigration, the European Union and welfare. The findings presented from below are primarily taken from the second round of interviews. In this chapter, we maintain that the areas of concern about integration and immigration draw on the same culturally racialised resources but are expressed differently, around classed experiences and inflected by personal biographies.

Class, whiteness and the 'Other'

The interviews produced material on the 'othering' process engaged in by White UK nationals. We note here some of the patterns this process threw up. The assumption behind opinion polling and government policy in recent years has been that working-class people are more likely to express racist ideas and their communities are more likely to be won over by the Far right's messages. Electoral successes of the British National Party in specific areas of the North, and in Outer London (Cruddas et al., 2005; John et al., 2006) may well have made government concerns about managing white responses to immigration more acute. Indeed, in the Commission on Integration and Cohesion's commissioned MORI attitudinal survey (CIC, 2007b) one sample group is effectively labelled 'Far Right Target Group'. The socio-economic groups most vulnerable to the BNP (Cruddas et al., 2005; John et al., 2006) are C1, C2 and D (skilled, semi-skilled and unskilled workers). However, further analysis of the polls suggests firstly, that the difference between working and middle-class responses is more relative than absolute, and secondly, that the traditionally liberal graduates who comprise a chunk of the Labour vote are becoming less liberal on immigration (McLaren and Johnson, 2007).

Our analysis takes place against a backdrop of a process by which social class is evacuated from British public culture (Skeggs, 2004). The erasure of class includes, paradoxically, an aspect of culturally pathologising working-class behaviour on a number of fronts (including racism). This can range from the televisual confrontation of good (middle-class) with bad (working-class) models of personhood in reality television shows (Skeggs and Wood, 2008); to the othering of white working-class students as less valuable agents of capital vis-à-vis BME children in school selection (Reay et al., 2007), and the development of the figure of the 'Chav' (Tyler, 2008), through which contemporary anxieties about disorder are focussed on white working-class bodies. Indeed, the trailer for the BBC's March 2008 season of films called 'White', showed social anxieties literally being inscribed on a white man's face, colouring it in until the face disappeared and was obliterated. The films showed exclusively working-class people, as if there is no need to examine middle-class attitudes, or that integration should happen only in working-class residential areas.

We argue here that such assumptions need rethinking. What we found was that working and middle-class interviewees were often concerned about similar things; competition for resources and what they see as the (negatively) changing face of British society on a number of levels. However, the emphases and the ways in which these topics were brought up are classed. Typically the working-class interviewees' opinions were framed by first-hand experience of competing for benefits, housing and/or skilled and semi-skilled employment (not necessarily with minorities), or had family members who were now in this position. This does not grant an insight into whether the perception of minorities getting unfair advantage is borne out, but it is knowledge of the relative powerlessness of being in that situation.

Nick (20s, WC) for example, is becoming aware of the difficulties accessing decent employment and housing in Bristol, which is an expensive city. (Note that in all the extracts in this chapter the speakers have been given pseudonyms.)

> Well, if you're a British citizen, as a British citizen, yeah, if you are a British citizen, then you should... I'm sorry... At the end of the day, if you're coming over from another country, you've got to understand how our country works, do you know what I mean, so you know, you should respect and understand what our law... you know what is acceptable and what is unacceptable. You can't come into another country and then get everything handed to you on a plate. I'm sorry, I just don't agree with that.

Nick conflates cultural integration with entitlement to welfare, a recurrent discursive association in our interviews. In Mary's case, her confrontation with Bristol City Council housing officers draws on images gleaned from media:

There was a case about an Indian family staying in a hotel and they just kept paying for them. And I said to them, if I was black or wore a sari and had half a dozen kids, I said, you'd put me in a place right now. They said, that's not very nice, Mrs. Butler. I said, 'no it isn't', but that happens to be true... And I'm not prejudiced, but we should come first, we are British, we are born here.

As can be seen from Mary's claim, an association we frequently found linked two groups that were undeserving of the priority accorded them: migrants/asylum seekers (or whoever were thought to fall into those categories), and 'indigenous' white British who are not pulling their economic weight (e.g. young single mothers and people getting benefit when they should be working). Mary's reference 'if I had six kids' is to single mothers. She and her husband live next door to one, whose boyfriend burgled their flat. They are dismissive in their interviews about the ease with which young single mothers access housing and boyfriends.

Kevin (50s, WC) here talking about his estate in Bristol, takes up the theme of the undeserving white poor:

Interviewer: How do you feel about things like the welfare system of the benefits system in Britain?

Kevin: There's definitely more going out than goes in to it. There's too many people on it, for a start. I see them in this area, people who shouldn't be on it, but they are.... I'm not on about the older ones who have retired. I'm on about the young ones who've never tried to get a job and things like that. It's too easy to get now.

This heightened sensitivity over entitlement is more acute for these working-class respondents than their middle-class counterparts, whose different life experiences allow them the distance to evaluate social problems from the outside. However, what we might call a discursive 'hinge' between working and middle-class accounts is the use of 'scripts' (Edwards, 2003) and 'commonplaces' (Billig, 1991), such as the 'when-in-Rome' argument. We found respondents from across the spectrum using 'when-in-Rome' as a clinching argument for why people should assimilate to British culture. This is predicated on the idea that if the speaker (a British person) went to one of the countries that problematic immigrants originate from (almost always an Islamic one in our sample, although James (below) also uses Japan), then he/she would not be able to pursue aspects of British culture. Typical examples given are to do with dress codes and building churches.

I feel to a certain extent that if people are going to be here, they should play by our rules rather than we should bend over backwards to let them play by their rules. I wouldn't expect to go to a foreign country and totally live out my culture if it wasn't the way people did things there (...) I just think it is the way the world works. You know, if I went to Japan I would expect to take my shoes off or whatever it is when you go into somebody's house, the same way. I think if people want to embrace our culture, they should embrace our culture and if they don't want to, then don't live here. It's simple (James, 50s, MC, Plymouth).

The establishment of a reasonable set of expectations regarding cultural adaptation is a device for highlighting the illegitimacy of the behaviour of people who do not assimilate. Yet the parallel is a false one, depending on the status of white UK nationals abroad being equivalent to that of the groups they are comparing themselves with – generally non-white migrants. While the middle-class sample shared this framing device, the individuals usually had little experience of being on housing lists or of understanding themselves as competing for employment with migrants and other minority groups: they were principally owner-occupiers with professional careers. Their concerns were more abstract, analytical and remote; cultural segregation, population density and its secondary effects were those most frequently raised.

Barry (20s, MC, Bristol) sums up the argument:

> I suppose I feel we're a small country trying to accommodate a lot of people. And I feel there must come a limit to how many people we can accommodate without everything going to pot (...) not so much from an identity point of view, but more from the point of view of sustainability of resources.

Another of the middle-class immigration topics is the development of linguistic and cultural segregation, as Martin (60s, MC, Bristol) asserts:

> Interviewer: What does the word immigrant mean to you?
> Martin: Not necessarily an ethnic thing. Basically someone from another culture who's come into our culture and who should adapt to our culture (...) If they want to integrate, they have to learn English. The idea of, you know, great swathes of people in Bradford or Southall or Birmingham or Bristol or wherever, not speaking English is absurd, if you're going to have integration. Otherwise, you do have cultural and racial ghettos, which is no good to anybody.

Most British Muslims agree with Martin. In the BBC's (BBC, 2005) poll, taken in the weeks following the London Bombings, 90 per cent of Muslims, compared to 82 per cent of the national sample agreed with the statement, 'Immigrants who become British citizens should be made to learn English.' Martin's assumption of linguistic non-integration by residential district alone is a problematic one, suggesting a collapsing of diversity into a distinguishing flaw.

Integration

With Martin's observations, we move into the territory of integration, which was a term the research team deliberately avoided using in questions (as we did with 'multicultural') to allow respondents to use their own categories. The example above shows one of the recurrent themes: self-segregating immigrants. In the British context, work on how residential segregation develops (Hussain and Bagguley, 2005; Phillips, 2006) suggests that it is a much more complicated phenomenon than this, with inter-related economic and cultural dimensions.[1]

Aside from this classed distinction over concerns came a shared (mis)understanding of integration. The policy term has been around for a decade and a half (Castles et al., 2002), and is usually loosely defined as involving a two-way process. However, it is clear from our fieldwork that the popular understanding is much closer to 'assimilation'. Individual integrators are held up as models by which the collective non-integrators are measured. Integration in this perspective is achieved by not trying to be different. James's friend is:

> going up to Liverpool on a stag weekend that he's organised because he's a passionate Everton fan, he's a second-generation Asian, but you just wouldn't know it because he's a Scouser, and he waves the flag for England for the cricket (...) That's my kind of immigrant. If everybody was like that, there would be no problem, you know, but they aren't. They want to have, they want to import somehow too much, and it's not their culture, it's their religion, and that's the problem.

The question of religion is important here, and identifies the problem as located away from blackness, which James is at pains to do throughout. However, James' positioning of his friend as an immigrant as well as a second-generation Asian reveals some of the ambivalence around this distinction. This 'Scouser' is not an immigrant at all. Moreover, the role of sport (enthusiastic local football supporter and follower of the national cricket team) and national identification through the flag bind him into an arena of masculinised competitive imagined community.[2] Denise (30s, MC, Plymouth) on the other hand, has two model women in mind:

> My husband's cousin is Indian. Her family are Indian and have been here nearly 40 years, but they're very westernised. They don't, you know, they do wear their saris at special occasions and things, but they're not here demanding to bring a bit of India or, you know, to be Indian in this country... The children's godmother is from Jamaica... Janine is just as English as I am because. Well, she was born here, but not because of that, because she's not, you know, they're just the same as me and anybody else. They're not trying to be different.

Minorities perceived as 'trying to be different' generate frustration in our sample. Jane forcefully expresses the comments of a number of respondents:

> And I still get that feeling of anger sometimes (...) and I think, *is it not because you disenfranchise yourself by demanding to be different?* You know, with Muslims, for example, they want their mosques, they want to keep their women at home, they want their girls to wear burqas and God knows what for school, well, okay, we've said they can do that, and then they say, we're different, you don't accept us, we're not integrated with you, and you think, well, just hang on a minute, you know, *you want your cake and eat it*, either you want to integrate and be part of the way this country lives or you don't.
>
> (our emphasis)

This form of logic sees integration as a set of individual choices, agency, and failings, rather than taking into account any systemic discrimination or obstacles placed in the way of it. In its US incarnation, this type of explanation (for racism, poverty and gender inequalities, for example) has been labeled 'power-evasive discourse' (PED) (Frankenberg, 1994). Such discourses, it is argued, have become the hegemonic ones for explaining the social world. These frames are much more freely available to individuals than those involving reference to structural disadvantage. While in some US fieldwork (Bonilla-Silva, 2006; Lamont, 2000) it is minorities who are more likely to hold counter-hegemonic understandings of structural impediments, they are not immune to the prevailing 'PED'.[3] Very few of our sample saw integration as anything but a simple choice.

One element feeding into the overall confusion around integration may well also be the lack of understanding of the different entitlements relating to the statuses of people as labour migrants, asylum seekers, refugees, and UK nationals who are not white. In our interviews, these groups tend to be amalgamated, or the lines between them blurred. As we have already seen, James's model integrator turns out to be born and brought up in Liverpool. As in the case of Denise's friend (above), born in Manchester of Jamaican parents, the generation for whom integration begins seems confused. Why think first of other UK nationals when giving examples of integration? Surely it is incoming people who are supposed to integrate? Others draw lines in different places, like Eric (below) who prefaced the following comments with the statement that there were a lot of Somalis in Cardiff:

> It (the word 'immigrant') conjures up spongers, people living off us who are not destroying our way of life, but having an effect on the British side, I suppose (...) This is why we're partly being diluted. It's not being diluted by Indians or Pakistanis who've been here for 55 years or whatever. It's by people coming in, and I've noticed it, I go to London once a month, and I do find it, I'll be honest, mildly irritating because you hardly see what you would call a normal white British person on the street, because it is just full of foreigners, Foreigners in inverted commas, sorry...

Indeed, in the talk about immigration and Britishness people regularly ended up with stories of first- or second-hand encounters with racialised others. Some were nuanced but many others showed no evidence that the object of conversation were migrants, merely that they were not white. This slippage is a pattern, borne out in Lewis's fieldwork (2005), in which people repeatedly lump all non-white people into the category of asylum seeker. Those who could be open to arguments suggesting an alternative to buying into the racialised discourse of immigration and asylum face major information deficits around what the distinctions are between the various statuses. It is absurd for example to expect asylum seekers to contribute through taxes when they are prohibited from taking paid employment, yet few know this condition is attached to that status. Beyond that there is an increasingly complex range of identifications of who is a migrant. Many recognise that they could now just as easily be white Europeans as brown-skinned non-Europeans. The problem lies where colour is read unproblematically as mapping someone into any of those categories without considering that they might also be UK nationals: this happens frequently. Whole towns and areas (Martin's 'great swathes' of Bradford, Southall, parts of Bristol) are read as codes for non-assimilation because they have relatively high proportions of BME residents, a minority of whom do not speak English.

To recap, we deliberately chose places where there were less than the national average BME populations because we wanted to see how white identities function in those urban settings rather than in more explicitly multicultural ones. What does living a convivial multicultural life (Gilroy, 2004) mean for people who have virtually no BME neighbours or colleagues? In the following section, we look at the identifications made by the White English respondents.

Who ticks the 'big box'?

> You know that big box for ticking 'White British' – it's as if you don't have to be analysed quite as much as everybody else does.
>
> (Lucy, 20s WC, Plymouth)

Lucy's upbringing as a white child in Asia has given her experience of being a minority and not calling England home until she was already 12. She has not grown up with the taken-for-grantedness of whiteness in Britain which we were trying to unpick in this project. She was now living on a small part of the estate in Plymouth where the most ideological work had been put into actively creating community. Indeed, in our exploration of community, it was the localness of the scale of people's identifications that was most striking. Understandings of community were focussed on relatively small units.

In three of the four areas in which we worked, the ideal size of community seemed to be the 'village'. Indeed while one of the middle-class areas heavily self-identified as a village, this idea was not class bound. We wonder if the attachment to ideas of village-ness that we picked up in all four of the sites are part of a yearning for a more coherent past, turning away from what some might see as the confusion and uncertainty of multiculturalism and Britain's declining place in the world. On one of the large estates, the constituent residential areas were seen as having their own identities, and the area in which a lot of proactive community-making had been going on was based on this model (annual fete, community events, a welcome pack for new residents). We think there is an emotional investment in a community whose members are known, even if only by sight. When we asked them for their thoughts on what a community should be, people's 'imagined' communities involved buildings and institutions (schools, churches, community centres) as well as friendly people and good amenities, but the qualities people sought were safety and trust. These may be better encapsulated in a geographically smaller area.

This focus on the local links into the way people seem to be evacuating from a British identity into an English one. The point of the nation as an 'imagined community' in Anderson's phrase (1983) is that there is an act of faith: you will never meet everyone else in that community because it is too big for that to be feasible. What we found was a nostalgic turn towards a smaller-scale community that does not have to be 'imagined' (of course 'England' is no less feasible than 'Britain' in this regard). The nostalgia emerged in some ways as what Les Back (1996) calls a 'Golden Age' that people refer to as having preceded the kind of social fragmentation forming the core of contemporary understandings of Britain: a time when you didn't have to lock your door, where people took care of other people's children, and looked out for each other as a norm.

From British to English: Englishness as beleaguered

The way in which Britishness is evoked by our interviewees is paradoxical. The direct question we asked about what Britishness means elicited relatively little in terms of definitions of Britishness *per se* as well as a degree of indifference. With the exception of significant moments of national history (World War II, the 2005 London bombings), or when they were abroad and had to define themselves nationally, people generally agreed that it was not something they had thought much about. Yet there was more identification at sporting events (the Olympics, football, rugby, cricket) at which point the focus was Englishness rather than Britishness. On one hand there are few accounts of substantive Britishness (giving the world the English language; wartime resilience; independence) but a strong narrative of whatever it did mean having been weakened in the post-war period. Britishness seems to be defined more by what it is not. Several expressed embarrassment about the behaviour of Brits abroad and anti-social behaviour at home. From this theme of plummeting standards came the thread that inspired most comment. People tended to talk more about the ways in which belonging to the nation related to feelings of injustice.

There was awareness that Englishness is seen and historically experienced by other groups as oppressive:

> 'I'm of an age', recalls Theresa (60s, WC, Plymouth), 'that can still remember the British Empire, and when we were at school, there was lots of pink on maps or atlases of the world (...) but again we exploited all these countries going back then, not that I feel in these days, that's history and we shouldn't have to be apologising to everybody all the time for what we did'.

We encountered ambivalence about the legacy of these historical relationships. Some agreed that the history of oppression should be ignored completely, left in the past, or the positive side of British history stressed more. Others felt Britain still erroneously sees itself as more powerful than it really is. However, the historical legacy haunts people's statements about the desire for a more tangible and substantial Englishness in the face of the 'dilution' of Britishness. Martin (60s, MC, Bristol) has adopted a long view:

> I think English is somewhat purer or somewhat filtered, I suppose.... I would say that English goes back to, you know, Norman times, whereas British might be a British subject from the Caribbean or the Far East or whatever. One is not making racist judgements, one is merely saying that English has a longer history in this island that British does.

Indeed, in post-devolution Britain, celebrations of Welshness, Scottishness and Irishness are viewed enviously by many who feel caught between the acknowledgement that the St George's Cross and the Union Jack have become symbols linked to the political right,[4] and the perceived political correctness that involves not celebrating Britain and England's imperial past for fear of offence. It is interesting that much of the anger expressed about 'political correctness' derived from the administrative banality of filling in forms and not having anywhere to stipulate an English identity. Denise (30s, MC, Plymouth) angrily recounts the story of how her son had brought a form home from school. It was:

> ... some census that they're doing and it had every nationality, every denominal (sic.) mixture, anything that you could possibly think of, except English. And I just think, the Scots can be Scottish, the Welsh, you know, they're Welsh, but we have to be British. And it is just because of everything else. I had never bothered about it before, but I am bothering about it now.

A key focus for the emotional identities of our group was the question of fairness, and this was invoked around resources (benefits and culture). Much of the resentment was expressed towards the idea of non-nationals accessing resources and cultural preference (as seen in the previous section). There is a clear strand of hostility towards people not pulling their weight, as Janice (60s, WC, Plymouth) comments, when talking about who should be let in as immigrants:

> I suppose if we've got a shortage of skills and they want to come here and work and again, it's being useful members of society, innit? And let's face it, there's plenty of white English people, or not just saying white, but English people in this country, or British people in this country who really, if you set the criteria of not being useful members of society, you'd kick out of the country anyway....

The annoyance, frustration and sense that the celebration of Englishness is judged according to different criteria permeate the interviews. There is a real sense that being English is a social location of relative weakness that now has to be defended.

In general then, the preference for developing Englishness as a point of reference seems tied to a sense of identity injustice and deficit compared to other more 'identity privileged' groups, which of course includes the 'culture-rich' BME. Perhaps this sense that English culture is somehow 'weak' drives the feeling some people have that it is being over-ridden. Denise again:

> ...I think that, you know, we should allow for different religions, but not when their religion takes precedence over ours, because we certainly can't go to a Muslim country and have the same rights. And to call, I think, was it in Leicester, I'm not sure, the Christmas lights winter lights because of an offence, see, and it's that that's becoming really annoying to most people that I have spoken to lately anyway.

The ever-present external force of 'political correctness' is used as shorthand to articulate a variety of English anxieties about losing ground, both economically and culturally, vis-à-vis other groups. The retreat into Englishness and the repeated reference, even by secular people, to Christmas as a festival that has to be defended, cropped up in the narration of distinctions between the majority and minority communities. However, even in areas were minorities were virtually absent the localness of identifications could lead to white territorial tribalism.

This was strongly influenced by emotional attachments to certain areas that others were not going to take over.

> You never saw, hardly ever saw foreigners here, so there was a very insular, and (...) Devonports regard themselves as separate, there's rivalry there. There's rivalry between Efford and Eggbuckland, they don't intermarry (...) They'll marry within Efford and... Swilley will marry in Swilley, you don't marry from St. Budeaux if you live in Swilley.[5]

Local residents acknowledge the importance of this emotional identity and the emotional sense of belonging to specific group and place. They were both critical and aware of outsiders, usually holding some power, who do not accept the conventions and importance in these constructions of identity.

The patterns we identified among the White UK nationals were to do with shrinking communities to a more immediate size, where they could be made sense of more readily: the village rather than the estate or the town; this estate rather than that one; Englishness rather than Britishness. In this process, of relational definition, as the 'us' gets smaller, so logically does the 'them' increase, and when the immediate context is virtually all white, the definition can easily assume racialised forms.

Sam: a psychosocial study of cultural belonging

We now turn to a case study of one of our interviewees, Sam, to see how drawing on the kinds of canonical cultural narratives described above cannot be separated from the ways in which an individual represents their own circumstances, and the kind of emotional work cultural belonging actually does.

Methodologically, we aimed to unravel some of the dynamics at work in identity construction by using an unstructured life history interview, where the respondent is encouraged to talk freely and openly about their feelings and ideas, to free associate (Clarke, 2008). This often leads to a description of the respondents' unconscious fears and phantasies that are frequently based more in fiction and fear than any kind of factual experience or physical interaction.

It is only by considering the psycho-social implications that we can fully understand some of the views and attitudes held by many of the people that we interviewed. The psycho-social has to be understood as both a method (Clarke, 2006), and tool for understanding emotional identifications alongside others, so in some sense, who we are as 'white' is always constructed in relation to some 'Other'. The present is also constructed in relation to the past, and as noted above, the notion of a time when social relationships were of a higher quality pervaded the narratives of our respondents. These strong attachments and identifications with ways of life often lead to the denigration of 'Others': newcomers and outsiders who bear the brunt of the established group's hostile projections. People felt particularly threatened by asylum seekers, Muslims and Eastern Europeans, even though they knew little about these groups, yet they represent symbolic threats to white English identity. The latter tends be constructed in a way that leads to exclusionary practices and racism. Sam, one of our working-class Plymouth respondents, had what appeared to be very clear views on immigration:

> I'm afraid because they're all coming in and we're taking a lot of asylum seekers and God knows what. The British people, I'm just speaking for British now, have lost a lot of things...because they're like some people, and always, what do you call, got a social security number or social service number, and they get away with murder. That's what I'm afraid of. Society is going to beat itself.

Sam's forthright feelings on immigration seem to be based on some fear of the 'Other' or the unknown. He seems to slip between issues of immigration as a social process and ethnicity as an identity borne by 'Others' that somehow endangers his. He also seems unaware that when he talks of British people 'speaking for the British now', that this category includes many different ethnicities and cultural identities. These thoughts are reinforced when he answers the question 'What are your feelings about immigration into the country?'

> Sam: Too many.
> Interviewer: Have your thoughts changed over time?
> Sam: Put it this way, be blunt, I've never liked Coloureds, all my life, I don't know why. I've never liked them.

Sam was trying to be honest, and in doing so, constantly contradicted himself. His life history revealed that he was brought up in a care home, had been illiterate for most of his life and had worked in one job in heavy industry his whole working life. He came across as tough and dispassionate, yet has cared for his disabled partner for many years. Sam's childhood of turmoil and uncertainty not only left him incredibly good at adapting to change and resilient in the face of redundancy and ill health, but also resistant and fearful of change. We think this is reflected in his comments about immigrants. In the second interview he is fearful of them, yet then goes on to say:

> But since I've joined this community thing we run here, I went up to a gym meeting with my grandchildren, now all at the gym meeting were coloured people, and I have never met such friendly people in my life. And I came away from there thinking I enjoyed that. I'm not joking, my view changed overnight. I'll be honest. I wouldn't talk to a coloured man, I don't know why, something may have happened, I don't know, but when I went up there... My attitude changed, completely changed; now I'll even give them a cup of tea or what, purely because maybe I was ignorant of the fact that they're the same as us.

Although we think Sam is confusing recent immigrants with minority ethnic groups, his tone has changed through his own experience. Although he doesn't like change he is adaptable, and learns through experience, something he has had to do because of his lack of formal education. His statements about immigration were peppered with comments like 'I'm talking blind because I don't know whether they do it or not'; 'We can only go on what we are told or hearsay'. In fact, Sam almost admitted that he didn't really know anything about immigration.

There were some strong psychological processes at work in this interview. On one hand we are identifying with Sam and projecting things into him, as someone who symbolises hope. Someone we want to protect from misinterpretation and misrepresentation. On the other hand, we see a reparative Sam, someone who has learned by experience and changed (like all of us) for the better. He is someone who contains both good and bad, the ambivalent 'Sam' in you and us. The problem is that these positions often become confused. Because Sam offers hope, there is a danger that he becomes an idealised good object, and that his blatantly racist views are just glossed over, to preserve him in this state. Yet Sam doesn't really initiate conversation or communication with other ethnic groups and indeed is fearful of 'Others'. While we can gain particular types of insight through psycho-social interpretation, we also have to be mindful of the strong counter-transference reaction that happens within certain situations. These are apparent in the previous sections of this chapter where there is a slippage between fact and reality, phantasy and fiction.

We can see from Sam's case study that patterns in people's responses can be related to their individual biographies: both in terms of the knowledge they bring to bear, but also emotionally in the kind of affective work that ideas of difference, otherness and community do for the individual.

Conclusion

While the white working class has become an actor of sorts in the government's thinking about community cohesion recently (CIC, 2007a), individual ministers may acknowledge publicly that class still matters (Russell, 2008), we think that this policy focus is still too narrow. We spoke to people representative of the vast majority of White UK nationals, who live in areas with very small proportions of BME neighbours. People from the middle as well as the working class are enmeshed in the kinds of racializing discourses we identified, but they emphasise different aspects of it that correspond to their own experiences. In the identity talk, a number of anxieties arose: the place of the English within a devolving UK; the place of the ethnic majority in an increasingly diverse nation; the shortage of public resources. There are points where these anxieties cross class lines, and it is more the immediacy of the experience than the actual themes that distinguishes working from middle-class respondents in this respect. Fairness and unfairness are the major themes in self-identifying as English and beneath this lies sensitivity to what is perceived as losing 'our' place, as the old certainties of welfare provision, a level of civility and a more homogeneous society are understood to be disintegrating. Hence the evacuation we found from Britishness as a focus of identity.

The scenarios of allegiance thrown up are complex but rely heavily on the local. If that local area is overwhelmingly white, this does not mean there is an absence of racialisation, but that it happens in a different way than in multicultural places where encounters happen frequently enough to reach the critical mass at which conviviality seem to assume its own life.

Notes

1. See Massey and Denton's (1994) work on segregation in the USA, which shows the extent to which white flight, informal exclusionary practices from lending institutions and real-estate agencies contribute to levels of black/white segregation.

2. This raises a lot of interesting questions about identification and sport in contemporary Britain such as the meaning of the Khan Army (followers of boxer Amir Khan), who combine the Union Jack with Pakistan cricket tops; the white English cricket fans who regularly go to international matches dressed as Monty Panesar (the first Sikh to represent England at cricket), complete with false beard and headgear.
3. See Bonilla-Silva's (2006) chapter 8.
4. Although the St George's Cross' exposure through international football tournaments since Euro 1996 might well have successfully dispelled some of this.
5. These are areas in Plymouth. 'Swilley' is the former name of North Prospect, but in conversation many Plymouthians still refer to the area using its old name.

References

Anderson, B. (1983) *Imagined Communities.* London: Verso.

Back, L. (1996) *New Ethnicities and Urban Culture – Racisms and Multiculture in Young Lives.* London: UCL Press.

BBC (2005) Multiculturalism Poll, 10 August 2005. http://www.ipsos-mori.com/_assets/polls/2005/pdf/bbc050809.pdf (accessed on 8 June 2009).

Billig, M. (1991) *Ideology, Rhetoric and Opinion.* London: Sage.

Bonilla-Silva, E. (2006) *Racism Without Racists: Color-Blind Racism and the Persistence of Racial Inequality in the United States.* Lanham, MD: Rowman and Littlefield.

Castles, S., Korac, M., Vasta, E. and Vertovec, S. (2002) 'Integration: Mapping the Field' Home Office Online Report 29/03.

Commission on Integration and Cohesion (CIC) (2007a) *Our Shared Futures.* Wetherby: DCLG.

Commission on Integration and Cohesion (CIC) (2007b) *Public Attitudes Towards Cohesion and Integration.* Wetherby: DCLG.

Commission for Racial Equality (CRE) (2007) *Race Relations 2006: A Research Study.* London: CRE. http://83.137.212.42/sitearchive/cre/downloads/racerelations2006final.pdf (accessed on 8 June 2009).

Clarke, S. (2006) Theory and Practice: Psychoanalytic Sociology as Psycho-Social Studies. *Sociology*, 40(6), 1153–69.

Clarke, S. (2008) Psycho-Social Research: Relating Self, Identity and Otherness. In: S. Clarke, H. Hahn and P. Hoggett (eds) *Object Relations and Social Relations: The Implications of the Relational Turn in Psychoanalysis.* London: Karnac Books.

Cruddas, J., John, P., Lowles, N., Margetts, H., Rowland, D. and Weir, S. (2005) *The Far-right in London: A Challenge for Democracy?* York: Joseph Rowntree Reform Trust.

Dorling, D. and Thomas, B. (2004) *People and Places: A 2001 Census Atlas of the UK.* Bristol: Policy Press.

Edwards, D. (2003) Analyzing Racial Discourse: The Discursive Psychology of Mind-World Relationships. In: H. Van Den Berg, M. Wetherell and H. Hootkoop-Steenstra (eds) *Analyzing Race Talk: Multidisciplinary Approaches to the Interview.* Cambridge: Cambridge University Press.

Frankenberg, R. (1994) *White Women, Race Matters*. Madison: University of Wisconsin Press.

Garner, S. (2007) *Whiteness: An Introduction*. London: Routledge.

Gilroy, P. (2004) *After Empire: Melancholia or Convivial Culture?* London: Routledge.

Hussain, Y. and Bagguley, P. (2005) Citizenship, Ethnicity and Identity: British Pakistanis after the 2001 'Riots'. *Sociology*, 39(3), 407–25.

John, P., Margetts, H., Rowland, D. and Weir, S. (2006) *The BNP: The Roots of Its Appeal*. Democratic Audit: University of Essex.

Lamont, M. (2000) *The Dignity of Working Men*. Cambridge, MA: Harvard University Press.

Lewis, M. (2005) *Asylum: Understanding Public Attitudes*. London: Institute for Public Policy Research.

Massey, D. and Denton, N. (1994) *American Apartheid: Segregation and the Making of the American Underclass*. Cambridge, MA: Harvard University Press.

McLaren, L. and Johnson, M. (2007) Resources, Group Conflict and Symbols: Explaining Anti-Immigration Hostility in Britain. *Political Studies*, 55, 709–24.

Phillips, D. (2006) Parallel Lives? Challenging Discourses of British Muslim Self-Segregation. *Environment and Planning: Society and Space*, 24(1), 25–40.

Reay, D., Hollingworth, S., Williams, K., Crozier, G., Jamieson, F., James, D. and Beedell, P. (2007) 'A Darker Shade of Pale?': Whiteness, the Middle Classes and Multi-Ethnic Inner City Schooling. *Sociology*, 41(6), 1041–60.

Russell, B. (2008) Harman in 'Class War' Row after TUC Speech. *Independent*, 11 September 2008. http://www.independent.co.uk/news/uk/politics/harman-in-class-war-row-after-tuc-speech-925571.html (accessed on 8 June 2009).

Simpson, L. (2004) Statistics of Racial Segregation: Measures, Evidence and Policy. *Urban Studies*, 41(3), 661–81.

Skeggs, B. (2004) *Class, Culture, Self*. London: Routledge.

Skeggs, B. and Wood, H. (2008) Spectacular Morality: 'Reality' Television, Individualisation and the Re-making of the Working Class. In: D. Hesmondhalgh and J. Toynbee (eds) *Media and Social Theory*. London: Routledge. pp. 177–93.

Tyler, I. (2008) 'Chav Mum Chav Scum': Class Disgust in Contemporary Britain. *Feminist Media Studies*, 8(1), 17–34.

YouGov (2007) Immigration. http://www.migrationwatchuk.org/pressReleases/01-November-2007#164 (accessed on 8 June 2009).

YouGov (2004) Attitudes to Immigration. http://www.yougov.co.uk/extranets/ygarchives/content/pdf/DBD040101004.pdf (accessed on 8 June 2009).

8

The Subjectivities of Young Somalis: The Impact of Processes of Disidentification and Disavowal

Gill Valentine and Deborah Sporton

The twin forces of the global economy and global conflicts have accelerated patterns of transnational migration at the beginning of the 21st century, raising questions about how such mobility might shape processes of identification. In this chapter, we focus on the experiences of Somali refugee and asylum seeker children aged 11–18 now living in Sheffield, UK. In doing so, we draw on narrative theories of identity (Somers, 1994). In outlining a narrative approach to identity, Somers (1994: 606) argues that 'it is through narratives and narrativity that we constitute our social identities . . . all of us come to be who we are (however ephemeral, multiple and changing) by being located or locating ourselves (usually unconsciously) in social narratives rarely of our own making'. In particular, we seek to understand how young Somalis negotiate and discursively position themselves within hegemonic social narratives that are not of their own making and which define what it means to be: British and Muslim; that are racialised and gendered. These hegemonic social narratives are very powerful in making certain subject positions available to be inhabited, even though the actuality of social categories are more contradictory, fragmented, shifting and ambivalent than dominant public definitions of them (Frosh et al., 2002).

At the same time, drawing on the work of Giddens (1991) and Beck (1992), we are also alert to the ways that Somali young people position themselves in relation to these dominant frameworks and produce their own narratives of the self, and the particular interpretative repertoires that they draw on within this process. Here, we understand identity not just to be about commonality; but also to be defined by difference: what it is not (Said, 1978). In doing so, we recognise that individuals' identities are never produced along one axis of difference (e.g. gender, class or age). Rather, as Crenshaw (1993) argued, we need to be alert to the intersection of differences. Social categories do not accumulate but rather inflect each other such that multiple social distinctions may amplify, contradict and shape one another (McCall, 2005). As such, we are concerned with the multiple, shifting and sometimes contradictory ways that individuals both identify and disidentify with other groups; and with their fluctuating emotional investment in different subject positions.

The social sciences have paid relatively little attention to space in processes of subject formation. Yet, we recognise that identity practices do not occur in a vacuum: who we are emerges in interaction but within specific spatial contexts and biographical moments. As such, we understand identities to be 'situated accomplishments' (c.f. West and Fenstermaker, 1995) in that they are performed in, and through different spaces (such as the home, the nation, the transnational diaspora, etc.), such that one identity category may be used to differentiate another in specific spatial contexts and particular subject positions may become salient or irrelevant in particular spaces (Valentine, 2007).

While, as Hall (1992) has argued, having 'an identity' is problematic because of the way different social (and we would stress spatial) contexts produce varied subject positions that may be occupied, nonetheless people still claim specific identities as a process of making sense of 'self'. Yet, a given identity is not just something that can be claimed by an individual however, it is also dependent, at least in part, on an individual's identity being recognised or accepted by a wider community of practice (Bell et al., 1994). Power operates in and through the spaces within which we live and move in systematic ways. One consequence of this is that a given identity in different contexts can define an individual as 'out of place' according to specific spatial norms and expectations (Cresswell, 1996), resulting in processes of exclusion which define 'the person not to be'. To-date, there is relatively little empirical work to show how such processes of disidentification impact on young people's subjectivities and are lived out in particular spaces. In the remainder of the chapter, we therefore focus on some of the ways Somali young people, currently living in the UK, move between different subject positions, highlighting how in particular spatial contexts arbitrary signifiers such as skin colour and dress assume particularly powerful meanings, defining and shaping experiences of disidentification.

The material presented here is based on multi-method qualitative research. Fifty Somali children and the majority of their parent(s)/

guardians (some of the children were unaccompanied minors who did not have an appropriate adult able to be interviewed) were recruited for interview as a result of snowballing through a school survey, homework clubs and a range of contacts and organisations. These interviews explored their individual histories of mobility, senses of attachment and understandings of their own identities.

Somali migration to the UK can be divided into different phases: around the turn of the 20th century, Somali seamen came to work in the British Merchant Navy, when this was run down in the 1950s, Somalis moved to work in industrial cities such as Sheffield. At this point, many of the seamen were joined by their families. From the late 1980s onwards, significant numbers of Somalis arrived in the UK seeking asylum because of the civil war. The last phase of migration began around 2000 when Somalis who had obtained refugee status and later citizenship in other European countries (e.g. Netherlands and Denmark) began secondary migrations to the UK. The Somali community in the UK is thus characterised by different arrival scenarios. The interviewees were therefore purposively sampled to include all major arrival scenarios, a range of ages (between 11 and 18) and an equal number of boys/girls.

The interviews were conducted in English, or with an interpreter at a place of the interviewee's choice. In addition, interviews were conducted with key stakeholders (e.g. representatives from local bodies dealing with asylum issues, various Somali education and community projects, etc.) about the broader contextual issues that may shape young people's everyday lives, and participant observation was carried out in local Somali community spaces. All of the interviews were taped, transcribed and coded. Quotations from the interviews that are used in this article are verbatim, spoken or grammatical errors have not been corrected.[1]

Skin colour: the denial and disavowal of the identities 'British' and 'Black'

Most of the young people interviewed argued that they had the right to occupy the subject position British because they live in the UK, speak English and share many things in common with other local children, including the same interests, aspirations and everyday practices at school. Yet, despite being able to position themselves as British in these ways, when some of the young people had actually claimed to be British in public space, their identity claims were rejected. In other words, it is not enough to claim an identity – it must also be recognised or ascribed by others as these interviewees describe:

> Ayaan: ...they go 'Oh you're not British, you're not from Britain, you're not British', but it's like 'I've got a passport, I've been here practically all my life'...I goes 'I bet I know more about Britain than your daughter who's white and British born and everything'. And they're like 'Oh no'. And I'm like 'I probably do'. And like...most of the time I'm always right (female 17, migrated directly to UK from Somalia).
>
> Labaan: Like being British is not that important cos if I'm British the other people won't recognise me, they don't think I am British...cos [of] what I look like. Being black, it's like the colour of my skin (male, 14, migrated directly to UK from Somalia).

In the 1980s, Gilroy (1987) demonstrated how Englishness and blackness were produced as mutually exclusive categories. Despite, subsequent political attempts to re-imagine what it means to be 'British' and the extension of equality legislation, nonetheless both English and British are still racialised as white identities, largely unfragmented by multicultural experiences (Valentine, 2008). As such, none of the young people claimed an English or a British identity even though some said they 'felt' British or English. Rather, the children recognised that the identity category 'black' overshadowed or undid their right to take up this particular subject position and that they were implicitly 'out of place' in the UK:

> Asad: I can't use that word I belong here...you can't use that for yourself...I belong in England...I would say this yeah...but usually I never see someone saying to me 'Oh you belong in England'. You know what I mean...English people I hear what they're saying to me, 'you belong in Africa...go back there'...and when people say 'Where you belong?' I just say 'Oh I belong in Somalia'...cos you've heard enough times 'you're not from England' (male 17, migrated directly to UK from Somalia).

Hall (1996) has pointed out that identity 'requires not only that the subject is hailed, but that the subject invests in the position'. Yet, despite being ascribed a black identity in everyday public spaces, the majority of the interviewees disavowed the identity 'black'. This was because it was not an identity that was either emotionally or politically salient for them. Rather, blackness was dismissed as just skin colour – an external veneer – rather than an emotional (inside) attachment as this interviewee explains:

> Abdikarim: When you think about black and white...it's just the colour of your skin, it's like the colour of your hair basically, really that's all it is. So it's just how other people see you, it's not nothing inside you...but it's just how other people see you on the outside (male, 17, born in UK).

Commentators (e.g. Bonnett, 2000) have critiqued whiteness as a monolithic identity which obscures the diversity of subject positions, experiences and cultural identities which constitute the category 'white'. In the same way, for the Somali interviewees, the identity 'black' equally represented an unexamined 'norm' ascribed to them by others, which erased their particularity. For the interviewees, 'black' signified a particular set of African Caribbean identities:

> Hassan 1:[2] Although I'm black, that's my skin colour there's not a lot of black people that are Muslims.... I grew up in South London and especially Brixton...90% are black...and what I found is that within that community there was so much different black cultures and yourself you had to think about what kind of black you are...then the English will say you're not English you're black, how can you be English? I feel I've got an identity being Somali so I always know where I'm from...My skin is black and that's what colour I am...but I see myself as Somali black. A white person will just see you as black...They see a black is black. Sometimes they think I'm Jamaican. I'm not Jamaican; I'm Somali (male, 17 migrated directly to UK from Somalia).

In an in-depth study of 11–14 year-old-boys in London schools, Frosh et al. (2002) demonstrated the power of a particular hegemonic social narrative of black masculinity as the 'boy to be'. This located African Caribbean boys as smart and tough: the 'cool pose'. In a finding that chimes with other studies (e.g. Connolly, 1994), Frosh et al. (2002) argued that some white boys, as well as Somali boys, were 'black wannabes' who aspired to the cultural trappings associated with being black. In contrast, Asian was the 'boy not to be': Asian boys were the focus through which other boys developed and asserted their masculinity. Black and white boys regarded themselves as more like each other than Asian boys who were picked on and disparaged in implicitly Islamaphobic ways because of perceived differences such as their language and culture, strong family ties and sense of togetherness.

The Somali boys interviewed as part of this study were caught between competing subject positions at school. On the one hand, by playing football, disrupting lessons and so on, many of them were implicitly positioned within hegemonic social narratives of 'cool' black masculinity. On the other hand, as Muslims, their faith, as well as their residential location – Somali families are concentrated in predominantly Pakistani neighbourhoods – positioned them in relation to Asian masculinities. Likewise, while hegemonic black femininity is associated with being loud, aggressive and assertive and is therefore variously admired, feared and disparaged (Frosh et al., 2002), Somali girls, as Muslims, predominantly wear the hijab and enact more modest femininities.

The Somali interviewees therefore took up complex and implicitly contradictory subject positions produced through intersecting disidentifications (Valentine and Sporton, 2009). They disidentified as black because they are not from the Caribbean and recognised their inability to fully accomplish hegemonic black masculinity/femininity (e.g. because of their Muslim names and religious observance), while also disidentifying with any attempts by their black and white peers to position them in relation to Pakistani Muslim cultural identities. Rather, in the context of the socio-spatial norms of the school, they asserted the specificity of 'being Somali'.

In highlighting the significance of their place of origin rather than a racial or cultural identity, they also disavowed the significance of racism despite describing a range of experiences in which they had patently been subject to racism in multiple forms. For example, when describing how their claims to be British had been denied in public situations many of the Somali interviewees failed to locate this as racism, rather accepting that such experiences were the 'norm' in public space and should be ignored; or de-racialised these accounts by labelling them as 'bullying'. Likewise, in describing being called a 'black bastard' on the street one of the interviewees disassociated this experience of racism from himself by projecting it onto the Pakistani community, claiming that he had only been abused in this way because he had been mistaken as 'a Paki'. Indeed, despite such accounts, the majority of the informants described feeling 'safe' in the UK. This perception of trust appears to stem from being part of a strong and stable local Somali Muslim community which gives its inhabitants a freedom to define their own narratives of identity beyond narrow prescriptions such as 'British' or 'black' (Valentine et al., 2009).

> Hassan 2: In the neighbourhood you feel Somali because there's a lot of Somalis around here therefore... Somali will be the only thing you will be speaking. That's when you most think you're a Somali... you're around people that are the same as you... that gives you the impression of being a Somali... being safe (male, 15, migrated to UK via Dubai in United Arab Emirates).

Indeed, despite the fact that Somali interviewees' described experiences strongly marked by racism – and numerous other studies (e.g. Frosh et al., 2002) have demonstrated the prevalence of racism in schools perpetrated by both teachers and children – the children adopted the language of multiculturalism to describe their everyday encounters. They argued that skin colour was unimportant in their everyday lives because it was not an emotionally salient identity for them because they believed that everyone should be accepted as equal, while simultaneously reproducing contradictory racist comments about other groups. This positioning shares striking similarities with the accounts of white boys as described in Frosh et al.'s (2002) study, and has obvious political significance, disconnecting Somalis from anti-racist movements.

Being 'in place' and 'out of place': the ambiguities of (dis)identifying as Somali

We all define ourselves, at least in part, by *where* we are from. Yet this was not a straightforward process of identification for the interviewees. The Somali community is fractured by allegiances to different Somali clans (Griffiths, 2002) and by cultural differences between the established Somali community, those who have newly arrived direct from Somalia, and those who are secondary migrants, having come to the UK via other countries where they have spent significant periods of time and in some cases acquired different nationalities and associated linguistic and cultural practices. As such, these different histories of mobility inflected the young people's self-identifications as Somali, and the degree to which they were ascribed a Somali identity by the local Sheffield Somali community.

Abdikarim, who was born in the UK, self-identifies as Somali. Yet, he simultaneously disidentifies with both new arrivals from Somalia because of what he perceives as their inappropriate cultures of interaction and public incivility, and older generations of Somalis in Sheffield who have not learnt to speak English and whose everyday lives are still heavily circumscribed by their Somali clan (which he refers to as tribes) identities.

> Abdikarim: I've noticed that people who have come direct from Somalia, they don't fully integrate into society. Like you'll see them walking around town ... they'll see another Somali far away and they'll shout in their language. [Whereas] when people from Britain, when they talk to each other they talk so they can hear each other not any more [louder] than that ... I find them [new Somali arrivals] quite embarrassing to be honest cos from experience when we go places people give you looks and think what are these barbaric people ... I feel these Somalis that have just come over ... they lack the characteristics of civilised people ... [Later he referred to the older generation] they still haven't integrated into society ... they can't speak English so they hang around with Somalis all day and they just speak Somali and they talk about tribal matters ... so it's the older generation they haven't integrated ... (male, 17, born in UK).

Yet, despite disavowing significant elements of Somali cultural identity and his own community in such ways, Abdikarim's self-identity as Somali remains untroubled.

Layla lived in Newcastle, predominantly a white northern UK city, for six years where she was isolated from a Somali community and spent most of her time in the company of a white majority peer group. When she moved from Newcastle to Sheffield she was called 'fish and chips' by members of the Sheffield Somali community, not only because of her lack of fluency in the Somali language but also because her identity was read by them as 'British'. The experience of being denied recognition as a 'proper' Somali by the community, rather than prompting Layla to disavow her identity as Somali, led her to reposition herself within hegemonic local community narratives by learning the Somali language, embracing other cultural practices and switching friendship groups from a predominantly white British social network to a Somali one as she describes

> Layla: The Somalis were surprised at me cos I didn't know none of the language [when she first arrived in Sheffield] and they like,

they have a word for certain people who are born in, like a name calling, if when a Somali person's lived in Britain their whole life they call them fish and chips, yeah. It's like a modernised person, so that's what I used to be called...Now that I know more of the language I tend to move towards Somali girls...cos its better like that so then all the people like family and like your uncles and that when they see you, it's better for them to see you with Somali girls than like another girl if you know what I mean (female, 16, born in UK).

For the majority of the interviewees being brought up within Somali households (a few of the unaccompanied children were living with white British foster carers), the importance of 'being Somali' was produced through everyday domestic practices from the language spoken, clothing worn and faith practised, through to the food eaten.

Hassan 3: At home, it's where I learnt most things about Somalia. From the moment I talked I speak Somali with my Mum and Dad so I feel Somali when I'm at home. It's like the food that we eat, it's traditional Somali food. Things such as that make you feel Somali (male, 18, migrated directly to UK from Somalia).

Indeed, most of the parents interviewed were concerned that because their children spent the majority of their time at school speaking English and conforming to everyday public narratives about what it means to be British they might begin to disidentify as Somali. As such, many explained that they had to use 'home rules', such as insisting that the children only spoke Somali at home, to reproduce and enforce the home as a Somali space, because they wanted to ensure that their children had a sense of belonging to Somalia and were ready to return either permanently or for a visit when peace is restored to the country (Valentine et al., 2008).

All of the young people interviewed were emotionally invested in this subject position. Indeed, the sense of displacement they experienced as the result of their own/families' mobility and sense of lost homeland only served to signify the importance of their emplacement as Somalis.

Ayama: I'm Somali. That means to me a lot actually because it's where I come from and where I belong and all my family belong there. Even though my skin colour is black my nationality is Somali and I am proud of that...I know where I belong and I know one day

> I will go back home (female 18, migrated as an unaccompanied minor direct to UK from Somalia to live with her uncle and aunts)

Yet, because most of the interviewees' families had fled Somalia when they were very young, or they had been born once their families were on the move, the majority of the interviewees had few direct memories of Somalia. Rather, the young people interviewed positioned themselves in relation to narratives of what it means to be Somali that as well as being not of their own making were predicated on sometimes contradictory second-hand accounts ('civil war' and 'beautiful country') of a place they do not know. Whereas media reporting of Somalia commonly creates negative representations of a country riven by war, famine and terrorism, most of our interviewees were offered more positive representations by their parents of a 'lost' family life. Pratt (2003/2004), drawing on research with Filipino immigrants to Canada, argues that parents' experiences of dislocation have an impression on their children's self-identities. She employs Hirsch's (1997) notion of 'postmemory' – the experiences that young people 'remember' only as the stories and images of past places/times instilled them by their parents – to demonstrate how negative experiences or traumas can be passed down the generations. However, the evidence of this research (Valentine et al., 2009) is that parents were anxious to protect their children from the burden of negative postmemories. Rather, they glossed over the hardships and violence that they, or relatives, may have experienced in order to protect their offspring from trauma.

Some however, have been able to make return visits to Somalia. Other studies (c.f. Mason, 2004) suggest that such 'return journeys' provide an important process through which migrants can reflect on their own identities and develop a sense of affinity with the country visited. For the Somali children, the journey was imagined as a homecoming: as an opportunity to experience a sense of identity. Yet, on arrival many of the children were shocked by the poverty they encountered as well as struggling to adjust to the heat, food, sanitation and lifestyle. Some of the interviewees were also troubled by the way their age positioned them differently in Somalia than the UK. While at first, the earlier school leaving opportunities and the possibility of taking on more adult-like responsibilities at an earlier age in Somalia were superficially attractive to some of the interviewees, others recognised the potential consequences of a lack of educational opportunities for their imagined future occupations and identities. The young women interviewed in particular disidentified with the gender roles that girls of their own age occupied in the more traditional patriarchal society of Somalia as this interviewee explains

> Nadifa: It's like there [in Somalia] it's just totally different. There' it's like women stay in the house, clean, cook and things like that. It's not like here where a woman goes independently to work and things like that. It's like there's two different roles for a woman, here and there... When we went home [i.e. to Somalia] most girls stayed at home, maybe played inside the house and the boys just went and played outside... It's totally different to here... Being a woman here it's like a guy. You have to go to school and study and everything like that. I don't think I've washed dishes since I came here [to UK] [laughs] (female, 17, migrated to UK via Ethiopia and Italy).

Such experiences of disidentification were compounded by the way that as visitors the interviewees were positioned by local people. As this interviewee describes, some found their claims 'to be' Somali were rejected by local people for whom their pale skin, language errors/accent and western dress, which we might summarise as embodied ways of being, marked them out as not belonging (Valentine et al., 2009). Others recounted how despite the fact that their families lived in the UK in low-income neighbourhoods where unemployment was high and housing standards were poor they were mis-identified in Somalia as 'wealthy' and as a consequence were hassled for money and favours, leaving them feeling uncomfortable and unsafe.

> Nadifa: When we used to go to Somalia a lot of people used to say 'oh you lot, people from England'. And I just said to my Mum 'how do they know?' And My Mum goes 'that's how they are because of your walk and the way you talk'. Cos I used to talk English to my brother in Somalia and they used to turn round and stare at us and they knew that we were not from here... That's how it is, that's how it is in Somalia... there's a lot of people now these days that are scared to go to Somalia because... people stare at you and they talk about you (female, 17, migrated to UK via Ethiopia and Italy).

In such ways, the interviewees simultaneously both identified as Somali yet also disidentified with Somalia and the age and gender subject positions available to them there. When their claims to Britishness were not ascribed by the white majority community, the interviewees accepted this denial or rejection of their self-identification. Yet, despite being similarly not ascribed a Somali identity in Somalia, the interviewees' self-identities as Somali, though shaken, were not over-turned by their experiences of being 'out of place'. This is because the young people retained their belief in their right to claim this identity because of the way that it is recognised or hailed within the spatial contexts of the family home and the local Somali community in Sheffield, UK, despite being misinterpellated in Somalia. As such, the identity 'Somali' remained emotionally salient for the interviewees notwithstanding their visits to, and reception in, Somalia. Rather, some of the young people managed their identity troubles by constructing an imagined future narrative of the self in which they would qualify as a doctor, or an engineer in the UK and 'return' to Somalia to help transform the economy and society to enable young people there to have a better standard of life.

Being Muslim: continuity and emotional investment in the context of mobility

Muslims are often located within an imagined Black or Asian community (Modood, 1992). Yet, all of the Somali young people interviewed defined themselves first, and foremost in relation to their faith, rather than their race, ethnicity or nationalities. For the young people interviewed, the subject position Muslim overcame some of the troubling aspects of the other subject positions available to them: notably the denial of their Britishness, disidentification as black and the complex ambiguities of their (dis)identifications as Somali. Moreover, it was a subject position which embraced the transnationality of *umma* and thus offered a stable, omni-available attachment which was rendered particularly salient by the young people's complex histories, and possible futures, of mobility. As such, an attachment to the identity Muslim offered the young people some temporal continuity – because they could build on this sense of self from memories of their past; while also imaging their future self as a Muslim (the person they wanted to be) whatever the past or future discontinuities in their location and their associated positionings as being 'in place' or 'out of place'. In part, this sense of continuity in this identity claim stemmed from the way that their faith powerfully shaped their everyday use of space (e.g. through the rituals of prayers, visits to the Mosque or Quranic education classes) wherever they happened to be living. Yet, it was also frequently described in implicitly essentialist terms.

Khatara: You've got to pray five times a day and read the Qu'ran. I read the Qu'ran. It's important to me because my religion comes before everything. Like first would be my religion and then my Mum and then my family, so it's very important to me because it comes before everything else... You pray wherever you are... If it means you have to pray in the street, you have to. It comes wherever you are [edit] I'm always aware of the fact that I'm a Muslim... you think about it everywhere you are (female, 18, migrated to the UK via a refugee camp in Djibouti).

Asad: Allah is watching 24 hours you know what I mean. And always when I'm sleeping, when I wake up, I know that I'm a Muslim and part of my heart and part of my body and part of me a Muslim always (male, 17, migrated directly to UK from Somalia).

Not surprisingly, all the young people interviewed had powerful emotional investments in the subject position Muslim. Yet, this is not to suggest that this always overrode all other forms of identification and was not also inflected by gender, age, nationality and so on. In particular, young people's degree of knowledge about their faith and the extent to which they put it into practice was shaped by specific 'community' norms in different geographical locations. The Muslim community in Sheffield, like others in the UK is made up of Muslims from Africa, the Middle East and South Asia as well as white British Muslims. As such it is bisected by doctrinal, as well as cultural/linguistic differences (c.f. Afshar et al., 2005; Vertovec, 1998). Likewise, as we observed earlier, the Somali community itself is also fractured by divisions between established Somalis, those newly arrived direct from Somalia and those who are secondary migrants. As such, these histories of mobility have inflected the young people's understandings of what it means to be Muslim.

Community 'norms' in Sheffield served as regulatory regimes, circumscribing gendered identities in particular ways. Young women therefore described wearing the hijab and behaving in modest ways in public space in order to maintain their own and their families' reputations within the neighbourhood. However, below Layla and Zeinab describe how Somali European migrants' different interpretations of the subject positions available to young women (which included dress, use of language, smoking and drinking alcohol) meant that their identities were read as not 'proper' Muslims by the local Sheffield Somali community.

Layla: People from European countries like Holland them girls like here now Sheffield people don't really like Holland girls you know ... the 'Dutch girls' [the nickname used for European migrants] they have it, have a hard time.

Interviewer: Why?

Layla: Because they're the free girls, they'll do anything ... They're up front they're aggressive yeah. They'll be out 24/7 they'll wear things that are forbidden like short skirts and things, the Holland girls. So like we do, we do think bad of them ... They're loose girls, yeah, we call them loose girls (female, 16, born in UK).

Zeinab: ... if I compare Sheffield with Holland, here it is like all eyes on you because there are so many Somali people here and they all talk about each other. In Holland we were just free. Do what you want, go where you want ... Here, you go outside, you do something and your Mum knows what you've been doing because there are a lot of people around and say 'oh I see your daughter and I've seen this' ... I've gone more religious [since moving to the UK] because I've started wearing the scarf and that. In Holland I never used to wear a scarf, because here, when I saw the Somali community, I thought I'd respect them, you can't go off like you're in Holland (female, 18, EU secondary migrant from the Netherlands).

While some of the young women, like Zeinab, modified their appearance and behaviour in order to conform to hegemonic local narratives about what it means to a Muslim young woman, others openly contested the local community 'norms' about Islamic dress or appropriate personal conduct, drawing on the local norms they had encountered when living in other Muslim communities/countries. Likewise, there were also differences between the young men interviewed in terms of those who were very observant of their faith and those who adopted a more flexible or lax approach towards the practices of the local Muslim community. Yet, despite in some cases drinking alcohol, clubbing, smoking and becoming involved in drugs and crime, none of the young men disidentified as Muslim or disavowed their faith. Rather, they argued that repentance would ensure forgiveness and that they would follow their faith more observantly when they were older and married.

The interviewees' consistent identifications as Muslim, despite the way interpretations of this subject position were inflected by local community 'norms', is significant. While the interviewees were willing to accept denials of their claims to be British, to disidentify as black and to negotiate the ambiguities of being positioned as Somali in the UK but British in Somalia, their continuous (across both space and time) emotional investment in the subject position Muslim (despite their mobility) was such that the young people were not willing to disavow their faith. In the conclusion, we reflect on the importance of emotional salience as an explanation for why the young people prioritise their faith above their racial, gender or ethno-national identities.

Conclusion

In this chapter, we have focused on young Somali refugee and asylum seekers, exploring their narratives of identity in the context of their complex histories of mobility. In doing so, we have focused in particular on how processes of disidentification or disavowal impact on young people's subjectivities and are lived out in particular spaces. We have argued that in different spatial contexts arbitrary signifiers such as skin colour, accent and dress assume powerful meanings, weighting the importance and availability of certain identities, such that they become particularly salient or irrelevant in specific spaces. These spatial norms regulate the subject positions individuals are able to occupy – defining who is out of place, the person not to be (i.e. it is not enough just to invest in or claim a particular identity, it must also be recognised by a wider community of practice).

Thus, while some of those interviewed 'felt' English or British, they implicitly recognised that the identity category 'black' overshadowed or undid their right to take up this particular subject position in the UK because of the racism which persists in public space. Yet, despite being denied a British identity and ascribed a black identity in everyday public spaces, the majority of the interviewees disavowed the identity 'black'. It was not an identity that was either emotionally or politically salient for them. This, they explained, was because they are not from the Caribbean and because as their accounts demonstrated they are unable to fully accomplish hegemonic black masculinity/femininity at school. At the same time, the interviewees also disidentified with attempts by their black and white peers to position them – laden with racist and Islamaphobic assumptions – in relation to neighbourhood Pakistani cultural identities. Rather, in the context of the socio-spatial norms of the school, they asserted the specificity of 'being Somali'.

Yet, those who had made a return visit to Somalia, while claiming a Somali identity, also disidentified with the age and gendered subject positions available to them in the more patriarchal culture there and disavowed the way their own identities were misread in Somalia, for example, as 'British' and as 'wealthy'. A skin read as too black in the UK was read as too pale in Somalia, and accents and dress considered too inflected by Somali and Muslim culture in the UK were read as too 'western' in Somalia. As such, these accounts demonstrate the importance of recognising that while individuals can actively produce their own lives, we should not underestimate how the ability to enact some identities/realities rather than others is highly contingent on the power-laden spaces, in and through which, our experiences are lived. While as individuals our identities might be multiple and fluid, power (here we have considered in particular racism, Islamaphobia and patriarchy) operates within the spaces within which we live and move in systematic ways to generate hegemonic cultures and spatial orderings that define who can claim a particular identity, where and who cannot; who is in place and who is out of place.

While the interviewees described complex and varying levels of emotional (dis)investment in a range of subject positions, one subject position – Muslim – offered them continuity (across both space and time) in the context of their complex histories, and possible futures, of mobility. For those interviewed, the subject position Muslim overcame some of the troubling aspects of the other subject positions available to them: notably the denial of their Britishness, their disidentification as black and the complex ambiguities of their claims to be Somali. It alone offered them a stable, omni-available attachment that powerfully shaped their everyday use of space wherever they happened to be living. Such was the strength of their emotional investment in this subject position that individuals were not willing to disavow their faith (in the way they were willing to do so in relation to being British or being black) even when they clashed with the way their identities were regulated by the local spatial norms of specific Muslim communities. Rather, it was the powerful emotional salience and continuity of the identity Muslim, in contrast to their more unstable racial and ethno-national identities that were only recognised or hailed in specific time-space contexts, which meant that young people prioritised faith in their narratives of the self. As such, while contemporary sociological emphasis is on ways to better theorise the fluidity and multiplicity of subject positions that individuals are able to occupy, this research also demonstrates the importance of *continuity* (across space and time) in understanding the more profound emotional investments that individuals/groups make in particular subject positions.

Acknowledgements

This chapter is a slightly edited version of a paper published in *Sociology* 2009, volume 43, issue 4 under the title: 'How other people see you, it like's nothing that's inside': the impact of processes of disidentification and disavowal on young people's subjectivities'. We are grateful to Sage for permission to reproduce this article here.

Notes

1. Three ellipsis dots are used to indicate a few words have been edited to remove repetitions or to clarify the meanings of confused speech. The term [Edit] is inserted where a more substantial amount of text has been edited out.
2. The names attributed to the quotations are pseudonyms. Some of the children had the same first name so to maintain the integrity of the anonymisation process they have also been given the same pseudonym but distinguished by a number: e.g. Hassan 1, Hassan 2.

References

Afshar, H., Aitken, R. and Franks, M. (2005) Feminism, Islamophobia and Identities. *Political Studies*, 53, 262–83.

Beck, U. (1992) *Risk Society*. London: Sage.

Bell, D., Binnie, J., Cream, J. and Valentine, G. (1994) All Hyped up and No Place to Go. *Gender, Place and Culture*, 1, 31–47.

Bonnett, A. (2000) *White Identities: Historical and International Perspectives*. Harlow: Prentice Hall.

Connolly, P. (1994) 'Boys Will Be Boys?' Racism, Sexuality and the Construction of Masculine Identities among Infant Boys. In: J. Holland and M. Blair (eds) *Equality and Difference: Debates and Issues on Feminist Research and Pedagogy*. Clevedon: Multi-Lingual Matters.

Crenshaw, K.W. (1993) Mapping the Margins: Intersectionality, Identity Politics and Violence against Women of Color. In: M. Albertson Fineman and R. Mykitiuk (eds) *The Public Nature of Private Violence*. New York: Routledge.

Cresswell, T. (1996) *In Place/Out of Place: Geography, Ideology and Transgression*. Minneapolis, MN: University of Minnesota Press.

Frosh, S., Phoenix, A. and Pattman, R. (2002) *Young Masculinities: Understanding Boys in Contemporary Society*. Basingstoke: Palgrave.

Giddens, A. (1991) *Modernity and Self-Identity. Self and Society in Late Modern Age*. Cambridge: Polity Press.

Gilroy, P. (1987) *There Ain't No Black in the Union Jack*. London: Hutchinson.

Griffiths, D. (2002) *Somali and Kurdish Refugees in London. New Identities in the Diaspora*. London: Ashgate.

Hall, S. (1992) The Question of Cultural Identity. In: S. Hall, D. Held and A. McGrew (eds) *Modernity and Its Futures*. Polity Press: Cambridge.

Hall, S. (1996) Who Needs Identity? In: S. Hall and P. DuGay (eds) *Questions of Cultural Identity*. London: Sage.

Hirsch, M. (1997) *Family Frames: Photography, Narrative and Postmemory*. Cambridge, MA: Harvard University Press.

Mason, J. (2004) Managing Kinship over Long Distances: The Significance of 'The Visit'. *Social Policy and Society*, 3, 421–29.

McCall, L. (2005) The Complexity of Intersectionality. *Signs: Journal of Women in Culture and Society*, 20, 1771–802.

Modood, T. (1992) British Muslims and the Rushdie Affair. In: J. Donald and A. Rattansi (eds) *'Race', Culture and Difference*. London: Sage.

Pratt, G. (2003/2004) Between Homes: Displacement and Belonging for Second-Generation Filipino-Canadian Youth. *BC Studies*, 140, 41–68.

Said, E. (1978) *Orientalism: Western Conceptions of the Orient*. Harmondsworth: Penguin.

Somers, M.R. (1994) The Narrative Constitution of Identity: A Relational and Network Approach. *Theory and Society*, 23, 605–49.

Valentine, G. (2007) Theorising and Researching Intersectionality: A Challenge for Feminist Geography. *Professional Geographer*, 59, 10–21.

Valentine, G. (2008) Living with Difference: Reflections on Geographies of Encounter. *Progress in Human Geography*, 32, 321–35.

Valentine, G. and Sporton, D. (2009) 'How Other People See You, It's Like Nothing That's Inside': The Impact of Processes of Disidentification and Disavowal on Young People's Subjectivities. *Sociology*, 43(4), 737–53.

Valentine, G., Sporton, D. and Nielsen, K.B. (2008) Language Use on the Move: Sites of Encounter, Identities and Belonging. *Transactions of the Institute of British Geographers*, 33, 376–87.

Valentine, G., Sporton, D. and Nielsen, K.B. (2009) Identities and Belonging: A Study of Somali Refugee and Asylum Seekers Living in the UK and Denmark. *Environment & Planning D: Society & Space*, 27(2), 234–50.

Vertovec, S. (1998) Young Muslims in Keighley, West Yorkshire: Cultural Identity, Context and Community. In: S. Vertovec and A. Rogers (eds) *Muslim European Youth: Reproducing Ethnicity, Religion & Culture*. Aldershot: Ashgate.

West, C. and Fenstermaker, S. (1995) Doing Difference. *Gender and Society*, 9, 8–37.

9
Living London: Women Negotiating Identities in a Postcolonial City

Rosie Cox, Sue Jackson, Meena Khatwa and Dina Kiwan[1]

Introduction

We are writing at a time when debates abound in the UK about notions of 'Britishness' and about how lives should be lived, including those around immigration and asylum or the incompatibility of the 'traditions' of Islam with 'modern' Britishness. More recent expressions of imperialism cannot be divorced from the long-standing antagonistic indifference towards the histories and legacies of empire which runs through British political discourses and underpins the casual racism that shapes lives in British cities. In this chapter, we explore how women negotiate lives which are truly liveable in the spaces of a postcolonial city; outlining ways in which women perform and (re-)iterate social identifications and manage 'liveable lives'. We explore the multiple points of intersection, convergence and divergence which together compose constellations of interviewees' identifications in a postcolonial social order, showing that 'liveable lives' are (re)produced and performed in complex ways. We also highlight the complexities of locality and belonging in place and show how London is made and experienced through relationships and connections inflected by its history and its contemporary connections.

In her 2004 collection *Undoing Gender*, Judith Butler explores the concept of 'liveability' and the relationship between gender norms and human survival. She suggests (2004a: 226) two senses of 'life': 'one which refers to the minimum biological form of living, and another, which intervenes at the start, which establishes minimum conditions for a liveable life with regard to human life.' Butler argues that liveability is comprised of each of these senses. Liveable lives involve both being able to be literally alive – that one's life is not ended, for example, through a violent homophobic or racist attack – and being able to live in a way that is not 'loathsome' (Butler, 2004a: 3, 2004b) to the individual.

We are interested in looking at the space between these two senses of 'liveable'; the space within which women make lives which are possible. This space is not empty but brimming full with the oppression, violence and prejudice, not only of gender norms, but also of racial/ethnic, class and other forms of discrimination. It is in this space of everyday inequalities, bracketed by threats of violence and fears of misrecognition on one side and hopes of safety and belonging on the other, that women do the routine work of creating lives which are liveable. Butler's ambivalent notion of liveability is important because it allows us to explore how people make lives that are really liveable without losing sight of the fact that such struggles are framed by very real threats, including violence.

This chapter focuses on one particular geographical expression of these struggles and one site for the negotiations of liveable lives – postcolonial London. It advances an understanding of contemporary London as an uneven landscape characterised by diverse, unbounded, transnational, local cultures and political communities. London is perhaps the postcolonial city *par excellence*. Its population and trading relations reflect centuries' old colonial ties as well as new forms of economic domination. It is described as 'hyper-diverse' (Benton-Short et al., 2005: 945), having over-taken New York now on most measures of population diversity, and is perhaps the 'most diverse city ever' (Benedictus, 2005: 1). Its 8 million plus inhabitants speak over 300 languages and there are at least 50 ethnic/national communities with over 10,000 members. Over 50 per cent of babies born in London in 2007 were born to women who were themselves born outside the UK (ONS, 2007).

London is not simply the location of our research, however, this chapter is about London as an experiential space; a space – or series of spaces – in which interviewees socialised and within which their identities were shaped by themselves and myriad others, known and unknown. London is understood not as a bounded, political entity but as a dense web of relations – personal, social, economic and environmental – that link people in one geographical location to the rest of the world and to other specific localities both near and far. As Massey states: 'places [...] can be imagined as articulated movements in networks of social relations and understanding' (Massey, 1993: xii). The everyday actions of women are part of this web of relations and understandings. The flow of connections which constitutes them constitutes the city as well.

The chapter is based on a discussion of the experiences of 42 interviewees who were located through semi-formal women's social groups. Some of the groups were organised on the basis of an activity (for example knitting or reading); some on the basis of an identity (for example a group for Asian lesbian and bisexual women); and some groups were a mix of both, such as a queer knitting group. The interviewees had a diverse range of social backgrounds, ages and identifications. Few had been born in London and they had lived in the city for very different lengths of time from just a few weeks to more than 40 years. Interviewees were asked about their experiences of socialising, of celebrations and about their neighbourhood in London.

The interviews presented rich arguments about the way women's sexual and ethnic identities engaged with and used localities and sites of sociality in London. The women in our study 'located' their identities and negotiated 'liveable lives' not through singular experiences but multiple belongings, creating fluid interactions and tensions both with and within the city. The chapter is organised into two main sections. The first examines the notion of 'multiculturalism' and looks at how discourses of multiculturalism are used by interviewees to negotiate their own identities and to understand themselves in relation to others. We argue that by viewing 'multiculturalism' through a postcolonial lens we can reveal how fluid, transitional and contested the notion is. The second section uses Fortier's (2003) concept of 'homelands' to reflect on the ways that women negotiate their own sense of belonging and identity in place, and at ways in which negotiations of self also (re)produce and are (re)produced by others. Throughout we explore commonalities and differences in ways in which the women who were interviewed construct and perform their gendered and sexualised, racialised, ethnicised and religious identities within the spaces of London.

Multipli/city: liveable lives and multiculturalism

In this section, we develop understandings of the ways in which liveable lives are made possible in the multipli/city of London, including through the complexities of intersectionality. In particular, we consider multiple and negotiated ethnicised, religious, gendered and sexualised identities and argue for different ways of understanding and engaging with 'multiculturalism' through the intersected identities of postcolonial lives. The lens of multiculturalism allows us to reflect on the ways in which the (re)production of the self and the search for 'home' also (re)produce others. The negotiation of liveable lives is always framed by power relations, by centuries of inequality and by real interactions between people in specific real places.

In our considerations of postcolonialism, we do not take the 'post' to represent merely 'after', but are more interested in 'post' as 'beyond'. Postcolonialism is about future possibilities as well as about past and present struggles: struggles with identities born out of imperialism and colonialism, both for the (previously) colonised and the (previously) colonisers. As Couze Venn suggests: '[t]he post-colonial can be understood as a virtual space, that is, a space of possibility and emergence. It is thus also potential becoming: it opens towards a future that will not repeat existing forms of sociality and oppressive power relations' (2006: 190). The future is, of course, in part determined by those who have the power to direct its possibilities. Nevertheless, we do not engage with postcolonialism through the binary oppositions of colonised and colonisers, but through postcolonial processes of power and intersectionality; processes which are fluid, transitional and shifting.

Foucault has described how the idea of power/knowledge is inextricably linked to any considerations of discourse:

> Power produces knowledge. Power and knowledge directly imply one another. There is no power relation without the correlative constitution of a field of knowledge, nor any knowledge that does not presuppose and constitute at the same time power relations.
>
> (1980: 93)

It is the constitution of claims to knowledge linked to systems of power that determines and legitimises 'truth' (Burke and Jackson, 2007). Here we are interested in the mechanisms by which claims to knowledge are exercised; the ways in which exclusionary discourses and practices are constructed and resisted; the ways in which hegemonic practices are normalised; and the effects of these on the ability to have a liveable life (see, e.g. Mohanty, 2003; Spivak, 1996). Here we explore issues of power, knowledge and resistances through the discursive, social, cultural and political site(s) of (postcolonial) multiculturalism.

The last few decades have seen growing debates about 'multiculturalism' (see, e.g. Alibhai-Brown, 2000; Blunkett, 2001; Phillips, 2004; Toynbee, 2004). 'Multiculturalism' is a contested term with no agreed definition. It is misconstrued as being about and for minority groups whilst supporting an image of a homogeneous majority with small pockets of 'unmeltable' minorities (Anthias and Yuval-Davis, 1993). This is sometimes referred to as 'mosaic' multiculturalism, where a number of different communities live together side by side with differences kept distinct (Joppke and Lukes, 1999). 'Culture' is conceptualised in a relatively bounded way. This is contrasted with 'hodgepodge' multiculturalism, which is conceptualised in terms of hybridity, with 'culture' seen as in a state of flux (Joppke and Lukes, 1999).

One way of making a liveable life in London has been for its inhabitants to embrace multiculturalism, ostensibly at least. For example, two-thirds of London's population say that multiculturalism makes Britain a better place to live, with 82% indicating a belief that everybody in London should be free to live their lives how they like (MORI, 2006). However, for some of the interviewees, as for many other Londoners, multiculturalism is understood through difference as exotic, and through cultures of consumption: multiculturalism brings a diversity which has less to do with the complexities of multiple identities or postcolonial spaces than it has with the pleasures gained in their own neighbourhoods linked to a perceived global consumerism derived from colonial histories. There is no indication of the power relations at play when migrant groups seek to survive, to find their own liveable lives, in new diasporic homelands. Instead, neighbourhoods are described through personal consumption:

> [Wood Green] is a really nice area. Restaurants, Indian Kebabs, Turkish, Greek, a bit of Thai, a bit of Chinese. Sunday nights at the friends. Go down to the Curry Leaf and stuff our faces with Sri Lankan. Very nice, very nice (SSG4, East African Asian, Lesbian, 40s)[2].

> Well I'm all for [multiculturalism] really, I mean pretty cheesy but um, but I love the fact that [Wimbledon]'s a diverse place, that it's so multicultural and that um you know the area where we live you walk up the high street... and it's all written in different languages and different kinds of foods and you know clothing from different countries and things – I love that (CLKG14, White American, Jewish, 30s).

Here we see the pleasures of multiculturalism described literally as the consumption of food, but also as the consumption of the languages and cultures of the 'other'. These interviewees' understanding of multiculturalism is based on their experiences as consumers and in framing such experiences as exotic.

Mosaic multiculturalism is conceptualised as tolerance of differently bounded groups with distinct cultures (Joppke and Lukes, 1999). Whilst 'tolerance' appears to be both neutral and benign, it is constructed in and through power relations. Those in positions of privilege determine which groups (and individuals) deserve toleration, whilst those in less powerful positions are not able to move beyond being merely tolerated. For some of our interviewees therefore, the benefits of 'hodgepodge' multiculturalism is that 'tolerance' enables them to 'fit in', to believe that they 'have a place' to live their lives:

> I do like Edmonton. [...] I really actually enjoy living in a diverse community, because I would not be happy to live in a monocultural one. That much I know. I need to be able to live somewhere where I feel I fit in, where I have a place. And so I like that about being here. And I like the fact that I have neighbours, er, who come from all over the place (SSG2, Mauritian, Lesbian, 40s).

However, for others, even hodgepodge multiculturalism does not provide sufficient security for a liveable life. Another interviewee talks about her overwhelming feeling of being a minority in her neighbourhood. She describes the unwanted attention she receives on the streets, and arrives at an answer as to why this is happening. First she concluded that 'this is what Peckham is like':

> But afterwards I thought about it and I think it was simply because Peckham is like 90, 99% black in terms of ethnic groups there and the 1% is made up of like white people, Chinese people, world cultures 1%, and they're just not used to seeing Asian women. I promise you they are really not. I think I'm the only Asian woman on like on 1, 2, 3, 4, 4, 5 streets (SSG5, British Indian, Lesbian/dyke, 30s).

Although there is a large Black community in Peckham (an area in South London) its population consists of 52% Black, 36% white, 4% mixed, 3% Asian, 3% Chinese and 2% other. For SSG5, her identity as British Indian is intersected primarily with her gendered and sexualised identities. Peckham has a population of around 25,000 with a higher proportion of females than males aged 25–59 and 65 and over (Southwark Council, 2008). The proportion of Asian women although not specified, will inevitably be low, and the numbers of lesbian Asian/Indian women even lower, and possibly hidden. Whilst this interviewee has little choice but to 'wear' her Asian-ness and her gender, she might feel safer keeping aspects of her identity, such as her sexuality, hidden. Living in a multicultural neighbourhood does not in itself guarantee liveable lives for minoritised groups.

Like those above, others of our interviewees have struggled with trying to live lives which are recognisable, validated and meet cultural norms and expectations. As we can see, BC02 is one of the few interviewees who problematises 'whiteness', describing how she is part of a minority struggling with an identity which is both white and minoritised:

> I do feel um that I am part of a minority and I am aware of that um I think it's a struggle to have an identity because it's, it's a mixture of things. [...] So me being Jewish because I'm white, most people you know don't know. Most people have no idea in England... what Jews are or who they are or whatever... (BC02, British Jewish, 40s).

Multiculturalism, whether 'mosaic' or 'hodgepodge', too often focuses on a discussion of identities as white or 'other'. However, here we see how 'whiteness' can be a problematic identity, also structured through the power relations of 'difference'. White women can occupy different racial consciousnesses (Frankenberg, 1993). BC01 also problematises minority groups in ways which move beyond black/white binaries. She recognises both similarities and differences between 'us lot' (British Asians) moving in, and the new migration from Eastern Europe. Here she identifies both with newer migrant communities and with more established communities in the ways in which she values multiculturalism:

> BC01: I like the fact that there's so many different people around. [...] A huge influx of people from um Eastern Europe. Polish, like one of the most common languages when you walk down my high street now is Polish [...] and that's been really interesting for me because it raises, it makes me wonder what it was like for the sort of indigenous white population when all of us lot moved in, because it raises some of the same feelings in me. [...] I know that lots of white people used to feel very weird about lots of Asians because they didn't say you know talk in a certain way or greet them in a certain way. [...] I suppose I do have some, um I'm aware of certain prejudice towards the Eastern Europe, Europeans who are there
> Interviewer: – On the part of?
> BC01: On the part of me
> Interviewer: – On your own part?
> BC01: Yeah of my own prejudice against them in terms of feeling uncomfortable (BC01, British Asian, 40s).

The interviewee has identified complex and shifting power relations and intersected identities. Describing herself as British Asian, her understandings of multiculturalism move beyond dichotomies of black/white or British/Asian, seeing the complexities of constructions of whiteness that abound in Britain, and especially in London, with regard to a perceived large influx of migrants from Eastern Europe.

The multiculturalism identified by this interviewee is not captured by definitions of 'mosaic' nor 'hodgepodge' identified earlier, although it may derive from concepts of hybridity (Joppke and Lukes, 1999), a metaphor crucial to postcolonial theory, although there are difficulties in finding appropriate language to capture the complexities of a postcolonial world (Phipps, 2004). Whilst for policy-makers as well as for many of our interviewees definitions of 'multiculturalism' are often opaque, what we are arguing here is for an engagement with a multiculturalism which recognises discourses of power and power relations. Like critical race theory (see e.g. Dixson and Rousseau, 2007) and critical post-modern discourse (see e.g. Giroux, 1992), critical multiculturalism includes critiques of power (Jackson et al., 2008).

Parekh (2000) argues that multiculturalism should be active rather than passive, and about the political restructuring of society, with the key to defining 'multiculturalism' being in the responses to multicultural society, and the meanings and significance attached to choice:

> Multiculturalism is not about difference and identity *per se* but about those differences that are embedded in and sustained by culture; that is a body of beliefs and practices in terms of which a group of people understand themselves and the world and organise their individual and collective lives. Unlike differences that spring from individual choices, culturally derived differences carry a measure of authority and are gathered and structured by virtue of being embedded in a shared and historically inherited system of meaning and significance.
> (Parekh, 2000: 23)

We have been arguing here that some of the meaning and significance of these derived differences and authority stem from the historically inherited system of colonialism; and that postcolonial lives are embedded, sustained and constructed differently in relation to histories, authority and power.

Living lives through the multiple identities of postcolonial urban spaces is challenging, sometimes seemingly impossible, sometimes hopeful and pleasurable. As our interviewees show, 'belonging' in postcolonial London is complex. For AWG1, her gendered Asian identity enables her to develop a sense of belonging.

> I enjoy a lot at Community Centres that we Asians have, where we have our celebrations, such as this Community Centre, or sometimes we go to other women's centres. I feel very free and relaxed, because it's our own people, and it's a carefree environment, be it a Hindus' party, one of Sikhs, Muslims, Christians, anyone. Religion is no constraint/restriction (AWG1, British Asian, 60s).

The Asian Women's Group to which she belongs, based on shared networks, values and practices, could be described both as multicultural and as postcolonial, and interviewees 'belong' in multiple spaces simultaneously.

Floya Anthias (2006) has argued that to understand identity formations under colonialism is also to 'read' and understand colonial powers, although the complexities of global capitalism make such readings more difficult. We argue that one way to understand 'multiculturalism' is to also read it through a lens of 'postcolonialism'. Mica Nava describes London's neighbourhoods as 'increasingly undifferentiated, hybrid, post-multicultural, lived transformations which are the outcomes of diasporic cultural mixing and interdeterminancy' (Nava, 2006: 50). Interviewees expressed a sense of 'belonging' in multiple localities simultaneously and could show strong ties to neighbourhoods they did not live in because of disparate social connections with them, as well as ties of memory (Tolia-Kelly, 2004) and diaspora (Brah and Phoenix, 2004; Hall, 1990). Interviewees also (re)produced a sense of belonging to neighbourhoods through multiple identities, for example neighbourhoods where there was recognition of 'queer' identities. It is to the lived experience of multiple belongings, intersected identities and questions of home and homelands that we now turn.

Locality and identification – multiple belongings

To explore the interplay of sexual, racial/ethnic and religious identities in place we use Anne Marie Fortier's concept of 'queer cultural homelands' (Fortier, 2003: 119). Building on Avtar Brah's notion of 'homing desires' (1996: 180), Fortier's work provides an insight into how the creation of 'homelands' becomes important for gays and lesbians. She states, 'narratives of queer migrations constitute different versions of [...] "homing desires": desires to feel at home achieved by physically or symbolically (re)constituted spaces which provide some kind of ontological security in the context of migration' (Fortier, 2003: 115). This resonates with Butler's notion of liveability but also signals the 'spaces' – both metaphorical and real – of searches for belonging. It is also a concept which has purchase beyond gay and lesbian communities. The idea of searching for and creating 'homelands' has clear echoes of the experience of exile and diaspora that make it relevant for understanding the lives of many people who find themselves 'out of place'. It reveals the relational nature of belonging and the ability of some groups to decide who does and does not belong. The search for cultural homelands is produced, at least in part, by exposure to dominant social norms and their expression within dominant communities; the quest for identity is about knowing ourselves in relation to others and in relation to our histories. As Stuart Hall suggests:

> Cultural identities come from somewhere, have histories. But, like everything which is historical, they undergo constant transformation. From being eternally fixed in some essentialist past, they are subject to the continuous 'play' of history culture and power. Identities are the names we give to the different ways we are positioned by, and position ourselves within the narratives of the past.
>
> (Hall, 1993: 394)

Our interviewees discussed the ways in which home is made through relationships to others and through the experience of space and place. The quotes below, from two members of the queer knitting group, reveal the intricate layering of scales that takes place when 'home' is built in a postcolonial city. They illustrate complex tensions between being accepted as a 'visible member of the community' and also fears of rejection:

> [M]y upstairs neighbours I know really well, you know, in a kind of lending, borrowing type scenario, but also the two children [laughing] come and call for me on their own. Um, yeah I think I'm not out to my neighbours but then I don't have that kind of conversation with any of them d'y'know what I mean? I would be reticent about holding hands with a partner on my street for safety reasons. Um, but apart from that, it's really important to me to have contact with people I live around and I feel like mutually people have a lot to offer each other and it just makes your day nicer you know? (KQKG8, White, Lesbian 30s).

> Stokey [Stoke Newington] is nice because you can walk down the street and you're bound to see some other lesbians which is always really nice in an affirmation sort of sense and also in a safety sort of sense. [...] It's got a very alternative hippyish sort of feel to it which I like. I used to live in Tottenham and that was a completely different atmosphere. You wouldn't, I mean you could still walk down the streets holding hands but you're a lot more likely to be stared at and harassed and all of that sort of stuff. And you certainly wouldn't see any sort of other readily identifiable lesbians walking down the street. So yeah it's, I feel really comfortable in Stokey. It's got a really nice feel to it, although I have been harassed quite a lot there as well, but you get that I guess (KQKG13, White, New Zealand Pākehā, Lesbian 30s).

These interviewees illustrate that the social norms that are possible within an area – whether you can hold hands in the street for example – are important in making a place a possible 'home', a location for a liveable life.

'Homelands' do not have to be created through residence in a place, but rather are produced through relationships and connections. Connections can be with people, but they are also mapped on to the city and produced through its physicality, for example, through transport networks or the location of regularly used facilities. The quote below reveals the intimate connections/relationships one woman has with parts of London, and how different types of belonging, attachment and detachment are experienced:

> It just feels like home to me and always has, although I'm not from London. I'm from um Loughton, which is actually in Essex, but there's a tube stop there. So kind of, it's always felt like I'm from London [...] I've kind of known places like Redbridge and Stratford and Walthamstow... had friends there when I was growing up. I would visit them, you know people from my college might have come from those areas, and then when I was at college, M my best mate, lived in Hackney, and so [I] became very familiar with that as a kind of area and... [...]. Like Bethnal Green is kind of a place that was... quite local to me, so I would have known fairly well... and it just kind of feels, it feels like the bit of London that I know the best and feels most like home (KQKG4, White British, Lesbian, 30s).

For this interviewee, multiple identities intersect with multiple localities in greater London. There is a strong sense of connection to places in London through her identification with particular areas where friendships and memories have been formed, expressing her own 'homing desires'. These experiences map multiple, simultaneous places of belonging, reflecting the notion of places as unbounded, networks of social relations (Massey, 1991). As Fortier writes with reference to autobiographies by queer writers:

> Rather than isolated sites of (un)belonging, 'homes' are locations criss-crossed by a variety of forces the authors had to negotiate again and again. Though all the texts begin with a story about the 'original' home, it soon becomes one among many other places that could be called 'home', even temporarily. Each is inhabited by different people – friends, colleagues, family, lovers – who touched the authors differently – in caring, friendly or even, but to a lesser extent, antagonistic encounters.
>
> (Fortier, 2003: 122)

The interviewees quoted above also reveal that 'home' is produced in response to fear and anxiety as well as love and caring and that liveability is negotiated in the space between Butler's two senses of 'life'. Women who are members of minority ethnic groups, disabled women and lesbians are particularly likely to consider home as a haven. Although violence and sexism exist in the home, these women feel they have 'less claim over the public realm than able-bodied, white heterosexual women, and thus denied the chance of an authentic selfhood in settings other than the home' (Valentine, 1989: 38; see also Darke, 1994). Different areas in London are imagined to offer different levels of safety, connectedness and belonging, depending on whether the neighbourhood is seen as 'gay-friendly'. Fear of harassment can overshadow exertions of ones own sexual identity, and adds to the inner conflict of 'coming out' not just to family and friends but also to neighbours, thus determining how individuals engage with their neighbourhoods.

Some expressions of identity, then, cannot always easily or safely be publicly displayed, including gay identities. In addition, in some neighbourhoods gay spaces can be hard to find, even those within a city as diverse as London. However, neither public nor private places/spaces are asexual, and the meanings of space are continually contested and (re)negotiated. Research by Gustav Visser (2007), for example, shows that the leisure spaces in which the gay men in his study 'felt free' were overwhelmingly heterosexual spaces rather than gay-coded. This was also the case for some of the women in this study, for whom the colonising of 'straight' spaces became a political act. Similarly, members of the 'queer' knitting group in our study stated that by holding their sessions in a cinema bar in Soho they are being politically active in creating their own queer space within a mainstream 'straight' space.

> It's interesting because [the queer knitting club] happens in a straight bar but there's so many of us that it's like we create our own queer space within, and that's a political act as well, kind of creating that safe queer space within the kind of wider straight space (KQKG4, White British Jewish, Lesbian, 30s).

However, other interviewees experienced 'gay' spaces differently, emphasising intersected commonalities:

> I do have a need in me to meet and to socialise with gay people. There is a commonality there. I mean, actually, [the social group] is that extra special cream on the top of the cake isn't it. That they're not only just gay, but they are also Asian women. And you just think, 'oh fantastic'. Because there is just that commonality and it just makes a huge difference' (SSG01, 30s, Asian, bisexual).

However, 'lesbian friendly' spaces were identified as difficult to locate by some of our interviewees. For example, whilst one interviewee lives in a locality where it is not difficult to find 'gay spaces', she says that these are not 'lesbian friendly':

> There's actually quite a lot of gay places, but they're more aimed at men, but there's sort of umm there is a pub, but I don't usually go there, I don't socialise in Vauxhall itself [...] the clubs are sort of very hard house techno and aimed at men (SSG3, British Asian Indian, 20s).

Sexual identities are neither separate from nor the same as gender identities. Another interviewee, who is a member of the same Asian lesbian and bisexual women's group as the interviewees above, explains how difficult it can be to find spaces that fit all the 'permutations of oneself'. The interviewee quoted below reveals both a struggle to find belonging with one's own identity to 'be me' and how dependent this is on relations with others. She describes her multiple identifications and how her identity shifts depending on who she is with and how open she is with them about her sexuality:

> I really compartmentalised my life yeah between Asian people, non-Asian people, white people, non-white people, family, non-family and this was a rare occasion where actually my brother was there, my queer Asian friends were there, my straight white friends were there, my straight Asian friends were there, you know? It was all permutations. [...] So I wanted to be in a space where I was me, yeah and I could talk about what's going on for me and what's difficult or what's great. To see that many Asian women who identify as lesbian or bisexual in a space celebrating, celebrating them, you know their sexuality but also the space that they've created (SSG6, British/Indian Bisexual, 30s).

'Homing desires' such as these do not have to be about the search for sameness: rather familiarity can be found amongst difference, and homogeneity can sometimes be stifling. For example, interviewees highlighted how recognition of past memories of space/place can resonate in present surroundings, somehow slotting into the now and fitting in even though they could be markedly different. In her interview, KQKG8 illustrates how an English white person can feel at ease in a multiethnic version of their past community:

> There's a huge influx of Eastern Europeans at the minute [...] I think it's partly, it feels very much like a multi-ethnic version of the community I grew up in. I grew up in a kind of um quite close-knit, white working-class community in Grimsby where we all lived in terraces, which is what I live in now... it feels very familiar to me 'cause it's like that really (KQKG8, White, Lesbian, 30s).

This contrasts with the experience of SSG2 who reveals internal conflicts with multiple identifications: although she is from an Asian Mauritian family, she feels out of place in a predominately Asian area. Her comments reflect the tensions that come from the 'too familiar' and rather than feeling part of the homogeneous microcosm of Southall she highlights the estrangement a 'non-straight' south Asian woman can feel. However she does assert her fondness for multicultural locations: 'different types of people that [are] quite vibrant, just people on different incomes, different classes, different backgrounds':

> [Southall is] sort of an odd place..., its sort of it feels very vibrant because of the shops and the restaurants and umm I suppose there's a different kind of uniformity there umm, also it's a very 'straight'

> Asian culture, which perhaps again I didn't feel totally at ease with...Just I don't know it's the kind of area that you feel trapped in and sort of there's sort of this high presence of Asian boys there that sort of walk past, and I was never quite at ease with that either. So it's like a little tiny microcosm of Asian culture that's quite sort of claustrophobic in a way. If you walk down the street you're bound to see someone who knew your auntie (SSG2, British Mauritian, Lesbian, 40s).

Southall is one of the most established Asian neighbourhoods in Britain. It could be thought of as representing a 'nation construct' where a communion has been formed with visible markers for an ethnic group. Places such as community centres and the temple become beacons of belonging that draw people together to re-create familiarity and traditions (Khatwa, 2004). The importance of such places is recognised by Lily Kong:

> [t]here is also the production of cultural landscape signatures (for example, residential architecture, houses of worship, recreation and commercial establishments, and street signage) in attempts to reproduce memory and experience, sometimes giving rise to little enclaves. (Kong, 1999: 578)

Such enclaves or 'microcosms' are the physical representation of the 'imagined communities' that Benedict Anderson (1983) discusses. For Anderson and theorists such as Iain Chambers (1994) and Russell King (1995a, b), notions of belonging, displacement, attachment and settlement are metaphors for nation and the nation is closely related to ideas of home. Areas such as Southall are the built expressions of attempts to create home in diaspora and to rejoin the community of the nation. However, as SSG2 makes clear, even in such well-established areas, not all members of the imagined community feel 'at home'.

The narratives of our interviewees reveal how women negotiate the multiple strands of their identities in place and through relations with others. The women who identify as lesbian or bisexual in particular have described their attempts to find liveable lives in a balance between 'blending in' and 'standing out'. However, sometimes being 'cloaked' is easier and safer and the different areas/spaces of London can determine how cloaked or visible they feel. For many women, there is a real attempt to forge multiple identifications but this can also conflict with being drawn into a broader, seemingly homogeneous group, which hides important differences. As Heidi Mirza notes:

> [A] reductionist notion of blackness erased religious and ethnic difference. The desire to be named according to (cultural) difference and not (racial) sameness, demonstrated the need for recognising the meaning of hair, skin and colour, the importance of shared history and religion, in the construction of identity and belonging.
>
> (1997: 4)

Yet, such tensions in identity and belonging do not have to be destructive but instead can lead to an openness that 'pave[s] the way [...] to the possibility of new forms of belonging that are not predicated on single unitary identities' (Fortier, 2003: 120). Fortier uses the model of 'two mindedness' to describe the multiple attachments and loyalties that gay and lesbian migrants can feel. She argues that:

> two-mindedness is about the everyday work of translation, and the opportunities of greater insight into the seemingly opposed worlds lesbian/gay migrants inhabit. It signals the openness, however fraught, about the multiple belongings that one negotiates in one's own life, rather than the concealment of one against the privileging of another.
>
> (2003: 120)

Conclusions: living London

We have argued throughout this chapter that identities are forged and liveable lives are built through the relationships of people and through and within specific places and spaces. The negotiation of multiple, intersected and fluid identities produces selves, others and the city. London was experienced by interviewees both as a series of places (neighbourhoods or villages) and as a whole city (see Massey, 1994). Interviewees appear to 'perform' or highlight different aspects of their identity in different places. These could be, for example, home town versus London, different areas within London, or work versus social space. Interviewees used space to negotiate and make comfortable the multiple aspects of their identities, although, as Crang (1998: 161) has shown, 'one's right to belong to a space is seen as dependent on possessing the culture that is also used to identify the territory'.

As interviewees indicated, identities in postcolonial London are intersected and distinctive, viscous and transitional and consistent and continuous, mobilised through different emphases and negotiations, 'subject to the play of history and the play of difference' (Hall, 1993: 17). In this light, postcolonial London can be understood as a dense network of connections: connections to surrounding areas, to other cities and to distant parts of the globe. It is connected through people, their movement, memories and trajectories, but also through the built environment, and the movements of things and ideas. London is also connected to its history – that which is normally understood to be its own – a history of global trade and exploitation, and also the histories of the people who make the city today, in its entirety and also its various unique and diverse components.

As we stated above, a prefix 'post' can be used both to indicate a process of ongoing transformation or change and to suggest something which supersedes, or at least comes afterwards (Jackson, 2008). Whilst it is not yet clear what, if anything, might be superseding multiculturalism, it is certainly the case – as we have argued here – that 'multiculturalism' is fluid, transitional and contested, and identity formations can thrive or whither under its auspices. Whilst we are not convinced that we are postmulticultural (Nava, 2006), we have been arguing for greater development of understandings of what we have named critical or postcolonial multiculturalism. Whilst the consumption of 'difference' and a 'multicultural' way of existing was cited by many interviewees as an appealing dimension of life in contemporary London, ideas of 'safety', 'danger' and 'belonging' are inflected by notions of the 'racial' difference of 'others' in the 'neighbourhoods' of our interviewees, and by prevalent homophobia in the 'local area'.

Within these contested spaces of the postcolonial city our interviewees built cultural 'homelands' as part of their search for belonging. These homelands were not simple reproductions of real or imagined places of 'origin' that authors such as Kong (1999) have highlighted. Rather our interviewees told us of spaces of belonging carved temporarily through the relationships and meanings brought to a place. These homelands did not have to relate to an ethnic identity or geographical 'origin' but could foster a sense of multiple belonging and recognise the multiple and intersected identities of the women who forged them.

As Butler states, liveable lives require at least a degree of stability: 'In the same way that a life for which no categories of recognition exist is not a liveable life, so a life for which those categories constitute unliveable constraint is not an acceptable option' (2004a: 8). Our interviewees carved this stability through their negotiation of self and their imagining of others. The facility or difficulty with which they could do this depends upon their race/ethnic identity and sexuality; the categories of recognition which were available to them. Through this chapter, we have shown particular understandings of culture and identity as unbounded and multilayered whilst avoiding 'the squeamishness of anti-essentialisms which are complacent about the continuing effects of racism' (Gilroy, 1993: 14) and other forms of inequalities. By exploring the space between Butler's two senses of 'life', we have shown how the vibrant, fluid, postcolonial space of London offers the possibility of multiple belongings while keeping in mind that these belongings must still be negotiated in a space which is bordered by the fear of violence and misrecognition as well as by the prospect of a liveable life.

Notes

1. All authors shown in alphabetical order.
2. Interviewees are identified by the group from which they are recruited and in the terms they identified themselves.

References

Alibhai-Brown, Y. (2000) *After Multiculturalism*. London: Foreign Policy Centre.
Anderson, B. (1983) *Imagined Communities*. London: Verso.
Anthias, F. (2006) Belongings in a Globalised and Unequal World: Rethinking Translocations. In: N. Yuval-Davis, K. Kannabiran and U. Vietem (eds) *The Situated Politics of Belonging*. London: Sage.
Anthias, F. and Yuval-Davis, N. (1993) *Racialised Boundaries*. London: Routledge.
Benedictus, L. (2005) Every Race, Colour, Nation and Religion on Earth. *The Guardian*: The World in a City, special supplement 21 January 2005.
Benton-Short, L., Price, M. and Friedman, S. (2005) Globalization from Below: The Ranking of Global Immigrant Cities. *International Journal of Urban and Regional Research*, 29(4), 945–59.
Blunkett, D. (2001) *Independent on Sunday*, 9 December, p. 4.
Brah, A. (1996) *Cartographies of Diaspora: Contesting Identities*. London: Routledge.
Brah, A. and Phoenix, A. (2004) 'Ain't I A Woman'? Revisiting Intersectionality. *Journal of International Women's Studies: Special Issue: Feminist Challenges: Crossing Boundaries*, 5(3), 75–86.
Burke, P. and Jackson, S. (2007) *Reconceptualising Lifelong Learning: Feminist Interventions*. London: Routledge.
Butler, J. (2004a) *Undoing Gender*. London: Routledge.
Butler, J. (2004b) *Precarious Life: The Powers of Mourning and Violence*. London: Verso.
Chambers, I. (1994) *Migrancy, Culture, Identity*. London: Routledge.
Crang, M. (1998) *Cultural Geographies*. London: Routledge.

Darke, J. (1994) Women and the Meaning of Home. In: R. Gilroy and R. Woods (eds) *Housing Women*. London: Routledge.

Dixson, A. D. and Rousseau, C. (2007) *Critical Race Theory in Education: All God's Children got a Song*. New York: Routledge.

Fortier, A. M. (2003) Making Home: Queer Migrations and Motions of Attachment. In: S. Ahmed, C. Castaneda, A. M. Fortier and M. Sheller (eds) *Uprootings/Regroundings: Questions of Home and Migration*. Oxford: Berg.

Foucault, M. (1980) 'Two Lectures'. In: Gordon, C. (ed.) *Power/Knowledge*. London: Harvester Wheatsheaf.

Frankenberg, R. (1993) *White Women, Race Matters: The Social Construction of Whiteness*. London: Routledge.

Gilroy, P. (1993) *Small Acts: Thoughts on the Politics of Black Cultures*. London: Serpent's Tail.

Giroux, H. (1992) *Border Crossings: Cultural Workers and the Politics of Education*. New York: Routledge.

Hall, S. (1990) Cultural Identity and Diaspora. In: J. Rutherford (ed.) *Identity: Community, Culture, Difference*. London: Lawrence and Wishart.

Hall, S. (1993) Cultural Identity and Diaspora. In: P. Williams and L. Chrisman (eds) *Colonial Discourse and Post-Colonial Theory: A Reader*. London: Harvester Wheatsheaf.

Jackson, S. (2008) Diversity, Identity and Belonging: Women's Spaces of Sociality. *The International Journal of Diversity in Organisations, Communities and Nations*, 8(3), 147–54.

Jackson, S., Kiwan, D. and Cox, R. (2008) Encounters, Intersections and Multiplicity: Women's Identities in Post-Colonial London. Encounters and Intersections: Religion, Diaspora and Ethnicities, St Catherine's College Oxford, 9–11 July 2008.

Joppke, C. and Lukes, S. (eds) (1999) *Multicultural Questions*. Oxford: Oxford University Press.

Khatwa, M. (2004) *Life Journeys: Narratives of Hindu Mothers and Daughters in British Homes*. Unpublished PhD Thesis. Queen Mary, University of London.

King, R. (ed.) (1995a) *Writing Across Worlds: Literature and Migration*. London: Routledge.

King, R. (1995b) Migration: Three Concepts. In: D. Massey and P. Jess (eds) *A Place in the World*. Milton Keynes: Open University Press.

Kong, L. (1999) Globalisation and Singaporean Transmigration: Re-imagining and Negotiating National Identity. *Political Geography*, 18(5), 563–89.

Massey, D. (1991) 'A Global Sense of Place'. In *Marxism Today* (June), 24–29.

Massey, D. (1993) In: E. Carter, J. Donald and J. Squires (eds) *Space and Place: Theories of Identity and Location*. London: Lawrence and Wishart.

Massey, D. (1994) *Space, Place and Gender*. Polity Press: Cambridge.

Mirza, H. (ed.) (1997) *Black British Feminism: A Reader*. London: Routledge.

Mohanty, C. T. (2003) *Feminism Without Borders: Decolonizing Theory, Practicing Solidarity*. Durham, NC: Duke University Press.

Market & Opinion Research International (MORI) (2006) Poll commissioned by Mayor of London, November. Available at http://www.london.gov.uk/mayor/consultation/docs/2006-11-poll.rtf (accessed 11 May 2008).

Nava, M. (2006) Domestic Cosmopolitanism and Structures of Feeling: The Specificity of London. In: N. Yuval-Davis, K. Kannabiran and U. Vietem (eds) *The Situated Politics of Belonging*. London: Sage.

Office of National Statistics (ONS) (2007) *Birth Statistics: Births and Patterns of Family Building in England and Wales*. National Statistics Online. Available at http://www.statistics.gov.uk/statbase/Product.asp?vlnk=5768&More=Y (accessed 15 December 2008).

Parekh, B. (2000) *Rethinking Multiculturalism*. Cambridge, MA: Harvard University Press.

Phillips, T. (2004) *The Times* (3 April 2004) *I want an Integrated Society with a Difference*, Interview with Trevor Philips. Online. Available at http://www.timesonline.co.uk/printFriendly/0,,1-2-1061080,00.html (accessed 21 July 2004).

Phipps, P. (2004) Hybrid identities and cosmopolitan community in an age of intensified globalisation. *International Journal of Diversity in Organisations, Communities and Nations*, 4, 1159–69.

Southwark Council Community Statistics: Peckham Community Council (2008) Available at: http://www.southwark.gov.uk/Uploads/File_20944.pdf (accessed 20 September 2008).

Spivak, G. C. (1996) *The Spivak Reader*. London: Routledge.

Tolia-Kelly, D. P. (2004) Landscape, Race and Memory: Biographical Mapping of the Routes of British Asian Landscape Values. *Landscape Research*, 29(3), 277–92.

Toynbee, P. (2004) *Guardian* (7 April 2004) *Why Trevor Is Right*. Online. Available at http://www.guardian.co.uk/columnists/column/0,5673,1187233,00.html (accessed 21 July 2004).

Valentine, G. (1989) The Geography of Women's Fear. *Area*, 21(4), 385–90.

Venn, C. (2006) *The Post-Colonial Challenge: Towards Alternative Worlds*. London: Sage.

Visser, G. (2007) Homonormalising (White) Heterosexual Leisure Space: The Case of White Gay Men in Bloemfontein, South Africa. *International Journal of Diversity in Organisations, Communities and Nations*, 7(1), 217–28.

Part III
Popular Culture and Relationality

10
The Making of Modern Motherhoods: Storying an Emergent Identity

Rachel Thomson, Mary Jane Kehily, Lucy Hadfield and Sue Sharpe

The increasing participation of women in further and higher education and the labour force since the Second World War has transformed the shape and meaning of women's biographies reflected in a trend towards later motherhood (Lewis, 1992). Yet stagnation in social mobility and widening inequality has also heightened differences between women, reflected in differential patterns of family formation depending on educational and employment status (Crompton, 2006). The transition to motherhood is not only an important site of identity change for women but also an arena where socio-economic differences between women are defined and compounded through the creation of distinct cultures of child-rearing (Byrne, 2006; Clarke, 2004; Tyler, 2008).

The Making of Modern Motherhoods research project funded under the Identities and Social Action Programme builds on existing qualitative investigations of the process of becoming a mother (Bailey, 1999; Miller, 2004), and negotiations of changing opportunities and circumstances over generations (Bjerrum Nielsen and Rudberg, 1994, 2000; Brannen et al., 2004). Bringing together a longitudinal and intergenerational research design with an analysis of popular culture, the study explores how contemporary motherhood is both a site of solidarity and division between women. Building upon previous work on the transition to adulthood (Henderson et al., 2007), we explore how the project of motherhood can be understood as an expression of social location – arrival and departure points within journeys of social mobility. This is an empirical project with the potential to speak back to dominant late modern theories which suggest a whole scale shift from biographies shaped by tradition to those shaped by choice (Beck, 1992). By focusing on the transition to first-time motherhood, we are able to contextualise and compare accounts of pregnancy and birth within and between generations. Our approach captures the interplay of historical, generational and biographical processes, connecting the subjective intensity of motherhood with the remaking of inequality and privilege (Smart, 2007).

In this chapter, we explore the ways in which the emergent identity of 'mother' takes shape for women in our study. We summarise and comment upon the main features of this identity shift in ways that make new motherhood intelligible to the self and to others. We begin by outlining a theoretical framework for locating these accounts before exploring the formal components of conception narratives. Our argument draws on an analysis of the full sample of 62, but is made through two contrasting case studies. These examples map the situated identity work that marks the opening gambit of the project of motherhood. They show how personal and popular narratives come together in concrete settings and moments in such a way that ensures that what it means to become an adult and live a good life continues to privilege middle-class experience.

Motherhood and recognition

Metaphors of communication are central to the ways in which theorists have attempted to capture the process of identity formation, and the relationship between the individual and the social. In recent work on the ways in which the performance of particular gender identities relate to broader configurations of class and gender, Judith Butler (2004) explores the 'social intelligibility of an action' (p. 41) that allows for 'certain kinds of practices and actions to become recognizable ... imposing a grid of legibility on the social and defining parameters of what will and will not appear within the domain of the social' (p. 42). Identities, practices and performances that lie outside of the norm are unrecognised, illegible and as such unliveable, yet there is always potential for recognition; and in lying outside the norm, such identities maintain a (troubling) relationship with the norm. Norms may not be obvious, but are most noticeable in what Butler calls an implicit *normalizing principle*, 'difficult to read, discernable most clearly and dramatically in the effects they produce' (p. 41).

Approaching identity as a communicative practice finds points of resonance with Volosinov's (1973 [1929]) concept of 'speech acts' in his study of language as a struggle for meaning embedded in the social world. For Volosinov, all speech acts are addressed to another's word or to another listener; even in the absence of another person, a speaker will conjure up the presence of an imaginary listener. In an evocative and much quoted passage, Volosinov conjures up the reciprocal relationship between speaker, listener and their social world:

> Each and every word expresses the 'one' in relation to the 'other'. I give myself verbal shape from another's point of view, ultimately from the point of view of the community to which I belong. A word is a bridge thrown down between myself and another. If one end of the bridge depends on me then the other depends on my addressee. A word is territory shared by both addresser and addressee.
>
> (Volosinov, 1973: 86)

Arguing that all forms of communication and social experience are dependent on social context, Volosinov identifies two poles: the 'I-experience', which tends towards extermination as it does not receive feedback from the social milieu, and the 'we-experience' which grows with consciousness and positive social orientation. From this perspective, self confidence, for example, can be viewed as an ideological form of the 'we-experience', deriving from positive and affirming social relations rather than individual strength and personality.

Echoing these themes of the storied and legible life, Plummer (1995) suggests that personal narratives remain an inherently conservative form, speaking to the past rather than the future. It is hard to tell new stories, which can only emerge in the confluence of developing identities and available resources that facilitate both the story telling and its reception. The transition from private story to the generation of a public problem involves struggle and recognition of subjecthood, and the privilege to narrate oneself (rather than to be narrated by others) reflects wider dimensions of social, cultural and economic status (Adkins, 2003; Skeggs, 2004).

Conception stories: remembering and forgetting

Motherhood is one thing and many. The subjective experience of pregnancy and birth are dependent on the personal and economic circumstances of expectant mothers, their positions within families and the intergenerational legacies that come into play as maternal subjectivities are formed. The social circumstances that structured women's options as well as the cultural resources that they draw on in order to imagine motherhood can be understood as part of a common culture (Willis et al., 1990) that women put to different use. Yet this common culture is also structured in such a way that affirms and recognises particular experiences which do not resonate with popular cultural resources or policy discourses and must be made sense of in more private, local and disjointed terms. In Judith Butler's terms, some women's experiences may be less 'intelligible' within the wider culture. If we look at the resources offered within families themselves, we can see how intelligibility may be secured in other less public ways, as well as how such identifications may be blocked or closed down, making individuals more vulnerable to the disciplinary effects of popular and public discourse.

Our starting point for exploring the relationship between the situations of first-time mothers and the common culture of motherhood was the stories that expectant first-time mothers told us about their pregnancies. Interviews were designed to elicit narratives using open questions such as 'Can you tell me the story of your life until now?' and 'Can you tell me the story of your pregnancy/How you found out that you were pregnant?' Discussing her longitudinal study of the transition to motherhood, Miller describes accounts produced in the antenatal period as 'tentatively constructed' (2005: 73) 'anticipatory narratives' (2005: 70), which are 'all about presenting an acceptable, culturally recognizable narrative of preparing appropriately and reasonably for motherhood' (2005: 88). We anticipated that women's accounts of their pregnancy might take the form of discreet narratives within the interview, defined in terms of having a beginning, middle and end, and by the sense that they had been forged and told outside the interview encounter. Our analysis confirmed our initial hunch that this aspect of the pregnancy is already 'storied' prior to the interview and that these stories are an important source for understanding the project that motherhood represents to individual women. We approach these stories as a record of and a response to the 'situation' that pregnancy poses for the woman concerned. The characteristic elements of conception narratives followed an identifiable pattern: knowing you are pregnant/finding out; identifying/remembering the moment of conception (including who the father is); telling others: the father, own mother, siblings or peers; public/private/exposure. Remembering and forgetting are explicit tools through which a narrative is forged, setting out the parameters of the project of motherhood and the characters included in the endeavour.

Memory (and its corollary forgetting) is integral to our research. We invited grandmothers to 'remember' their first pregnancy and birth. We found that for both expectant mothers and grandmothers, late pregnancy and early motherhood are suffused with powerful evocations of the embodied practices of mothering and being mothered. The preservation and passing on of special objects (books, baby clothes, health records, toys, cots, blankets or talismans to ensure safety) can be seen as a memorialising and materialising of these intergenerational connections. Yet, as Annette Kuhn (2002) observes when considering the family photograph album, the staging of memory through such material practices always also involves an editing out. The partial, constructed and staged character of memory has become an accepted part of historical scholarship: what is remembered is not simply understood as a record of the past but rather a representation of the past in the present that must be accounted for, shedding light on the identities, anxieties and situations of those involved. Ricoeur (2004) talks in terms of a 'reciprocal relationship between remembering and forgetting' which shapes both the perception of historical experience and the production of historical narrative. But can this approach help us in making sense of small-scale, intimate yet nevertheless historical narratives: the stories that women tell about becoming pregnant?

In the following sections, we present two examples, both strong narratives involving an explicit staging of memory. The first is a story told by a Jade, a 17-year-old woman, and is an ensemble piece involving many characters and detailed yet obscure plot lines. Here remembering and forgetting are staged to achieve ambiguity in terms of agency, causality and outcome. The second example is told by 33-years-old Deborah, whose pregnancy is planned and desired yet also involves complex negotiations with her partner and friends. Although her story appears at first sight to be polished and contained, we can also see the intensive work that her narrative is doing for her as she negotiates boundaries between the private intimacy of the couple and the public declaration of pregnancy. Although we sought stories of conception, we found within them stories of telling/revelation/and exposure. The staging of remembering and forgetting that is so central to conception narratives is integrally related to the exposure of the self to others that pregnancy involves.

Conception as survival

We met Jade at an educational project for young mothers. She was four months pregnant and had been evicted from her mother's house following conflict arising from her pregnancy. As her account indicates, the project of becoming a mother is contoured differently depending on resources and circumstances. Jade provides a detailed account, in which agency and the sequence of events are dissected and confirmed to moral effect. It is important to know who did what, to whom and when. Yet Jade has relatively little economic, social or interpersonal power and struggles to be heard and believed by others. She is faced with the problem of transgressing norms, thus becoming an object of gossip and rumour within her wider peer group. Her conception story has to do some very particular work, to establish her integrity as the narrator of her own life, in the face of both popular discourses that might pathologise her as 'too young' but more immediately, local discourses within which her 'story' becomes subject to the normalising effects of local value systems.

Jade's story was not 'typical' of the accounts that we gathered from the younger mothers, which were in general rather taciturn and cautious. She tells her story in a flood of words, episodes of uninterrupted narrative. The interviewer (Lucy Hadfield, herself a young woman) provided an audience; Jade addressed her as a supportive 'bridge' for the reception of the tale. The story of conception is marked by an intense and continuous flow of narrative detail. This part of the interview is framed by two episodes: first, an account of her mother's violent reaction to her pregnancy and her resulting homelessness, and second, a romantic description of how she met the baby's father and developed a sexual relationship. She then embarks on the following complex account, explaining how he disappeared for three months after she had told him that she was pregnant, and how her mother had intervened to inform his family. Unusually, Jade's conception story begins with 'telling others' rather than the story of conception:

> when I first told him I was pregnant he wasn't there for me for 3 months and I was very very upset and I was like, I wanted him there and stuff, but because we wasn't together it was just a casual thing er ... he was too interested in his life and he didn't want anybody to know. And one night I went round to my mums house, me and my mum spoke for quite a few hours which was quite shocking. And er ... she asked me for his house number so I gave my mum his house number and she spoke to his step mum and told his step mum because he hadn't told his parents, and an hour after she spoke to his step mum, his dad rang, and his dad said I'll get Darren to ring so ... an hour after that he rang and then he started coming in to me and the baby's life basically for 3 months, well 6 weeks. And then he told me he was going in to the army, went 3 days after my birthday,

> I didn't know he was going he just disappeared, and I rang up his dad and his dad told me he's gone in to the army, and I've not, I've only just recently got hold of him and that was two weeks ago. [...] his dad was lying for him saying he was in the army... and then two weeks ago I thought oh I'll try and ring him because he'd always, his phone was always on, but he doesn't answer the phone to me. So I tried ringing him and he answered to me and he goes ring me back in 15 minutes, so I left it 20, 25 minutes and ring him back and we had a good conversation, because I was actually falling in love with him, and I was like really upset how he was treating me, and I told him on the phone that I'm not in love with him anymore, I just really care for him and I don't want anything to happen, and er... he'll try turning it around and say he could change that and I turned round and said what do you mean you can change that? He says I can change you falling back in love with me. [...] Because he knows how to work my mind and he knows what changes me cos if he was to turn up he would know, that the way I was with him before, because that's what use to happen, we never use to see each other for months on end and then I'd meet up with him and I'm like I'm glad he's here and he knows that, that's why... But he's just he's too interested in his personal life... I don't count anymore, I don't rely on him anymore, so I don't need him now. I just want the baby to know he's got a dad, because he didn't grow up with a dad, from 5 years old he didn't grow up with a dad so if he wants to be the same with his child then let him. But rumours were going around that it wasn't his kid, it wasn't his baby.

This is an incredibly dense passage of speech, including a great deal of crucial and conflicting information. Although it does not have narrative slickness, it does manage to convey all the key characters involved (herself, Darren, her mum and his dad) along with the problems (her lack of influence and his own ambivalent feelings about fatherhood) and the context (a situation devoid of privacy in which communication is difficult and mediated by rumour). Jade's narrative communicates a very personal story: the patterning of an intense but intermittent relationship and the chaos of conception as she forges an account that speaks to an imaginary audience of parents and peers likely to comment on her pregnancy and speculate on matters of paternity. In keeping with many other women in our study, men are central to the shaping of a maternal identity, even when marginal or absent. For Jade, Darren is the absent centre; his role as the baby's father counts but cannot be counted upon.

The final comment, that Darren might believe that the child was not his provides the 'complication' on which the narrative turns. It is at this point that remembering becomes important and Jade's account turns to a reconstruction of the past.

> I fell pregnant on the 17th April, and I slept with someone two months previous. And she [friend] thought she worked out the dates and she thought I was pregnant with the other persons baby. And I was like no, because I fell pregnant on this time and I know I fell pregnant on this time because I had a period whatever, and I thought I could trust her and I told her and then she went back and told him that I'd slept with someone a month before I slept with, so basically I slept with someone in March, so it looked like it was the person's I slept with in March and not his, but I didn't sleep with no one in March if you know what I mean, so she made it out as if, I didn't know who the baby's dad was. So I asked him and he said no he's not heard anything about it whatever, but he turned round and said if the baby isn't mine, keep it quiet. And that was ticking over in my head, and I put the phone down to him and it was ticking over in my head what does he mean by that, does... if the baby isn't his, does he still want anything to do with it, do you know what I mean? And it was like, confusing so I rang him back a couple of days later, and I asked him and he just said if the baby isn't mine to keep it quiet. But I said the baby is yours.

It is not until this point that Jade tells the story of finding out that she was pregnant. The story that emerges suggests that from the very beginning the experience was 'public', 'shared' and contested. As with many other conception stories, her account begins with mistaken embodied symptoms.

> Jade: I'm just being sick cos I've still got a hangover and it comes up positive and I'm crying and I'm really upset cos I'm saying I don't know what my mum's going to be like, and er... I got my mate to come in, so the lady went and got my mate, and my mate's cuddling me and I'm crying more because she was cuddling me and comforting me. And I was just worried about what my mum would say. And then the lady at the clinic advised me to get rid of the baby. And I was really angry because I was shocked, just found out, worried, and she was advising me to get rid of the baby.
>
> Lucy: What did she say then?

Jade: Well me and my mate were sitting there and she turned round and said, if you're so worried about your mum, or my parents cos I still weren't speaking to my dad, if you're so worried about what your parents are going to say I really do recommend, advise you to have an abortion and she goes come back in a week and let me know and then we'll sort it out from there... I need a fag, so I had a fag and I was like how am I going to tell him? How'm I going to tell the baby's dad? And I was thinking it over and over in my head, how'm I going to tell him? And I went to my best mate how'm I going to tell him I don't know what to say? And she was like I'll tell him, I was like alright then, I was shaking and I was crying, and all upset... I text him saying, just casually hi what are you up to? We need to talk. And he didn't text me back... So we rang from the pay phone and she turned round and said er... Jade's just been to the clinic and he went yeah, she goes she's just found out she's pregnant and he goes you're joking... he thought she was lying and I turned round, I was angry and I was really mad, I says does he think I'm lying? And she goes yeah, so I said give me the phone, so I took the phone and he goes stop crying, I says I'm upset, I just found out I'm pregnant. And I said we need to meet up and he says alright I'll meet up on Saturday, 3 months later he finally met up with me and that's what's shocking because I was like, he's going to be a dad and he left it 3 months to meet up with me and I was always on his back saying come and meet me and stuff. Yeah... I'll never forget the day I found out.

This final episode in Jade's conception story can be seen as a condensation of what comes before. The setting and the conversation are described graphically, almost cinematically. As readers we can also imagine being there, or at least watching. The difficult decision of whether or not to keep the baby is dispersed and Jade's ambivalence expressed in several ways: shocked by the counsellor's advice, having the fag and insisting on telling immediately yet passing responsibility to her friend. In observing that she would 'never forget the day' that she found out, Jade is also positioning this story as emblematic of the way in which she is imagining her project of becoming a mother: with herself as an ambivalent yet active agent within a wider dramatic landscape, with a present yet absent father and grandmother. Almost by default, the counsellor plays a critical yet 'off stage' role. In voicing the possibility of a termination it becomes possible for Jade to turn away and engage in the drama that is the pregnancy.

Conception as inevitable

The second conception story is told by Deborah, a woman who is well-resourced, secure and unlike Jade, the conception described was planned. Nevertheless the core components of the narrative: finding out, 'knowing', remembering and telling still structure the account. Deborah was nine months pregnant with her first child when we met her. Until that point she had been working full time as an information worker in a large public sector organisation. The pregnancy she describes was a shared project between herself and her partner. She too was interviewed by Lucy Hadfield who described her as being friendly and co-operative interviewee, yet noting there were issues concerning the couple relationship that are 'too complex to be articulated in interview'. Deborah's conception story begins with the relationship

> Bit disorganised really because we have been together eleven year, well seven years before we got married erm and we were engaged for about six years something like that, just not very, we didn't really have any big plans or anything like that about where we wanted to be or whatever but I think we always knew that we wanted to be together, we wanted to have a family and then I guess a couple of years ago, about a year ago probably, we said, 'right are we going to do this baby thing?'. And so, I came off the pill and erm we said 'Right in the next two years we will see what happens and if it is meant to happen it is meant to happen and if it doesn't happen it won't'. So we were sort of using other forms of birth control whilst we were trying to come to terms with the fact that if we do it now we might have a baby in nine months time and erm ended up getting really drunk one night and forgetting! (hearty laugh) That was really the first time that I could have got pregnant because I had been secretly doing the maths and counting the days so yes in September within about two weeks of trying properly it was just the first time (laughs) really funny!!...I didn't find out that I was pregnant for about six weeks and it was a really big shock. And then I thought oh ok well it is meant to be then, that's fair enough. My mum had had problems conceiving my sister and she said to me, 'Well if you are going to do it you better get on with it because if you take as long as I did to have your sister, if you have the same kind of problems..', erm I think she had a blocked fallopian tube or something like that so there is a six year age gap between me and my sister erm, 'You better get on with it'. So we did and it took six weeks

instead of six years! (laughs) But there you go! That's just one of those things.

Deborah's description of herself and her husband as 'disorganised' appears ironic, in that the pregnancy is planned and appropriately synchronised within the norms (i.e. after marriage, in stable emotional and financial circumstances). Yet as the narrative unfolds the 'disorganisation' emerges in the form of uncertain communication between the two. The initial narrative episode articulates a simple story that allows both for them to be planners (coming off the pill) and to be more romantically caught by fate (forgetting one drunken night). Yet in mentioning her 'secret calculations' and her mothers warnings about infertility we get a sense of a more anxious and individual account beneath the surface. On Lucy's prompting, Deborah airs some of these feelings in a much less articulate manner.

Lucy: So you came off the pill but you still kind of backed it up a bit?

Deborah: Yeah, yeah (coy). I mean my husband was not... I mean did I make him aware that I was doing the counting? I mean, (laughs nervously) I was thinking 'Do we need to use a condom now or do we not?' And then sometimes I would go, 'Yeah I think it is alright' but then sometimes I would go 'I am not quite ready yet, not quite ready.' So we had some kind of..., it was kind of... I don't know really. I think, well I am just trying to remember, we didn't really ask questions about are we really going to do this now it was just kind of we will see what happens but I knew in the back of my mind when wasn't a, when it was like days 14–17 I was thinking, 'Well, maybe not.' Not that anything really happened between days 14–17 anyway because we were both too knackered (both laugh).

She then goes on immediately to narrate the experience of discovering that she was pregnant. Despite all the secret calculations, this is constructed as a story of shock, and returns to a more assured and rehearsed story telling style.

Lucy: So you say you felt really shocked when you –

Deborah: Yes I was really, really shocked. Erm I think I was shocked because I had been out on several drunken weekends (laughs) in the first sort of five weeks which was erm and actually we were away for a weekend with friends and one of my friends, she had her baby in December so it was last October, that's right. She said to me, 'Are

> you sure you are not pregnant you have been to the loo about six times in the last hour.' She said, 'I have got a pregnancy test upstairs go and do it.' And I said 'No I am not doing it, I am not doing it. I feel fine!'. Oh yes I am about a week late but I think my period is coming you know and I've got the cramps and whatever and she said, 'You should probably do a test you know. I had that when it was like an implantation so you should probably do a test'. So I thought well you know I better do one and I did it and I didn't tell my husband I was doing it and I came downstairs into the kitchen and I just handed him the rest of the bottle of wine and showed him the test. And we were both standing there in the kitchen going, 'Oh my god, oh my god, oh blimey, oh my god!'. I don't know I felt kind of caught out. I mean I am thirty three (laughs) and I felt like how I would imagine a seventeen year old would feel cos it had just been the first time and I hadn't thought it would happen. But it did and it was like, blimey and I have got to do something about this. So I did, I made an appointment with the doctor and erm we confirmed it and did all the dates and it was just a question of keeping it all quiet then from work because I think I was about six weeks something like that.

In contrast to the earlier 'we' ness of her account of planning to get pregnant, Deborah's story of finding out is characterised much more by a sense of herself in relation to her peer group. She talks of friends having babies and encouraging her to think that she might be pregnant. Again alcohol features prominently: and a drunken weekend with the girls is juxtaposed with the drunken night when they had not used contraception. It is fascinating that Deborah describes herself as feeling like a 17 year old when she realises that she is in fact pregnant: citing the well-worn clichés of feeling 'caught out' and it 'not happening the first time'. Both give us insight into the extent to which women are aware of and fluent in a wide range of narratives of motherhood, but also might help us see how exposed Deborah feels by the experience of becoming pregnant. It is instructive then to see how Deborah's narrative turns, and relates the experience of pregnancy back into the couple and the private. The care that Deborah and her partner take in regulating who is told, when and in what order, suggests that 'telling' involves important work in the process of constructing a new identity and relationships. Perhaps the most important part of this is to forge the pregnancy as shared enterprise for the couple. Lucy asks Deborah why she waited to tell everyone.

> Deborah: Well just the twelve week thing really. I wanted to leave it just to be safe erm cos ... I mean a few of them have had miscarriages and whatever and I just thought I knew that for my parents it was their first grandchild. For my husband's parents it is less of an issue because it will be their third erm and I thought when I start on the whole I am pregnant thing I am going to get the phone calls like every second day like, 'Are you all right? Are you okay? Are you feeling sick?' And I thought, 'I think I will just keep this special time just for me and Partner to tell everyone'. We would sort of grin at each other and make excuses about why we are not eating pate and whatever (laughs). Which was quite hard actually.

The final episode in Deborah's conception story is the stage at which she is ready to 'go public' to the group of girlfriends who form the audience for her account, all now mothers, egging her along, waiting impatiently. Here she returns to the opening motif of organisation/disorganisation

> I think I did a mass e-mail to everyone actually saying, 'We finally got ourselves organised and Junior is on its way'. And the particular friends, the weekend I think it happened the friends that were here, we were having a girly weekend and I sent my husband to bed and we were [doing here] watching Bridget Jones and drinking several bottles of Chardonnay – it was dreadful and I had to e-mail them and say 'You know that weekend when you were here and I got really, really drunk well I think it may have been then. That could be too much information for you but' (laughs).

This final sentence serves to tie all of Deborah's key themes and characters together, and implicate them in the moment of conception. It is a moment of deliberate and controlled exposure of the self to others, the intimate to the public and the sexual to the social. If conception is a moment in which individual agency is relinquished (and marked as such by alcohol), then the re-staging of this memory, both in the email and its subsequent re-telling, can be understood as an articulation of a new identity settlement, the beginning of the project that is motherhood.

The identity work of new motherhood

Remembering and forgetting are parts of the substance of these tales, pointing to the importance of securing paternity, and a normative sequence of respectable reproduction within the western late modern culture that these women share. Forgetting also plays an important role in the way that women narrate the profound change in their situation. Alcoholic confusion, fatalism, incompetence and misrecognition are all performed in these stories enabling the self and the intimate to be opened to the view of others. 'Telling' can be a way of seeking to control this exposure and to regain control. Selective remembering is the process through which a narrative is forged. Yet what is not told can still be present in its effects, a lingering feeling left with the interviewer and the reader.

Conception stories are part of the identity work of new motherhood and give insights into the necessary features of the changing identity and the nature of the project. The way in which women narrate this situation has common elements: with recurrent motifs around 'knowing', 'remembering/forgetting' and 'telling'. Yet, each also shows how women encounter motherhood in extraordinarily different circumstances. While it is productive to read these examples against each other, comparison should remain cautious. We are not seeking to identify ideal or typical narratives of early/late or planned/unplanned motherhood. Rather, we want to capture something of the paradoxical nature of motherhood that is both one and many things. The women in these examples are fluent in the popular narratives of motherhood. Both are aware of the need to construct an acceptable narrative that is recognised in the local culture of their lives and the wider cultural community to which they belong. Their accounts are highly moral tales, constructed heteroglossically in relation to broader narratives and normative expectations as well as personal fears and individual circumstances. They are aware of and position themselves in relation to the 'shame' of pregnancy and work to narrate themselves within the boundaries of normalising principles. Irrespective of their situations, both women struggle to make motherhood intelligible and their narratives bear the marks of a search for audience and for others to witness, affirm and react to this change.

Understood in narrative terms, these are both extraordinarily rich and inventive accounts – harnessing and shaping meaning, attributing responsibility and inventing causality. Their comparison is productive, enhancing an appreciation of form as well as the ways in which context shapes the narrative challenge. Yet reading these accounts together can also be uncomfortable, revealing a stark inequality of security and resource between the women. It is hard to hear these voices without also evoking a wider welfare discourse that places Jade's story safely beyond intelligibility and recognition. This does not mean that Jade does not claim recognition – her account is dominated by them, yet these claims have no purchase on public morality. Where Deborah's story employs the ironic comic form of Bridget Jones's diary, Jade's story can too easily be stripped of pathos by hearing it through the voice of Little Britain's Vicky Pollard – the increasingly acceptable popular portrayal of the 'undeserving' poor. A theoretical focus on intelligibility such as that argued in different ways by Butler and Plummer encourages us to understand the cultural realm as a site of politics and potentially of social change. Yet, a focus on norms and normalisation can also impoverish our understanding of the social world. To call certain lives unintelligible or unliveable may well reveal the operation of normalising principles and the paradoxical contingency and continuity of privilege, yet it does not provide us with many tools for appreciating the forms of recognition and sustenance that are always in play, however marginal and fragile.

References

Adkins, L. (2003) Reflexivity: Freedom or Habit of Gender. *Theory, Culture and Society*, 20(6), 21–42.

Bailey, L. (1999) Refracted Selves? A Study of Changes in Self-Identity in the Transition to Motherhood. *Sociology*, 33(2), 335–52.

Beck, U. (1992) *Risk Society: Towards a New Modernity*. London: Sage.

Bjerrum Nielsen, H. and Rudberg, M. (1994) *Psychological Gender and Modernity*. Stockholm: Scandinavian University Press.

Bjerrum Nielsen, H. and Rudberg, M. (2000) Gender, Love and Education in Three Generations. *The European Journal of Women's Studies*, 7(4), 423–53.

Brannen, J., Moss, P. and Mooney, A. (2004) *Working and Caring over the Twentieth Century: Change and Continuity in Four Generation Families*. Basingstoke: Palgrave Macmillan.

Butler, J. (2004) *Undoing Gender*. Boca Raton, FL: Routledge Taylor and Francis.

Byrne, B. (2006) In Search of a Good Mix. Race, Class, Gender and Practices of Mothering. *Sociology*, 40(6), 1001–17.

Clarke, A. (2004) Maternity and Materiality: Becoming a Mother in Consumer Culture. In: J.S. Taylor, L.L. Layne and D.F. Wozniak (eds) *Consuming Motherhood*. New Brunswick: Rutgers University Press.

Crompton, R. (2006) *Employment and the Family: The Reconfiguration of Work and Family Life in Contemporary Societies*. Cambridge: Cambridge University Press.

Henderson, S., Holland, J., McGrellis, S., Sharpe, S. and Thomson, R. (2007) *Inventing Adulthoods, a Biographical Approach to Youth Transitions*. London: Sage/The Open University.

Kuhn, A. (2002) *Family Secrets: Acts of Memory and Imagination*. London: Verso.

Lewis, J. (1992) *Women in Britain Since 1945*. Oxford: Blackwell.

Miller, D. (2004) How Infants Grow Mothers in North London. In: J.S. Taylor, L.L. Layne and D.F. Wozniak (eds) *Consuming Motherhood*. New Brunswick: Rutgers University Press.

Miller, T. (2005) *Making Sense of Motherhood: A Narrative Approach*. Cambridge: Cambridge University Press.
Plummer, K. (1995) *Telling Sexual Stories, Power, Change and Sexual Worlds*. London: Routledge.
Ricoeur, P. (2004) *Memory, History, Forgetting*. Chicago: University of Chicago Press.
Skeggs, B. (2004) *Class, Self, Culture*. London: Routledge.
Smart, C. (2007) *Personal Life: New Directions in Sociological Thinking*. Cambridge: Polity Press.
Tyler, I. (2008) Chav Mum, Chav Scum: Class Disgust in Contemporary Britain. *Feminist Media Studies*, 8(4), 17–34.
Volosinov, V.N. (1973 [1929]) *Marxism and the Philosophy of Language*, trans. L. Matejka and I. Turner. London: Seminar Press.
Willis, P., Jones, S., Canaan, J. and Hurd, G. (1990) *Common Culture: Symbolic Play at Work in the Everyday Cultures of the Young*. Buckingham: Open University Press.

11

The Allure of Belonging: Young People's Drinking Practices and Collective Identification

Christine Griffin, Andrew Bengry-Howell, Chris Hackley, Willm Mistral and Isabelle Szmigin[1]

Introduction

Drinking to intoxication now forms an increasingly normalised part of most young people's social lives. Research on young people's alcohol consumption indicates a pattern of increased sessional heavy drinking in the UK from the early 1990s, although there is some recent evidence that this trend is starting to level off (Measham, 2008). We have explored this issue in a recent study that examined the role of drinking in young adults' social lives in relation to the diverse ways in which alcohol is now marketed and advertised to young people. In this chapter, we focus on the significance of belonging to a social friendship group for young people's drinking cultures. Young people's alcohol consumption revolves around a collective culture of intoxication that is based firmly in informal mixed and single-sex friendship groups (Griffin et al., 2009). Drinking, as many alcohol researchers have pointed out, is a practice through which we are located (and locate ourselves) in terms of gender, class, age, religion, ethnicity and national identity (Wilson, 2005).

Alcoholic drinks are heavily promoted and a substantial proportion of advertising and marketing expenditure is targeted at young people (Smith and Foxcroft, 2007). Our analysis of a selected sample of 216 alcohol adverts aimed at young people shown during 2005–2006 on TV, radio, magazines and the internet indicates that many adverts associate drinking with 'having a laugh' and as integral to sociability (see also McCreanor et al., 2008). One example is the Carling 'Belong' adverts, featuring a group of male astronauts (the 'Space' ad), a group of men in a desert (the 'Out' ad). Each advert ended with a picture of five men standing close together in silhouette with the strap-line 'you know who your mates are' alongside the 'Belong' logo. The most minimalist version of this advert featured a flock of birds flying in unison above a rural winter landscape with the refrain 'Going out tonight' from the song 'Living for the weekend' by Hard-Fi on the soundtrack. At the end of the advert the familiar Carling logo appeared (gold lettering between two red slashes on a black ground) with the word 'Belong' substituted for the ubiquitous Carling brand name.[2]

A minority of alcohol adverts involve all-female friendship groups, such as the 'Lambrini girls' series which were first shown in the UK during 2004.[3] These adverts represent a group of young white women in all-female spaces such as women's toilets or a bedroom getting ready to go out, involved various humorous scenarios. The strap-line 'Girls just wanna have fun', the title of a Cyndi Lauper song from the 1980s, is linked to the brand name 'Lambrini' in these adverts.

Adverts of this kind 'hail' a particular drinking subject that is constituted around a gendered youth friendship group rather than an individual consumer. They hold out the promise of sociability as a treasured prize that is inextricably associated with a 'good night out'. The ultimate prize on offer is to belong. The use of space is significant, since the male 'mates' in the Carling 'Belong' adverts (and many other similar adverts) go out into the world to engage in risky and exciting adventures; whilst the female friends in the Lambrini adverts let themselves go and behave outrageously in far more confined and all-female domestic spaces (c.f. Hunt et al., 2000). In both cases, alcohol consumption is constituted as enabling and enhancing a (gendered and classed) sociability that is located within young people's friendship groups.

Friendship, belonging and collectivity in contemporary society

There is long-standing evidence that peer groups form an important part of young people's social lives (Kehily, 2007). Youth sub-cultural research has focussed on the importance of style and the political and social significance of 'having a laugh' and 'hanging out' for young people (Hodkinson and Deicke, 2007). Feminist youth researchers have also identified girls' and young women's friendship groups as sources of intimacy and care (Hey, 1997). Social groups are also central to young people's drinking cultures (Sheehan and Ridge, 2001; Tomsen, 1997; and Workman, 2001).

However, recent social theories on individualisation (Beck, 1992), late modernity (Giddens, 1992) and neo-liberalism (Rose, 1989) have lead to a reassessment of the significance of social and personal relationships. Such theorists have all – in different ways – devoted considerable attention to the emphasis on autonomous individuality manifested through consumption that is viewed as the cornerstone of contemporary identity and social life. This has produced some stark – and memorable – pronouncements. Beck and Beck-Gernsheim's influential work on the 'individualisation thesis' argued that

> Each of us is both expected and forced to *lead our own life* outside the bounds of any particular community or group.
>
> (2002: 46, original emphasis)

As Beck put it in an earlier text, 'community is dissolved in the acid bath of competition' (1992: 94). Although the work of these social theorists has been subject to substantial critique, research evidence supports some (but not all) of their key arguments (Furlong and Cartmel, 1997; Pahl and Pevalin, 2005). However, close mixed and single-sex friendship groups still play a central role in young people's social lives, and forms of collectivity and community have far from disappeared. They may, however, take on a different significance in the context of late modernity, with its emphasis on individualism, self-surveillance and responsible consumption.

For example, the past 40 years have seen a decentring of the family as a primary source of intimacy and care in contemporary British and US society. Pahl and Pevalin (2005) draw on data from the 1991 and 2001 British Household Survey to argue that younger (18–25) people are most likely to nominate their closest friends as being outside the family, although families are still viewed as important. Roseneil and Budgeon (2004) have argued that amongst the most 'individualised' sector of the British population (adults who are not living with a partner), primary sources of intimacy and care are found outside the family in networks and partners who are not living together as family. Research on friendship indicates that informal, private social relationships are likely to take on increasing significance as marriage is a less stable institution and employment is more 'flexible' and uncertain (Allan, 1989). So what are the implications of the shifting social meanings of friendship, collectivity, intimacy and care for young people's cultures of 'determined drunkenness' in the neo-liberal social order?

Alcohol consumption and neo-liberal subjectivity

Belonging to a social collectivity has a particular significance in relation to the compulsory individualism that characterises social relations in the neo-liberal social order (Cronin, 2000). A key element of neo-liberalism is the attempt to constitute new forms of subjectivity, especially around a particular form of individualism that carries with it a powerful (and new) form of governance (Rose, 1989). Contemporary discourses of individual freedom, self-expression and authenticity demand that we live our lives as if this was part of a biographical project of self-realisation in a society in which we all appear to have 'free' choice to consume whatever we want and to become whoever we want to be (Walkerdine, 2003). The neo-liberal social order puts pressure on all of us to act with moderation as active, rational individuals who are likely to be held responsible and accountable for our actions (Steinberg and Johnson, 2003).

Measham and Brain (2005) cite several key developments over the past 20 years as contributors to what they term the 'new' culture of intoxication amongst young drinkers in the UK. The emergence of rave and dance culture in the late 1980s saw a shift from the use of alcohol to dance drugs such as ecstasy. The alcohol industry responded by recommodifying alcohol as a psychoactive product targeted at a more diverse group of young consumers. From the early 1990s, a wider range of products appeared, designed to appeal to young adults as 'psychoactive consumers' (Brain et al., 2000). These include FABs (flavoured alcoholic beverages); RMDs (spirits-based ready-to-drink mixers such as Bacardi Breezer, the market leader); 'buzz' drinks based on legally available substances such as caffeine (e.g. Red Bull); and, more recently, cheap 'shots' of spirits and liquor, usually downed in one for an instant 'hit' (Measham, 2006). This coincided with an increase in the strength of traditional products such as wine and beers, and the increased availability of cheaper alcohol in promotional deals aimed at young drinkers. In addition, the retail trade has been transformed, with the emergence of café bars, dance bars and themed pubs in most city centres, broadening the traditional customer base well beyond the traditional pub clientele of white working-class heterosexual men to include more culturally and sexually diverse groups in the 18–35 range (Chatterton and Hollands, 2001).

The night-time economy also commodifies the pursuit of pleasure and hedonistic excess in bounded urban 'wild zones' that target a predominantly young adult consumer demographic (Hayward and Hobbs,

2007). Young people's consumption practices have been referred to as a form of 'calculated hedonism' (or 'controlled loss of control'), within the boundaries of a specific time (the weekend); place (a private party or a club or bar within a 'wild zone'); company (a supportive friendship group); and intensity (Measham, 2004). The concept of 'calculated hedonism' combines discourses of discipline, (self-)control and enjoyment to mobilise pleasure as a governing category (Szmigin et al., 2008). What Measham and Brain (2005) have termed the 'new culture of intoxication' operates in the context of simultaneous seduction and repression, such that young people are viewed as being seduced into a culture of normalised excessive drinking, whilst simultaneously being pathologised as disordered and disorderly 'binge drinkers' (Szmigin et al., 2008).

In the neo-liberal social order, there is an imperative on individual subjects to construct and display themselves as distinctive, authentic selves, discerning consumers and as ethical, responsible moral subjects. If one behaves in ways that are taken to be excessive, unhealthy, irresponsible or undisciplined, then this is constituted as a moral failure of the self (Croghan et al., 2006). Young people's public displays of drunken excess are constituted in governmental discourses as volitional acts of irresponsible excess, a willed entry into the realm of chaos, risk and danger and away from the rationality, self-control and moderation that is at the heart of neo-liberal subjectivity (O'Malley and Valverde, 2004), and this process is also classed and gendered (Skeggs, 2004).

'Binge Nation': constituting 'Britain's Boozy Youth'

Contemporary popular culture in the UK is suffused with narratives of young people drinking to excess. Health education initiatives generally constitute young people's alcohol consumption as a potential source of risk and harm, representing young drinkers as in need of help and treatment (e.g. http://www.knowyourlimits.gov.uk/; Hackley et al., 2008). Most advertising and marketing campaigns by the major drinks manufacturers represent young people's drinking as a source of pleasure, camaraderie, fun and adventure (e.g. http://www.thechoiceisyours.com; Nayak, 2006). More voyeuristic narratives in TV programmes such as 'Britain's Streets of Booze' (Woolwich, 2005) or 'Booze Britain' (Kattenhorn, 2005–2006) constitute young people's drinking as a source of entertainment and as a spectacle of excess. There is also a pervasive representation of 'drunken celebs' in print media and the internet, and a substantial focus on young women in states of distress and disarray (Davies and Hill, 2008).

The recent discourse of anxiety and censure over young people's alcohol consumption revolves around a particular concern with 'binge drinking' amongst 18–25 year olds. Although the academic and policy literatures draw on several different definitions of the term 'binge',[4] this lack of consensus over what constitutes a 'binge' has scarcely impinged on the force of the term in official discourses of youthful excess (Szmigin et al., 2008). The main onus is on young drinkers, rather than the alcohol industry or the retail trade, to change their drinking practices and reduce their alcohol consumption (Measham, 2006).

Drinking to excess, and especially public displays of drunkenness, are also heavily marked by gender, class and culture (Skeggs, 2005; Wilson, 2005). Although young women's reported levels of frequent drinking and drunkenness are still less than that of their male peers, young women's rate and level of alcohol consumption has increased over the past 15 years (Plant, 2008). However, drinking to excess is still associated with traditional and working-class forms of masculinity (De Vissier and Smith, 2007; Tomsen, 1997). Although there is a long history of ritualised drinking to excess amongst upper-class young men, this often takes place in the more secluded spaces of university colleges or private school grounds. In the event of more public displays of drunken excess, this elite group have the money to buy themselves out of trouble (Ronay, 2008). The upper class as a whole is seldom subject to the same level of horrified moral outrage and disgust that has been directed at the drinking practices of white working-class youth (Nayak, 2006; Saner, 2008). Public displays of determined drunkenness by young working-class men, and especially young working-class white women, are frequently constituted as the epitome of feckless excess (Skeggs, 2004, 2005).

What, then, is the significance of young people's cultures of 'determined drunkenness' in the context of neo-liberal discourses of individual freedom and consumerism, pervasive panics over youthful 'binge drinking' and the ubiquitous advertising and marketing of alcohol with its central place in the night-time economy? How do young people construct a 'liveable life' in such circumstances, negotiating their relationships and identities within their social worlds?

'We have such a laugh . . . together': belonging, friendship and the culture of intoxication

The 'Young People and Alcohol' study explored the relationship between consumption and identity for young adults aged 18–25, focusing on accounts of 'everyday drinking' by ordinary consumers in three geographical locations, via 16 informal focus group discussions with 89 young adults in three geographical locations: a major city centre in the English Midlands with a diverse population ('Rowchester'); a seaside town; ('Seatown') and a small market town ('Bolston') in the English West Country with more homogeneous populations and a more limited range of drinking venues. 'Rowchester' has a substantial night-time economy dominated by a wide range of bars and clubs aimed at a young adult clientele. It is ethnically and culturally diverse with a large student population and a degree of separation between the leisure spaces of predominantly white middle-class 'students' and more ethnically diverse but predominantly working-class 'locals' (Holt and Griffin, 2005).

Below we present an analysis of selected transcribed extracts from a series of focus groups conducted at Further Education colleges at 'Seatown' and 'Bolston', and with students at a nearby university in the small city of 'Avon' during 2005 and 2006. The 'Bolston' and 'Seatown' participants were white British (self-definition) and working class (by occupation and educational background), and the university students were white and middle class. We also include extracts from a discussion with students at a vocational nursing college in 'Rowchester', involving young white women from working-class backgrounds. Participants were recruited through contacts with local colleges, and in most cases, they were interviewed in friendship groups. Not all participants drank alcohol. Focus groups were facilitated by researchers in their twenties and thirties, with a view to putting participants at their ease when talking about their drinking practices,[5] although the interviewers were still older than the respondents, most of whom were in their late teens or early twenties. Focus group discussions lasted between one and two hours and were recorded and subsequently transcribed.[6]

Drinking was mentioned by participants as an important (although not essential) aspect of their social lives at an early stage in all the interviews. This is not to imply that drinking and socialising were treated as equivalent or coterminous. The common phrase 'you don't have to be drunk (to have fun)' acted as an implicit challenge to the notion of drinking as an essential component of a 'good night out'. This also held at bay the possibility that participants might rely on alcohol to have fun. This avoidance of any assumption of an (over-)reliance on alcohol was frequently linked to the construction of drinking as 'just fun', minimising any potential risks and harms connected with drinking to excess.

In extracts from two interviews with groups of young white working-class women from 'Rowchester' and 'Seatown' quoted below, our participants distanced themselves from any association with being reliant on alcohol:

Nicki: We have such a laugh getting ready together (.) that's like part of the night y'know (.) everyone's around you getting (.) you don't have to be drunk to do that but (.) it's just fun
ABH: So is it the getting together that's (.) what's the most important part of going out?
Anne: Bein being in a group is (inaudible) n having a laugh
(**Extract 1**: Rowchester nursing college, Nov 2006)

Helen: I think the whole point of going out is socialising (.) innit (.) and then the drink is next (.) well [(...)
Sara: [yeah
Helen: If I did go on my own (.) just to drink on my own (.) that's a bit (2) alcoholicky...I don't see the point
(**Extract 2**: Seatown FE college, June 2006)

In Anne's comment in Extract 1 (p. 220) above, drinking is represented as secondary to the more important 'bein in a group...and having a laugh'. In Extract 2 (p. 220), Helen gives top priority to 'socialising' as the primary reason for 'going out'. Drinking as part of a friendship group epitomised 'having fun', in contrast to drinking on ones' own, which Helen, in common with most of our participants, associated with being 'a bit (2) alcoholicky' and as a practice that was widely viewed to have no entertainment value ('I don't see the point'). By holding at bay the suggestion that drinking might be of primary importance in their social lives, these young women are also representing themselves as 'respectable' drinkers. The constitution of 'being in a group' and 'socialising' as an important source of fun and an integral part of a good night out operates in both extracts to mitigate against any possibility that these young women might *need* to drink.

As the group that is most commonly represented as feckless irresponsible 'binge drinkers' in popular cultural discourse, young working-class women have particular reasons for not wishing to be positioned as reliant on booze. However, the predominant tone of their talk about the role of drinking in their social lives was celebratory rather than defensive.

Risk, fear and safety in numbers

The friendship group was characterised as offering a number of specific functions. In addition to providing a source of fun and sociability, it also appeared as an essential source of protection in many young people's accounts – especially for young women.

Vicky: Cos there's so many of us and there's... I don't walk anywhere on my own I'm always with a group of people that I know really well (.) so I don't (.) like there nothing would happen to me (.) cos they're all with me and my Dad makes sure they'd walk me to my front door
ABH: Okay
Vicky: So I'm alright (1) if I was going out on my own (.) I wouldn't like if it was me on my own (1) I wouldn't go and like (.) if I had to walk on my own or something I'd phone my dad (.) or get a taxi or something like that I wouldn't walk on my own
ABH: Okay
Nikki: No when I'm with people I'm not scared
ABH: Right
Nikki: Just on my own I don't really like it
(**Extract 3**: Bolston FE college, May 2006)

In Extract 3 (p. 221), another group of young white working-class women discuss their personal safety strategies. Vicky and Nikki represent their nights out as shaped by the fear of being alone in the public space of the night-time economy – and here they are referring to a small market town in the English West Country, not a major conurbation like 'Rowchester'. Their movements are represented as so restricted by the avoidance of being on their own that a series of strategies must be mobilised to avoid this situation at all costs. The group (along with Vicki's father, and calling a taxi) is constituted here as a secure space that will guarantee that 'nothing would happen'. The zone of risk and danger is represented as beginning literally outside Vicki's front door.[7] In common with our other female participants, the nature of this danger remained largely unspoken, but the gendered nature of the accounts leads us to speculate that these young women are most likely to be referring to the spectre of sexual assault (Griffin et al., 2009).

Listening to – and ignoring 'The Voice of Good Reason'

Constituting oneself as fearful in public spaces and amongst the unnamed risks stalking the chaotic streets of the night-time economy (even in 'Bolston'), also operated to position young women as responsible, epitomising respectable (if somewhat enervated and passive) femininity. However, not all of our female participants presented their social lives or their relationship to drinking in this way. Extract 4 (p. 222) below involves the same group of young women as those quoted in Extract 1 (p. 220). Here their discussion of the role of the friendship group as an insurance against the dangers associated with getting (very) drunk constituted their own drinking practices as a potential source of risk.

Rose: I'd say that drinking is like counting the bruises the next day thing
ABH: Really (laughter)
Rose: Where did I get that one (laughter)
Julie: That's really scary that if you don't remember what you've done (.) that's really scary
Anne: If we're in a big group of us
Rose: Exactly
Anne: We wouldn't wouldn't ever let any anything happen
ABH: Right
Rose: That's why we always go out in such a big group (.) because we always *know* that there'll be someone that doesn't drink (.) because there's always somebody (.) who if (.) coz there's always (...) we all keep a watchful eye on em
(**Extract 4**: Rowchester nursing college, Nov 2006)

Rose in particular laughs as she associates drinking with 'counting the bruises the next day', and appears to accept the possibility of not being able to remember what she did while drunk (c.f. Griffin et al., 2009). There is no attempt here to avoid the position of irresponsible (and unfeminine) drinker reflected in Extract 1 (p. 220), as Rose produces a traditionally masculine account of her alcohol consumption (Gough and Edwards, 1998).

Julie's reference to losing one's memory through drinking balances Rose's humorous account by highlighting the 'scary' nature of the experience – and indicating to the researcher that they are aware of the risks. Anne and Rose emphasise this with their explanation that by going out in 'a big group' they 'wouldn't ever let anything happen'. The friendship group provides a sort of mobile private space, protecting its occupants from the risks of drinking to excess in the night-time economy and providing a cocoon of intimate shared 'fun' as the group moves around various drinking venues.

For Vicky and Nikki in Extract 3 (p. 221), the risks associated with drinking were located in unnamed threats outside the friendship group (and the family home and the taxi cab). For participants quoted in

Extracts 4 and 5 (pp. 222–23), their own uncontrolled behaviour when (very) drunk could be a source of potential danger, and their safety strategies involved a reliance on an unspecified and relatively sober person within the group. The safety of individual drinkers was represented as being guaranteed by the presence and size of the group itself, and also via references to one member of the group who 'doesn't drink' as Rose puts it in Extract 4 (p. 222). It is worth noting that our participants' definitions of 'not drinking' did not necessarily equate with abstinence. The term usually referred to not drinking to excess or extreme intoxication, or being able to consume alcohol but not be 'affected' by it, as in Joe's account below.

Joe: I think it's good sometimes to have a mate who goes out (.) who is not affected by alcohol and that (1) cos he's like a voice of good reason or something (1) so say you're going a bit over the top and he'll come along and he's like that and 'you're a bit over the top mate, calm it down a bit'

Callum: Usually (.) usually though if you say that (.) they'll go 'fuck off' (laughter)

Joe: ...because when you're drunk you tend to get a bit (.) some people tend to get a bit lairy (1) I know I've (...) I've been and (...) a person who's like sober or like only had a couple of drinks (.) they can like diffuse the situation better than you could (1) cos you'd be just giving it all that

ABH: So you think they could be helpful

Joe: Yeah (1) stopping me getting my head kicked in

(**Extract 5**: Seatown FE college, May 2006)

For the group of young white working-class women at 'Seatown' FE college quoted in Extract 4 (p. 222), Rose's reference to 'someone that doesn't drink' has its equivalent in Joe's reference in Extract 5 (p. 223) to the (male) 'mate...who is not affected by alcohol'. The latter position is gendered as acceptably masculine, in that this unidentified 'mate' is someone who can handle their drink without losing control. However, drinking until one is sick and obviously very much affected by alcohol is also a traditionally masculine drinking practice (Tomsen, 1997).

For Joe, the main risks associated with being drunk in the night-time economy are located outside the friendship group, not in the silent and unnamed spectre of sexual assault that haunted the young women's accounts, but in the possibility of 'getting my head kicked in'. In Joe's account, alcohol was represented as inducing an almost inevitable tendency to become 'lairy' in himself, although this was immediately hedged into a reference to the more general 'some people'. The association between fighting and (working-class) masculinity is a close one (Tomsen, 1997), and Joe's account represents these risks as inevitable but best avoided, with alcohol appearing as an incitement to the foolish and excessive activities reflected in the phrases 'going a bit over the top' and 'giving it all that'. The (relatively) sober 'mate' who can act as 'a voice of good reason' is constituted as a balancing force that counters the inevitable excesses, foolish and risky activities that occur during bouts of extreme intoxication.

Drinking in a friendship group then is represented here as a relatively safe base from which young men can engage in irrational, excessive and intense practices that risk the possibility of physical assault. The 'reasonable' voice that is located (somewhere) within the group is represented as being on hand to calm the agitated and 'lairy' male drinker and prevent trouble. Callum's wry comment that 'usually' anyone in that state may well not heed the sage advice of such a 'voice of good reason' and is more likely to tell them to 'fuck off' appears as a more 'realistic' and less optimistic note.

'Stupid' drinking practices as routes to belonging and exclusion

Elsewhere we have referred to male participants' accounts of drinking combinations of drinks (e.g. sambuca and lager) until they are sick (Griffin et al., 2009). Such practices are referred to as group activities, and the consumption of unpleasant combinations of noxious substances to the point of vomiting has long been a focal point of male drinking culture, notably in initiation rituals linked to college and sports events (Workman, 2001).

Conversely, not being part of such drinking practices was constructed as a source of social exclusion or marginality in some cases. Extract 6 (p. 225) involves a group of young white middle-class university students, and Jude represents her lack of access to 'funny stories' about 'stupid' drunken exploits as preventing her from developing a friendship with her flatmates during her first year at college. Carrie, Jude and Toni mobilise this argument as part of their objection to what they constitute as the compulsory nature of drinking to intoxication amongst their peers in university student culture. They are also able to differentiate themselves from the conformist mass of other students who drink to such excess.

Carrie: ...you feel like you almost have to get drunk in order to (1) share the funny stories (1) cos next day you have them to talk about
Toni: Yeah
Jude: I never really got on with my flat mates in the first year because (1) they had all these funny stories about their drinking nights and I thought (2) here we go (right) (1) erm (2) and because of that (1) I was really kind of (1) separate (1) separated (1) and it was horrible (hmm hmm)
Carrie: Yeah it's very much like that I think (.) it's all about like (.) what they (1) what everyone did last night (1) so in order to be in (.) if you like (.) you have =
ABH: = to have done something last night (laughter)
Jude: Something stupid
(**Extract 6**: Avon University students, Dec 2005)

This position is not held without a tinge of regret. Jude represents her marginal position on the fringes of her flat-mates' social life as 'horrible', feeling 'separate' and 'separated' from their friendship group. Her lack of a fount of 'funny stories' about doing 'something stupid' that could only have been gleaned from active engagement with the student culture of determined drunkenness marks her out as unable to belong. She lacks a passport to enter and join in the group sociality of her peers, and the latter cannot be rejected as completely worthless.

Conclusions

In many young people's accounts, drinking was represented as central to their social lives, which revolved around mixed and/or single-sex groups. Our participants refuted any suggestion that they might rely on drinking or getting drunk in order to 'have fun', but drinking in a social group was constituted as an important source of fun, laughs and enjoyment. Drinking as part of a group appeared to insulate them from the disavowed position of the 'alcy' or problem drinker, since the latter was constituted, above all else, as a 'lone' drinker. The group was also represented as a place of safety in a potentially dangerous world, on nights out when most other people were (also) drunk. Drinking groups moved around frequently in the course of their nights out, so 'keeping tabs' on one another, especially when drunk, was not a straightforward process. For young women, these risks were partly constituted with reference to the threat of sexual assault, whilst for young men they were more often constructed via discourses of physical assault. Young drinkers all recounted strategies for taking care of (or 'looking out for') one another on nights out, although young men could also represent themselves as able to 'handle themselves', and not in need of this type of protection, in displays of normative masculine prowess.

We have little space here to examine the gender and class dimensions of young people's drinking cultures in any depth. There remain relatively few in-depth studies of women's alcohol consumption, and researchers tend to treat drinking culture as effectively equivalent to male culture (see Ettore, 1997; Hunt et al., 2000; and Sheehan and Ridge, 2001 for exceptions). Drinking to intoxication in public is still viewed as a sign of disreputable femininity and 'loose' behaviour that is closely associated with white working-class heterosexual femininity (Skeggs, 2005). As Geoffrey Hunt and colleagues have argued, societal concerns about young women drinking appear to 'have less to do with worries about the pharmacologic impact of alcohol and more to do with political and symbolic concerns about the position of women within society' (Hunt et al., 2000: 332; c.f. Jackson and Tinkler, 2007).

The drinking subject hailed in much of the alcohol advertising and marketing aimed at young people frequently takes the form of a (gendered) collectivity. This has significant implications for health education campaigns aimed at reducing young people's levels of alcohol consumption or encouraging healthier and more 'responsible' drinking practices. Such campaigns generally focus on attempts to change individuals' behaviour, often failing to appreciate the positive significance of friendship groups for young people's social lives (Hackley et al., 2008). The most recent version of the UK government Alcohol Strategy refers to the need to change young people's drinking cultures as well as individuals' attitudes to alcohol consumption, which is a laudable shift away from a highly individualised focus (Cabinet Office, 2007). However, if such initiatives do not also impact on the licensed retail trade, the drinks industry and the advertising and marketing of alcohol, they are unlikely to have any substantial impact.

Structural changes brought about by neo-liberalism have created a context in which the 'culture of intoxication' amongst young people has emerged and thrived: indeed it has become an all but compulsory aspect of many young people's leisure. Indeed, Hayward and Hobbs view such practices as not simply allowed but mandated by corporate economics in the neo-liberal social order (2007). Paradoxically, this has also strengthened the importance of friendship groups as sites of collective identity, community, care and support, as well as of fun and enjoyment. Such pervasive and highly visible collective cultural practices are usually viewed as evidence of the pressure on young people to consume alcohol or a sign of their irresponsibility and moral degeneracy (O'Malley and Valverde, 2004). Official discourse focuses on the 'trouble' posed by young people's drinking for the health services, policing and social order, and for the health of young drinkers themselves. Less obvious, perhaps, is the possible trouble that such collective cultural practices might pose for the neo-liberal project itself, and especially for the rational flexible responsible individual neo-liberal subject.

We are not arguing that the neo-liberal social order is 'causing' young people to value their friendship groups more or in a different way compared to previous eras. Rather, we argue that the pervasive force of what Beck has termed 'individualisation' and the moralising consumer discourse of neo-liberalism lends a particular significance to the discourses around care, solidarity, fun and intimacy associated with social friendship groups for young people. Drinking is central to many young people's social lives, so these processes are played out in the night-time economy on a regular basis.

Notes

1. The four co-authors are all equal contributors to this chapter, and David Clarke and Louise Weale were also involved in some of the data collection and analysis.
2. Minimalist adverts using strongly branded icons are not unknown, for example the Nike 'tick'.
3. Lambrini is a sparkling white wine brewed to 5.5% proof, less than half the strength of most white wines, that is closely associated with young white working-class women and presumed to be their preferred drink of choice.
4. The UK National Alcohol Strategy cites research that defines 'binge drinking' as 'feeling drunk at least once a month', and identifies 'binge drinkers' as 'those who drink to get drunk, (…) likely to be aged under 25' (Cabinet Office, 2007: 4). See Martinic and Measham (2008) for a detailed exploration of different definitions of 'binge drinking'.
5. In all the extracts quoted in this chapter, Andrew Bengry-Howell was the interviewer (designated as 'ABH' in quoted interview extracts).
6. All the names of individuals and locations mentioned in this chapter have been changed. Transcription conventions adapted from Potter and Wetherell (1987).

   = Indicates the absence of a discernable gap between speakers
   (.) A pause of less than one second
   (1), (2) A pause of one second, two seconds and so on
   (…) Some transcript has been deliberately omitted
   [ABH laughs] Material in square brackets is clarifying information
   <u>They</u> A word or phrase underlined indicates additional emphasis
   [as you can see, Left square brackets indicates overlapping speech.

7. In common with many of our younger participants Vicki lived with her parents and went to a local Further Education college.

References

Allan, G. (1989) *Friendship: Developing a Sociological Perspective*. Hemel Hempstead: Harvester Wheatsheaf.

Beck, U. (1992) *Risk Society: Toward a New Modernity*. London: Sage.

Beck, U. and Beck-Gernsheim, E. (2002) *Individualization*. London: Sage.

Brain, K., Parker, H. and Carnwath, T. (2000) Drinking with Design: Young Drinkers as Psychoactive Consumers. *Drugs: Education, Prevention and Policy*, 7(1), 5–20.

Cabinet Office (2007) *Safe, Sensible, Social: The Next Steps in the National Alcohol Strategy*. London: HMG Cabinet Office.

Chatterton, P. and Hollands, R. (2001) *Changing our 'Toon': Youth, Nightlife and Urban Change in Newcastle*. Newcastle: University of Newcastle upon Tyne.

Croghan, R., Griffin, C., Hunter, J. and Phoenix, A. (2006) Style Failure: Consumption, Identity and Social Exclusion. *Journal of Youth Studies*, 9(4), 463–78.

Cronin, A. (2000) Consumerism and 'Compulsory Individuality': Women, Will and Potential. In: S. Ahmed, J. Kilby, C. Lury, M. McNeil and B. Skeggs (eds) *Transformations: Thinking Through Feminism*. London: Routledge.

Davies, C. and Hill, A. (2008) Anger Grows over Katona 'train wreck' Interview, *The Observer*, 26 October, p. 25.

De Vissier, R. and Smith, J. (2007) Young Men's Ambivalence Toward Alcohol. *Social Science and Medicine*, 64, 350–62.

Ettore, E. (1997) *Women and Alcohol: A Private Pleasure or Public Problem?* London: The Women's Press.

Furlong, A. and Cartmel, F. (1997) *Young People and Social Change: Individualization and Risk in Late Modernity*. Buckingham: Open University Press.

Giddens, A. (1992) *The Transformation of Intimacy: Sexuality, Love and Eroticism in Modern Societies*. Cambridge: Polity Press.

Gough, B. and Edwards, G. (1998) The Beer Talking: Four Lads, a Carry Out and the Reproduction of Masculinities. *The Sociological Review*, 46(3), 409–35.

Griffin, C., Szmigin, I.T., Hackley, C., Mistral, M. and Bengry-Howell, A. (2009) 'Every Time I do it I Absolutely Annihilate Myself': Loss of (Self)-Consciousness and Loss of Memory in Young People's Drinking Narratives. *Sociology*, 43(3), 457–76.

Hackley, C., Griffin, C., Szmigin, I., Mistral, W. and Bengry-Howell, A. (2008) The Discursive Constitution of the UK Alcohol Problem in *'Safe, Sensible, Social'*: A Discussion of Policy Implications. *Drugs: Education, Prevention and Policy*, 15(S1), 65–78.

Hayward, K. and Hobbs, D. (2007) Beyond the Binge in 'Booze Britain': Market-led Liminalization and the Spectacle of Binge Drinking. *British Journal of Sociology*, 58(3), 437–56.

Hey, V. (1997) *The Company She Keeps: An Ethnography of Girls' Friendships*. Milton Keynes: Open University Press.

Hodkinson, P. and Deicke, W. (eds) (2007) *Youth Cultures: Scenes, Subcultures and Tribes*. London: Routledge.
Holt, M. and Griffin, C. (2005) Students Versus Locals: Young Adults Constructions of the Working-Class Other. *British Journal of Social Psychology*, 44(2), 241–67.
Hunt, G., Joe-Laidler, K. and MacKenzie, K. (2000) 'Chillin', being Dogged and Getting Buzzed: Alcohol in the Lives of Female Gang Members. *Drugs: Education, Prevention and Policy*, 7(4), 331–53.
Jackson, C. and Tinkler, P. (2007) 'Ladettes' and 'Modern Girls': 'Troublesome' Young Femininities. *The Sociological Review*, 55(2), 251–72.
Kattenhorn, L. (2005–2006). Booze Britain [Television series]. Bristol: Granada Production for Bravo Satellite Channel.
Kehily, M.J. (ed.) (2007) *Understanding Youth: Perspectives, Identities and Practices*. London: Sage in Association with the Open University.
Martinic, M. and Measham, F. (2008) Extreme Drinking. In: M. Martinic and F. Measham (eds) *Swimming with Crocodiles: The Culture of Extreme Drinking*. London: Routledge.
McCreanor, T., Moewaka Barnes, H., Kaiwai, H., Borell, S. and Gregory, A. (2008) Creating Intoxigenic Environments: Marketing Alcohol to Young People in Aotearoa New Zealand. *Social Science and Medicine*, 67, 938–46. doi.10.1016/j.socscimed.2008.05.027.
Measham, F. (2004) The Decline of Ecstasy, the Rise of 'Binge' Drinking and the Persistence of Pleasure. *Probation Journal*, 5(4), 309–26.
Measham, F. (2006). The New Policy Mix: Alcohol, Harm Minimisation, and Determined Drunkenness in Contemporary Society. *International Journal of Drug Policy*, 17, 258–68.
Measham, F. (2008). Turning the Tides of Intoxication: Young People's Drinking in Britain in the 2000s. *Health Education*, 108(3), 207–22.
Measham, F. and Brain, K. (2005) 'Binge' Drinking, British Alcohol Policy and the New Culture of Intoxication. *Crime, Media, Culture*, 1(3), 262–83.
Nayak, A. (2006) Displaced Masculinities: Chavs, Youth and Class in the Post-Industrial City. *Sociology*, 40(5), 813–31.
O'Malley, P. and Valverde, M. (2004) Pleasure, Freedom and Drugs: The Uses of 'Pleasure' in Liberal Governance of Drug and Alcohol Consumption. *Sociology*, 38(1), 25–42.
Pahl, R. and Pevalin, D.J. (2005) Between Family and Friends: A Longitudinal Study of Friendship Choice. *The British Journal of Sociology*, 56(3), 433–50.
Plant, M.L. (2008) The Role of Alcohol in Women's Lives: A Review of Issues and Responses. *Journal of Substance Use*, 13(3), 155–91.
Potter, J. and Wetherell, M. (1987) *Discourse and Psychology: Beyond Attitudes and Cognition*. London: Sage.
Ronay, B. (2008). Young, Rich and Drunk. *The Guardian*, 9 May 2008, pp. 8–9.
Rose, N. (1989) *Governing the Soul: The Shaping of the Private Self*. London: Routledge.
Roseneil, S. and Budgeon, S. (2004) Cultures of Intimacy and Care beyond 'the Family: Personal Life and Social Change in the Early 21st Century. *Current Sociology*, 52(2), 135–59.
Saner, E. (2008). The Women? They're Far Worse in Fights'. *The Guardian*, 9 May 2008, pp. 12–14.

Sheehan, M. and Ridge, D. (2001) '"You become really close...you talk about the silly things you did, and we laugh": The Role of Binge Drinking in Female Secondary Students' Lives. *Substance Use and Misuse*, 36(3), 347–72.

Skeggs, B. (2004) *Class, Self, Culture*. London: Sage.

Skeggs, B. (2005) The Re-Branding of Class: Propertising Culture. In: F. Devine, M. Savage, J. Scoot and R. Crompton (eds) *Rethinking Class: Culture, Identities and Lifestyle*. Basingstoke: Palgrave Macmillan.

Smith, L.A. and Foxcroft, D.R. (2007) *The Effect of Alcohol Advertising and Marketing on Drinking Behaviour in Young People: A Systematic Review*. European Centre for Monitoring Alcohol Marketing (EUCAM): http://www.stap.nl/eucam/home/smith_foxcroft_2007.html (accessed 9 June 2009).

Steinberg, D.L. and Johnson, R. (eds) (2003) *Blairism and the War of Persuasion: Labour's Passive Revolution*. London: Lawrence and Wishart.

Szmigin, I., Griffin, C., Bengry-Howell, A., Weale, L., Mistral, W. and Hackley, C. (2008) Re-Framing 'Binge Drinking' as Calculated Hedonism: The View from the UK. *International Journal of Drug Policy*, 19, 359–66.

Tomsen, S. (1997) A Top Night: Social Protest, Masculinity and the Culture of Drinking Violence. *British Journal of Criminology*, 37(1), 90–102.

Walkerdine, V. (2003) Reclassifying Upward Mobility: Femininity and the Neo-liberal Subject. *Gender and Education*, 15(3), 237–48.

Wilson, T. (ed.) (2005) *Drinking Cultures*. New York: Berg.

Woolwich, P. (Executive Producer). (2005, October 3–7). Britain's Streets of Booze [Television Series]. London: BBC One.

Workman, T. (2001) Finding the Meanings of College Drinking: An Analysis of Fraternity Drinking Stories. *Health Communication*, 13(4), 427–47.

12
The Transformation of Intimacy: Classed Identities in the Moral Economy of Reality Television

Beverley Skeggs and Helen Wood

Introduction

This chapter reports on a project which set out to see if the ethical dramas and emphasis on self-work offered by the expanding number of reality television formats might influence current articulations of identity. Reality television is generally deemed a valueless pursuit, a form of 'trash' television and is often used to represent a crisis in civic public culture locating participants and viewers at the bottom of a hierarchy of taste classification.[1] By using reality television as a barometer of current moral value, taste and authority, the project explored how television, as part of a wider symbolic process, attaches value both to practices and people. We investigate how circuits of value are mobilised around reality television and theorise their relationship to the changing discourses and practices of class.[2]

Our initial motivation was to empirically interrogate contemporary theories that argue individualisation has led to the demise of class and the rise of the reflexive self. For instance, Anthony Giddens (1991) and Ulrich Beck (1992) propose that the project of the reflexive self is non-exclusionary and a universal imperative. Yet previous research suggested that theories of individualisation may be describing the re-making of, rather than the decline of, class (Adkins, 2002; Skeggs, 2004). Against the growing popularity of the individualisation thesis, others have charted the increased symbolic denigration of the working class in law (Garland, 2001), political rhetoric (Haylett, 2001) and popular culture (Lawler, 2002; Mount, 2004; Skeggs, 2005). In light of these conflicting theoretical tendencies, our project aimed to 'test' the demise of class hypothesis by studying reality television programmes that dramatise self-transformation and reflexivity.

That the majority of reality television programmes interrogate and often demand self-transformation might be seen as evidence that we are experiencing a period of 'compulsory individuality' (Strathern, 1992; Taylor, 1989). Here the terms of moral legitimacy have shifted from traditional sources of authority (religion, the patriarchal family and the state) to the ability of the self to tell itself as a source of good. Jon Dovey (2000) in his work on 'first person television' documents how this is reflected in changes in documentary, factual television and talk show formats which visualise 'extraordinary subjectivities' where the basis for truth claims transfers from grand narratives to an emphasis upon personal statements about the world. Similarly, John Hartley (2004) argues that 'the self' is very much at stake in every aspect of television as matters previously considered private are represented as public concerns. These shifting contours of the boundaries of the public and private are central to Lauren Berlant's (2000) account of 'intimate citizenship' where the self has to perform its own value through self-disclosure and displays of intimate literacy, reliant upon access to a pseudo-psychological discourses of an 'inner' experience to authorise an 'outer' identity. To be a true American citizen, one has to reveal a dramatic-traumatic experience to be overcome in order to be a full member of the nation. A process which she argues eclipses stories of everyday poverty and suffering, and thereby class.

Such accounts of oneself abound in reality television where the personal revealing of trauma is sometimes the qualification required for the rewards offered by television. (For instance families who lost loved ones in hurricane Katrina recall their individual trauma whilst the television team from *Extreme Makeover Home Edition* builds them a mansion, usually with a swimming pool, and throws in college education for their sons.) Across the range of reality television, formats draw upon a number of psychological techniques whereby participants are called to display their moral value, they discuss weight problems, family breakdowns, financial dilemmas, self-esteem issues and so on to experts, to other 'competitors' and, importantly, directly to the camera. But we argue that it is important to identify the historical precedents of the 'telling self' in order to account for how they are renewed through reality television and as clues to how they are embroiled in class practices. Carolyn Steedman (2000), for instance, details how the historical development of the 'telling self' was established as a precedent in sites like poor relief where redemptive narratives became a measure of a good respectable and worthy citizen. Eva Illouz (1997) charts how during the 1940s the belief in the positive value of verbalising emotions developed as a way of revealing a true self and solving conflicts, enabling middle-class women to make demands of relationships and partners. And now Valerie Walkerdine (2003) proposes that the grammar of psychology has replaced the grammar of exploitation, closing down the space to speak of wider structural inequalities as focus intensifies on the self.

Explanations of this current 'transformation of intimacy' suggest the extension of domination and capital to domains hitherto out of reach (Illouz, 1997). Because the promise of normalisation is no longer trusted to the family, kin groups and other institutions of civil society, the self has to learn to authorise itself, but this authorisation, no longer reliant on the institutions of religion and state, must access other forms of capital (Clough, 2003). Reality television therefore enters into this climate by representing and sensationalising aspects of everyday lives, displaying the new ways in which capital extends into the 'private' by mobilising affective capacities and using emotional performance as a mechanism for entertainment and profit. What is therefore new is the mediation of this process which can be seen to be part of a more general trend of subsumption, whereby capital exploitation seeps into intimate areas and the accumulation of wealth can be drawn from the immaterial. For instance, Nick Couldry (2003) argues that we are all increasingly encouraged to generate a 'media self' accumulating knowledge on how to 'represent' oneself and perform to the camera. Thus, amongst other sites like knowledge, education, communication, caring and taking care of the chain of services, reality television becomes central to a new form of economy where the moral and the economic are intimately linked.

Reality television and the opening out of intimacy

Debates about what exactly constitutes reality television are extensive within television production, journalism, marketing discourse and academic analyses. Su Holmes and Deborah Jermyn (2004) suggest that the output is now too diverse for the generic category to hold. Many of its forms, particularly the make-over, have evolved from daytime TV and from talk-shows, and the term 'lifestyle television' has also been used as a catch-all phrase. The tensions between documentary filming techniques and melodramatic 'staging' have led some to use the term 'docu-soap', but the event-focussed narrative structure and short timescale of many programmes questioned the soap element, whilst the formatted, and contrived generation of drama questioned the documentary elements (Bruzzi, 2000; Dovey, 2000; Kilborn, 2003). It is precisely the continuing hybridity and the speed with which reality television formats mutate that make the category difficult to define, influenced by a changing television economy where the demand for skills in television production shift from direction to casting and editing.[3] John Corner (2002) proposes that reality television is best viewed as part of television's 'post-documentary context', a contradictory cultural environment, where viewers, participants and producers are less invested in absolute truth and representational ethics, and are more interested in the space that exists between reality and fiction, foregrounding new forms of representational play and reflexivity. We take up Nick Couldry's argument for maintaining the generic category 'reality television' because of what it suggests about the myth of the mediated centre: 'the media constructs and maintains a symbolic hierarchy between media/ordinary worlds, presenting itself as the privileged "frame" through which we access the reality that *matters to us as social beings*' (2003: 58 emphasis added).

One consistent feature of reality television is that issues of cultural value have always defined the form as public discourse associates it with low quality and poor taste. These claims are partly related to the emphasis on 'ordinary' people (as opposed to trained actors), the 'everyday' and the 'domestic', representing a tide of 'ordinary everydayness' across television (Bonner, 2003). Mischa Kavka (2006) refers to this as always the 'national ordinary' which deals with mundane, routine and uneventful lives made extraordinary by the dramatic techniques of production. The hybridity and 'leaky' textual characteristics of the genre coupled with the focussing in on the details of everyday life offer a winning formula. In one week in November 2005 we counted 92 possible reality television programmes from 'free to air' channels (not satellite). We mapped a taxonomy of these programmes showing how a number of technical narrative devices, including swaps, tests of passing, challenges, gameshows, make-overs and expert interventions can be multiplied by the number of intimate arenas available for examination, food and health (*You Are What You Eat*), parenting (*Supernanny*), sex (*Sex Inspectors*), relationships (*Honey We're Killing the Kids*), careers (*Apprentice*), finances (*Bank of Mum and Dad*) and so on. Thus the economic imperative for formats in the multi-channel television economy provides the momentum behind the opening out of intimacy across our screens. Our textual analysis focussed on holding together the characteristics of phenomenon of the opening out of intimacy on television inhabited by non-actors. Our map indexed production techniques against areas of intimate life interrogated, charting 42 programmes aired in 2004 and 2005 and we focussed closely on 10 'self-transformation' style programmes selected to represent the range.

Whilst intimacy, self-authorising and morality are key staples of reality television there is clearly an over representation of working-class participants on these programmes (White, 2006). Class is often a central theme of dramatic tension as class distinctions are played out particularly in swap life-style programmes (*Wife Swap, Holiday Showdown*) or in Pygmalion narratives (*Ladette to Lady, Asbo Teen to Beauty Queen*). But across all formats our textual analysis demonstrated how class figures in potentially more subtle ways, tied to the contemporary politics of self-reflexivity. Elsewhere we have charted how the individualising and de-historicising of personal dilemmas in reality television evade socio-economic contexts transforming classed distinctions into personal failure (Wood and Skeggs, 2008). We discuss how the representation of this process mirrors trends in other social spaces concerned with behavioural micromanagement, such as education (Gillies, 2005), national social policy (Social Exclusion, ASBOs and the Respect Agenda) and national political rhetoric (Haylett, 2001), where inequalities have been re-invented as behavioural and psychological malfunction.[4] This might indeed be part of what Marilyn Strathern (1992) identifies as a broader social process towards making middle-class values the national-normative, what Mike Savage (2003) identifies as the new 'particular–universal' class.

These trends take shape in reality television through the hybridity of the format. The traditions of melodrama (happenstance, crisis or sensation) and documentary (realism, observation or talking heads) are integrated into the reality format which help the reproduction of classed forms of self-telling. By placing television participants in situations outside of their experience, particularly in the swapping and passing formats, the actualisation of reflexivity is made difficult: reaction rather than reflection is required, making dramatic responses signal moral value, supporting Linda Williams' (2001) analysis of melodrama as a national 'moral structure of feeling'. We identified how techniques such as the voice-over, advice, castigation, established authority and the terms of judgement, and how psychological discourse was central to establishing 'expert' authority. We tracked the ways in which television participants were encouraged to narrate themselves 'to camera', recording definitions of appropriate and inappropriate behaviour, and how participants struggled to account for events beyond their control. Self-reflexivity in these programmes is therefore contrived, mediated, edited and subject to approval whereby some seem to fail if they cannot account for themselves in the most appropriate fashion.

Metonymic morality

Whilst reality television represents the opening out of intimacy, it is accompanied by a focussing in on the minute details of daily existence. Our analysis showed how close-up-long-held filming was constantly used rhetorically to illustrate failure – dirt, chipped nail varnish, plates of food and symbolised key problems. This forensic detailing we suggest constitutes a metonymic morality, whereby parts of a body, home or a particular or practice stand in for the whole person. Again the metonym plays out class on the surface as a spectacular problem removed from its social context. Therefore, by mapping out how intimacy is opened out and made subject to scrutiny and organised into practices and routines, we were able to identify the circulation of value on reality television. We identified how specific aspects of behaviour are designated as immoral (for the self and/or the family and/or the nation), and how bodily parts are used to figure previously accumulated bad behaviour (e.g. fat). In this visual attribution, each behavioural or bodily part metonymically represents the 'whole' immoral person – 'the subject without value'. In this process we documented how

- Good communication is promoted as the key to a better and happier life; improving communication 'would improve everything else' (Cameron, 2000). For example, in '*Honey We're Killing the Kids*' watching television, not speaking and not eating around a dining table together as a family come in for substantial critique.
- Parenting practices were organised into component parts: feeding, play, discipline and so on as 'methods' taught for the public good (Gillies, 2005). Motherhood, in particular was opened out to scrutiny and judgement. In *Supernanny*, for instance, bad practices are identified, mothers called to account and then shown how to develop new practices through behaviour modification techniques, such as the use of the 'naughty step'.
- Performing emotional labour and management, socialising affective capacities, paying attention to others, servicing, learning, caring and making an investment in one's family and one's self were consistently advocated as essential skills of 'good people' (subjects with value). So for example in *Wife Swap*, the dramatic conflict engineered at when the wives meet at the end of the programme often

takes the form of one woman accusing the other of being a 'bad mother' due to lack of attention to the child, and the other making accusations of 'bad housewife' due to a lack of cleaning. That such defensive dichotomies of women's domestic labour are made in the 21st century are shocking.

- Any form of excess (clothing, eating, drinking, etc.) was allocated negative value and in need of improvement. For instance *What not to Wear* is the epitome of 'toning down' any form of physical or aesthetic excess which indicates working-class taste. One participant, Michalena, a large woman, who enjoyed bright colours, elaborate hair and jewellery is 'moderated' and normalised, being told in the process by one of the 'experts': 'you shock me as a woman'. In the reality food programmes, such as *You Are What You Eat*, excessive eating is visualised via strategies such as displaying a week's food consumption across a car and emphasis upon self-restraint and responsibility to others stretches into mention of the nation as the ultimate site of responsibility.

Future potential and self-reflexivity

As we focused on self-transformation programmes, the impetus for improvement was essential to the format, highlighting rather than evading the barriers to social mobility. The *potential* for transformation was identified and offered assistance through psychological techniques. Behaviour modification through rule-based learning, and psychoanalysis-lite – where the inner self has to be told, performed and made subject to accountability and scrutiny in order to be improved – were often used interchangeably. Yet, the transformation demanded and/or encouraged was often made difficult by divorcing skills from knowledge of *how* to put them into effect (what Bourdieu calls the logic, or episteme that underpins them). For example, in an episode of *Faking It*, Mick, the contestant, a factory worker, learns and is very good at dressmaking and fashion design skills, but when he has to convince the judges that he is a 'real' fashion designer, he cannot make the speech required and has no confidence in its delivery. Socialised dispositions such as confidence and entitlement underpin how to put skills into effect, and these cannot easily be learnt through a week of skills training when they are based on a lifetime's occupation of social position.

Likewise, proposed improvements were frequently divorced from the conditions by which they could be achieved, as Sylvie notes in *What The Butler Saw*: 'It showed me a whole new world and all the things I could be doing, **but I just can't**'. By moving participants into unfamiliar social settings and providing skill-based training, participants are offered a glimpse of social mobility, making it appear meritocratic, but in fact have no access to the cultural resources necessary for inhabiting these new spaces. Because all the assessments made on the programmes by experts are based on performance, it appears as if failed performance is a problem of individual or psychological disposition 'I just can't', rather than about cultural and social capital. Therefore, through a variety of means participants on 'reality' television appear as historically reified; drama is played out in the present, occluding social relations and material conditions. Any failure appears as personal rather than social or cultural, limiting the presentation of a more complete 'architecture of the self' (Bennett, 2003).

The process of responsibility-attribution, revealing-talking, performing, measuring, advising and improving and judgement gave us a basic framework for understanding the moral scheme of 'reality' television. If we see the extension of subsumption into hitherto unknown areas of affect and emotion, alongside a strong moral agenda based on the dramatisation of self-transformation, we can see how 'reality' television with its predominantly working-class participants offers a means for understanding some of the current possibilities for the identification of class and self.

The circulation of value: audiences speak

The use of 'ordinary' people on reality television helps to erode the distinction between the audience and performers, generating one of the key elements in the pretension to 'reality' (Biressi and Nunn, 2005; Dovey, 2000). This, and the genre's use of actuality, have led authors to suggest that the audience is positioned differently in relation to reality television than to other forms of fiction – not as a 'reader' of a representation, but inhabiting part of the interactive social space which the form has come to occupy. To understand this relationship with audiences, alongside our textual analysis, we used a multi-method approach to researching the audience: interviews, 'text-in-action' viewing sessions and focus groups. We drew our sample of women from locations around South London and with difficulty recruited 40 women from four different family/friendship groups: New Addington (white working class), Forest Hill (mostly white middle class), Brockley (black and white working class) and Clapham (South Asian mainly working class).

Our interviews about general media use, work and leisure activities generated a picture of the women's different types of capital: employment, education, housing, habits, taste and motherhood. Participants found it difficult to respond to direct questions about class position and so we asked instead whether they felt they 'had a fair deal in life'. We also recorded their television viewing habits and knowledge of 'reality' television. We then conducted 'text-in-action' viewing sessions with 36 of our respondents. They decided to take part in this stage alone or in groups of two or three. This method relies on linguistic responses to television, but we found that our women often also responded to the sensational intensity of 'reality' through affective 'para-linguistic' responses: tuts, sighs, groans, laughter and so on. With some groups we have long periods of what at the time we experienced as silences and a potential limitation to the method. However, after re-listening to tapes, we realised the significance of many of the affective responses that were elicited at key moments in the structure of the text. Our method evolved with our theoretical thinking as we began to see the connections between theories of affective economies (e.g. Ahmed, 2004) and the incitement of affect by textual techniques on television. We described these moments as 'affective textual encounters' (ATE's), which were crucial to the moments where moral judgement was made in relation to television.

Finally, we conducted focus groups to see how 'reality' television was addressed in a public forum. We generated questions from our interviews and viewing sessions and used prompts from programmes to generate feedback loops with the different stages of the research. Our multi-method approach allowed respondents access to different modes of articulation and authorisation: the middle-class women consistently produced distanced reflexive critique across all methods, whilst Black, white and South Asian women displayed maternal moral authority in their responses in the text-in-action sessions and focus groups. The three methods generated very different performances through the use of cultural resources, leading us to propose that methods may 'make', rather than 'find' class (Skeggs et al., 2008).

Moral judgements and emotive reactions

To begin to interpret our audiences' responses to reality television, we might draw from Tom Mathiesen's (1997) challenge to Michel Foucault's (1977) analysis of power. He suggests that the panoptical governance structure of the few watching the many has now been replaced by a synoptical structure in a surveillance culture where the many watch the many. On television we have discussed the extension of intimate performances into the public domain and the obvious invitation to moral judgement generated through the techniques we described above in our textual analysis. Our findings reveal how the participant and audience members at home are locked into an immanent circuit of judgement of which they are all part.

Our respondents made a range of general connections to 'reality' television programmes. We noticed how television participants were subject to performance review both on the programme and by our respondents. They all took pleasure in the intimate details of others' lives, especially in attempting to understand how other people lived different types of intimate relationships. As Annette Hill (2005) has also shown, viewers took pleasure in the anticipation of 'moments of authenticity' where television participants emotionally reveal 'their true selves' as well as revelling in detecting fake performances. When those on television displayed a too self-conscious display of Couldry's 'media self', they were often considered by our respondents to be 'too knowing' or 'inauthentic'.

Whilst respondents were very media savvy in terms of knowledge about the manipulation of events, editing and the presence of the camera, they still enjoyed engaging in the immanence of the drama. Our text-in-action method revealed the exact places where respondents felt compelled to make statements about, and sometimes directly addressed, television participants. They keyed into the same moments with surprising regularity. Affective reactions (aah! ugh!) were converted into moral shock statements 'Oh my God!' then converted into moral judgements, 'How can they behave like that'. These incitements enable moral judgements to be made, moral positions to be taken and moral authority to be tested, resisted or legitimated.

As we might expect from older traditions in audience research in relation to soap opera, comparisons with the lives of others were constantly made. Our methodological design however allowed an extended platform for these types of articulations to take place. The performances of television participants illuminated aspects of our respondent's lives as the respondents took great pleasure in making assessments of television characters' personalities, often inventing psychological stories to redeem or criticise their behaviour, such as 'they have had a difficult life', or 'they don't understand how other people live'. This often involved taking on the role of the expert or the voice-over or directly giving advice 'you shouldn't do that' or even spontaneously re-staging and performing dramatic scenarios from the programme. Through the text-in-action method the immediate and affective reactions were played out demonstrating a gamut of emotions, empathy, disgust, hate and also care. In Wood, Skeggs and Thumim (2008), we document how the word 'sad' is used simultaneously to evoke both empathy and contempt in judgements of television participants' behaviour.

Whilst moments of misanthropy were recorded, we also recorded many instances where our audiences made great efforts to pursue care for television participants. Gendered emotional labour enabled connections to be made across the groups as the women identified with their own relationship labour. The performance of care by television participants was central to their assessment. All participants at some points read through the negative value loadings of abjectness, to find 'genuine care' and 'real relationships'. Making what Vivien Sobchack (1999) calls a 'constitutive ethical actualisation', that is placing oneself in the ethical scenario, enables respondents to immanently connect across emotional labour experiences (Skeggs and Wood, 2008).

Programmes were also used pedagogically for tips and advice, often relayed through an interest in how people 'cope' with relationships, children, appearance, weight, clutter and domestic organisation. However, our audiences were highly selective about which expert 'tips' to use. A circuit of audience respondents alongside television participants and television 'experts' assessed television relationships via a consideration of investment (time, care and love) and returns (time, care, love and sometimes money). We think the scale and range from our responses and their relationship to the things that really matter to our audiences about their relationships, families, children, opportunities and so on challenge some of dominant fears about the impact of 'depthless specularity' of 'reality' television on public culture (Nichols, 1991). Instead, we would suggest that these programmes are central sites for national moral dialogue. This became increasingly apparent when we realised that – much more than we would have anticipated – class differences were being performed in the judgements of 'reality' television and its participants.

Relationships to television: a classed moral economy

As described above, there were a lot of similarities in the ways in which our audience participants deployed both judgement and care in relation to those taking part on television. In this sense we suggest, echoing Biressi and Nunn (2005), that reality television is experienced as an 'extended social/public realm'. However, not all our participants are situated equally within such a realm and unsurprisingly some scenarios on television struck chords more deeply with some than others. What marked out social identity was the ways in which our respondents could resource their moral reactions, depending upon the proximity of their own life experiences to the programmes and to the forms of capital to which they had access. These cultural resource issues were also bound up with expectations of television as a medium and reality television as a genre in quite complicated ways.

We found radically different approaches not just to the 'text' but also to the actual object of the television. For some of our middle-class participants, the television was given the status of a bad, powerfully corrupting object that could make them addicted, out of control and waste their time. They were conscious that they could be doing 'something useful', in other words, investing in the development of cultural or social capital. In some cases, their television had to be locked away and hidden from view and in most cases, television content was carefully controlled through taste (quality programmes only allowed), education (those from which they thought they or their children could learn) and political knowledge (demonstration of knowledge of media bias and political economy). By contrast, our working-class participants (South Asian, black and white British) did not attribute power to the object of television, nor felt required to control it, nor felt that it made them 'waste-time'. Television was a ubiquitous presence, part of the domestic architecture of which they demanded 'something compelling' that they would be drawn into, but also 'just fun' 'good to shout at' and part of their social and domestic relations. These radically different modes of attention organised around moral classifications of television as an object and mapped directly onto the class divisions of our respondents. We had not anticipated just how much television itself, before we entered into discussion of the programmes, would enter into the moral framework. Classed identities were therefore articulated through subject/objects relations with the television set. Given this finding, it is hardly surprising that we found stark divisions occurring when we asked them about participating on 'reality' television.

Our middle-class participants thought television exploited uneducated vulnerable people, who were not equipped with a sophisticated enough understanding of the media economy to defend themselves against trash television, deploying a typical critique of false consciousness. Yet they also maintained that participants were a particular type of person: 'desperate for celebrity', 'generally trashy people'. Some had been asked and had thought about participation, but decided against it. Our South Asian groups evoked an honour hierarchy, expressing concern about participants' allowing themselves be shamed. By contrast, our black and white working-class respondents saw 'reality' television as an opportunity structure, providing an alternative route to money, or as an opportunity for the public humiliation of badly behaved male partners. One of our white working-class respondents had appeared numerous times on talk-shows to discuss being a teenage single-mum – she liked the experience of a radically different world (hotels, champagne and taxis).

Working-class respondents were therefore clear in their respect for reality television participants who had 'made good'. Our black and white working-class respondents, in particular, took a great deal of pleasure from television participant's resistance to authority and refusals to take advice. In particular, even though we did not ask about celebrities Jordan and Jade Goody (who are represented as the epitome of abject subjects in public culture and generate a huge amount of tabloid contempt), they kept appearing as reference points for the black and white working-class groups, who wanted to defend their positive value against all the negative attributions that are made of them. Whereas our middle-class groups had referred to 'reality' television as 'stupid people doing stupid things', our working-class respondents talked of 'people doing well for themselves'. Such judgements can be seen on a scale of symbolic violence, or its defence, as Bourdieu notes 'nothing classifies somebody more than the way he or she classifies' (1989: 19). Therefore class (and race) place(s) participants in differing relationships to the form of reality television through its now relatively 'ordinary' accessibility. It is discussed as a real opportunity and a route to material rewards that are potentially otherwise beyond their means. In this sense, Couldry's notion of a 'media self' routed through the increased 'celebrification of culture' (Turner, 2004) has a tangible impact upon classed identity.

Proximity and distance: resourcing moral reactions

These differing relations therefore lead our participants to articulate their moral reactions through alternative means of propinquity. Our black, white and South Asian working-class respondents immanently placed themselves within the action: 'this is what I would do/did'; whilst our middle-class respondents made a distanced critique using resources of wider cultural explication, taste hierarchies and political/cultural knowledge, such as reflexivity and irony (see Skeggs et al., 2008).

Generally our middle-class participants authorise themselves through an educated critique: 'the programme represented people in a racist format in order to generate anxiety', 'I'd never watch something that humiliated people in that way', 'It's just part of the government trying to win support for its bankrupt ideas' and so on.

Our working-class participants instead used their immediate experience as mothers to resource their responses: 'you'd never be able to work those hours and look after your kids properly', 'she'd never be able to look smart all the time with three young kids', 'she's in that mess because she's exhausted, poor thing' and so on. Yet, proximity and identification through motherhood did not necessarily create empathy with television participants: of the working-class respondents all but the South Asian group were often highly critical of other mothers, displaying strong emotions of antipathy, disgust and/or anger towards 'experts' *and* participants. Middle-class mothers who sent their children 'away', came in for strong critique, repeating a long history of moral class critique (see Lawler, 2000; Reay, 1998). Occupying the moral high ground through motherhood was the major source of authority for working-class respondents, displaying to us their knowledge and value.

Class differences also emerged in the research through definitions of what counts as labour and knowledge. Our middle-class group thought 'reality' television participants did not deserve to 'get something for nothing' because they did not have any education or skills (not 'working hard at things') other than performing ('cheap celebrity'). This was in contrast to our black and white working-class respondents who assessed television participants on the basis of the specific type of labour they performed: 'just getting on with it' and 'not moaning' were identified as key values enabling worth to be attributed to those who would display the same criteria as they would apply to themselves, thus reproducing indefatigability as a moral value. This suggests that labouring and 'making an effort' is a key moral value in middle- *and* working-class culture, but is defined differently. In this sense, traditional relations of labour and class are reproduced in terms of middle-class terms of investment and working-class terms indefatigability, but what is interesting is how these relations are re-newed through the media's role in the transformation of intimacy.

Conclusions

Our tracking and mapping over time showed that there were few areas of life into which 'reality' television had not intervened. The opening out of people, their bodies, practices and performances for scrutiny was a staple of the self-transformation programmes we studied, which require detailing the person with the 'problem' in need of improvement. The emphasis on performing the self does suggest that individualisation, 'compulsory individuality' and intimate citizenship is indeed occurring in spectacular detail, in which matters previously considered private are presented as public and moral concerns, not just as matters for the self, but for the health of the nation more generally. That 'reality' television spectacularly visualises the micromanagement of behaviour that is promoted across other social sites of governance suggests that this is more than a matter of televisual entertainment. The transformation of intimacy through its detailing and publicising does suggest that the promise of normalisation is no longer left to be a family or private matter, but is a national collective responsibility for each individual.

If we had only analysed programmes, we could show that the middle-class particular was indeed becoming universally normative, that neo-liberal techniques were ubiquitous, intimacy had extended into a profit-making performance review and misanthropy was rife, with the working class being subject to a level of symbolic violence and affective contempt never previously seen. Whilst all this is clearly evident, its impact is not predictable. The symbolic detailing of the individual on reality television does not wrestle free material and cultural constraints. The attempt to promote middle-class standards as the new 'universal particular' shows that individualisation and so on depend upon a performance that is reliant on access to resources accrued from a social position. Whilst social mobility might be promoted, the genre abuts against the reality that mobility rates are lower than ever.

As reality television locates our viewers in a circuit of value, the audience responses show how the invitation to judge (the many watching the many) is also an invitation to display one's social position and access to cultural resources for authorisation. People are incited to make judgements about the micromanagement of their lives, but these incitements address people already positioned by other value strata (work, taste, education, bodies and money) that unevenly combine to produce their overall person value as a good/bad subject. Our research showed that the supposed universal moral values are often highly contested as both moral and particular (e.g. motherhood). Value-defences and value-promotions are thus tied to classed, gendered and raced experiences where traditional forms of moral value, for example around labour, are re-newed through relations to the notion of the 'media self' and performance. 'Performing oneself', or doing self-reflexivity, to generate self-worth only makes sense if there is consensus about what constitutes self-worth, if the measurement is agreed (Sayer, 2005). We found therefore that classed identities are reworked through the mediation of selfhood and articulated through relations of proximity. It is therefore the *value* attached to performances of personhood that is important in the construction of classed identity. How people connect or detach from others across the television frame depends on where and how they are positioned within circuits of value. In charting the mediated transformation of intimacy, we found a struggle over value and a reworked set of classed relations around the new conditions of the performance of selfhood.

Notes

1. See McTaggart Lecture by Lord John Birt, ex-BBC Director's speech to the Edinburgh Festival, 26 August 2005.
2. Our model of class was taken from Bourdieu (1979, 1985, 1986, 1987) who identifies four main types of capital: economic, cultural, social and symbolic. People are distributed in social space according to the following: the global *volume* of capital they posses; the *composition* of their capital; *evolution* of the volume; and composition according to their *trajectory* in social space. By *using* Bourdieu's metaphoric model of capitals (economic, cultural, social and symbolic), we trace different types of value and how they convert into the different fields of exchange. We also wanted to examine moral value as a specific element of cultural capital: the domains of and relationship between moral and economic value have historically been notoriously slippery as David Graeber (2005) charts, but can be explored through the resourcing of different types of personhood (see Skeggs, 2004).
3. There has been substantial restructuring of television since the 1990s across the globe with the introduction of numerous cable and digital channels requiring programmes, accompanied by the decreased role of national television, and in the UK a specific remit to use 'independent producers' to cut in-house costs (Raphael, 2004).
4. The government also recognised the potential of 'reality' television by developing its own 'ASBO TV', a £12 million project undertaken under the UK government's 'New Deal for Communities' established to regenerate poor districts (Swinfold, 2006).

References

Adkins, L. (2002) *Revisions: Gender and Sexuality in Late Modernity*. Buckingham: Open University Press.

Ahmed, S. (2004) Affective Economies. *Social Text*, 22(2), 117–39.

Beck, U. (1992) *Risk Society: Towards a New Modernity*. London: Sage.

Bennett, T. (2003) The Invention of the Modern Cultural Fact: Toward a Critique of the Critique of Everyday Life. In: E.B. Silva and T. Bennett (eds) *Contemporary Culture and Everyday Life*. Durham: Sociology Press.
Berlant, L. (2000) The Subject of True Feeling: Pain, Privacy, Politics. In: S. Ahmed, J. Kilby, C. Lury, M. McNeil and B. Skeggs (eds) *Transformations: Thinking Through Feminism*. London: Routledge.
Biressi, A. and Nunn, H. (2005) *Reality TV: Realism and Revelation*. London: Wallflower Press.
Bonner, F. (2003) *Ordinary Television: Analysing Popular TV*. London: Sage.
Bourdieu, P. (1979) Symbolic Power. *Critique of Anthropology*, 4, 77–85.
Bourdieu, P. (1985) The Social Space and the Genesis of Groups. *Theory and Society*, 14, 723–44.
Bourdieu, P. (1986) *Distinction: A Social Critique of the Judgement of Taste*. London: Routledge.
Bourdieu, P. (1987) What Makes a Social Class? On the Theoretical and Practical Existence of Groups. *Berkeley Journal of Sociology*, 32, 1–17.
Bourdieu, P. (1989) Social Space and Symbolic Power. *Sociological Theory*, 7, 14–25.
Bruzzi, S. (2000) *New Documentary: A Critical Introduction*. New York and London: Routledge.
Cameron, D. (2000) *Good to Talk? Living and Working in a Communication Culture*. London: Sage.
Clough, P. (2003) Affect and Control: Rethinking the Body, Beyond Sex and Gender. *Feminist Theory*, 4(3), 359–664.
Corner, J. (2002) Performing the Real: Documentary Diversions. *Television and New Media*, 3(3), 255–69.
Couldry, N. (2003) *Media Rituals: A Critical Approach*. London and New York: Routledge.
Dovey, J. (2000) *Freakshow: First Person Media and Factual Television*. London: Pluto.
Foucault, M. (1977) *Discipline and Punish: The Birth of the Prison*. London: Allen Lane/Penguin.
Garland, D. (2001) *The Culture of Control: Crime and Social Order in Contemporary Society*. Oxford: Oxford University Press.
Giddens, A. (1991) *Modernity and Self-Identity; Self and Society in the Late Modern Age*. Cambridge: Polity.
Gillies, V. (2005) Raising the Meritocracy; Parenting and the Individualisation of Social Class. *Sociology*, 39(5), 835–55.
Graeber, D. (2005) Value as the Importance of Actions. *The Commoner*, 10, 4–65.
Hartley, J. (2004) 'Kiss Me Kat': Shakespeare, *Big Brother* and the Taming of the Shrew. In: L. Oullette and S. Murray (eds) *Reality TV: Re-making Television Culture*. New York and London: New York University Press.
Haylett, C. (2001) Illegitimate Subjects? Abject Whites, Neoliberal Modernisation and Middle Class Multiculturalism. *Environment and Planning D: Society and Space*, 19, 351–70.
Hill, A. (2005) *Reality TV: Audiences and Popular Factual Television*. London: Routledge.
Holmes, S. and Jermyn, D. (eds) (2004) *Understanding Reality Television*. London: Routledge.

Illouz, E. (1997) Who will Care for the Caretaker's Daughter? Towards a Sociology of Happiness in the Era of Reflexive Modernity. *Theory, Culture and Society*, 14(4), 31–66.

Kavka, M. (2006) Changing Properties: The Makeover Show Crosses the Atlantic. In: D. Heller (ed.) *The Great American Makeover: Television, History, Nation*. New York: Palgrave.

Kilborn, R. (2003) *Staging the Real: Factual TV Programming in the Age of Big Brother*. Manchester: Manchester University Press.

Lawler, S. (2000) *Mothering the Self: Mothers, Daughters, Subjects*. London: Routledge.

Lawler, S. (2002) Mobs and Monsters: Independent Man Meets Paulsgrove Woman. *Feminist Theory*, 3(1), 103–13.

Mathiesen, T. (1997) The Viewer Society: Michel Foucault's 'Panoptican' Revisited. *Theoretical Criminology*, 1(2), 215–34.

Mount, F. (2004) *Mind the Gap: Class in Britain Now*. London: Short Books.

Nichols, B. (1991) *Representing Reality*. Bloomington: University of Indiana Press.

Ouellette, L. and Murray, S. (2004) *Reality TV: Re-making Television Culture*. New York and London: New York University Press.

Raphael, C. (2004) The Political Economic Origins of Reali-TV. In: S. Murray and L. Oullette (eds) *Reality TV: Re-Making Television Culture*. New York: New York University Press.

Reay, D. (1998) *Class Work: Mother's Involvement in their Children's Primary Schooling*. London: UCL Press.

Savage, M. (2003) A New Class Paradigm? Review Article. *British Journal of Sociology of Education*, 24(4), 535–41.

Sayer, A. (2005) *The Moral Significance of Class*. Cambridge: Cambridge University Press.

Skeggs, B. (2004) *Class, Self, Culture*. London: Routledge.

Skeggs, B. (2005) The Making of Class and Gender through Visualising Moral Subject Formation. *Sociology*, 39(5), 965–82.

Skeggs, B. and Wood, H. (2008) 'The Labour of Transformation and Circuits of Value 'around' Reality Television', *Continuum: Journal of Media and Cultural Studies*, 22(4), 559–72.

Skeggs, B., Wood, H. and Thumim, N. (2008) 'Oh Goodness I am Watching Reality TV': How Methodology Makes Class in Multi-Method Audience Research. *European Journal of Cultural Studies*, 11(1), 5–24.

Sobchack, V. (1999) Towards a Phenomenology of Nonfictional Film Experience. In: J. Gaines and M. Renow (eds) *Collecting Visible Evidence*. Minneapolis, MN: Minnesota University Press.

Steedman, C. (2000) Enforced Narratives: Stories of Another Self. In: T. Cosslett, C. Lury and P. Summerfield (eds) *Feminism and Autobiography: Texts, Theories, Methods*. London: Routledge.

Strathern, M. (1992) *After Nature: English Kinship in the Late Twentieth Century*. Cambridge: Cambridge University Press.

Swinfold, S. (2006) ASBO TV Helps Residents Watch Out. *Timesonline*, January http://www.timesonline.co.uk/tol/news/uk/article/786225.ece.

Taylor, C. (1989) *Sources of the Self: The Making of the Modern Identity*. Cambridge: Cambridge University Press.

Turner, G. (2004) *Understanding Celebrity*. London and New York: Sage.

Walkerdine, V. (2003) Reclassifying Upward Mobility: Femininity and the Neo-Liberal Subject. *Gender and Education*, 15(3), 237–48.

White, M. (2006) Investigation Cheaters. *The Communication Review*, 9, 221–40.

Williams, L. (2001) *Playing the Race Card: Melodramas of Black and White from Uncle Tom to O.J. Simpson*. Princeton: Princeton University Press.

Wood, H. and Skeggs, B. (2008) Spectacular Morality: Reality Television and the Re-making of the Working Class. In: D. Hesmondhlough and J. Toynbee (eds) *Media and Social Theory*. London: Routledge.

Wood, H., Skeggs, B. and Thumim, N. (2008) 'It's Just Sad:' Affect, Judgement and Emotional Labour in 'Reality' Television Viewing. In: S. Gillis and J. Hollows (eds) *Feminism, Domesticity and Popular Culture*. New York: Taylor and Francis.

Appendix A: List of the Economic and Social Research Council Funded Projects Informing the Volume

Simon Clarke (University of the West of England, Bristol) and Steve Garner (Aston University) **Mobility and Unsettlement: New Identity Construction in Contemporary Britain**. Research Fellow: Rosie Gilmour.
RES 148-25-0003

Christine Griffin (University of Bath), Chris Hackley (Royal Holloway), Isabelle Szmigin (Birmingham University) and Willm Mistral (University of Bath) **Branded Consumption and Social Identification: Young People and Alcohol**. Research Fellows: Andrew Bengry-Howell and David Clarke.
RES 148-25-0021

Anthony Heath (University of Oxford), John Curtice (University of Strathclyde), Miranda Phillips (NatCen) and Robert Andersen (McMaster University, Canada) **Are Traditional Identities in Decline?** Research Fellow: Gabriella Elgenius.
RES 148-25-0031

Sue Jackson, Rosie Cox, Dina Kiwan and Yasmeen Narayan (Birkbeck, University of London) **Intersecting Identities: Women's Spaces of Sociality in Postcolonial London.** Research Fellow: Meena Khatwa. [Building on Avtar Brah (Birkbeck, University of London) **South Asian and White Women's Spaces of Sociality and Celebration**. Research Fellows: Clare Roche and Sadhana Sutar]
RES 148-25-0022

Coretta Phillips (London School of Economics) **Ethnicity, Identity and Social Relations in Prison.** Research Fellow: Rod Earle.
RES 148-25-0053

Ben Rampton, Roxy Harris, Alexandra Georgakopoulou, Constant Leung (Kings College London) and Caroline Dover (University of Westminster) **Urban Classroom Culture and Interaction**. Research Fellow: Lauren Small.
RES 148-25-0042

Diane Reay (Cambridge University), Gill Crozier (Roehampton University) and David James (University of the West of England, Bristol) **Identities, Educational Choice and the White Urban Middle-Classes**. Research Fellows: Phoebe Beedell, Sumi Hollingworth, Fiona Jamieson and Katya Williams.
RES 148-25-0023

Ben Rogaly (University of Sussex) and Becky Taylor (Birkbeck, University of London) **'Deprived White Community'? Social Action in Three Norwich Estates, 1940-2005.**
RES 148-25-0047

Beverley Skeggs (Goldsmith's College, University of London) and Helen Wood (De Montfort University) **Making Class and Self through Televised Ethical Scenarios.** Research Fellow: Nancy Thumim.
RES 148-25-0040

Deborah Sporton (University of Sheffield) and Gill Valentine (University of Leeds) **Post-Conflict Identities: Practices and Affiliations of Somali Refugee Children.** Research Fellow: Katrine Nielsen.
RES 148-25-0028

Rachel Thomson, Mary Jane Kehily (Open University) and Sue Sharpe (London South Bank University) **The Making of Modern Motherhoods: Memories, Representation, Practices.** Research Fellow: Lucy Hadfield.
RES 148-25-0057

Valerie Walkerdine and Peter Fairbrother (Cardiff University) **Regeneration Identities: Subjectivity in Transition in a South Wales Workforce.** Research Fellow: Luis Jiminez.
RES 148-25-0033

For a full list of the research projects making up the ESRC Identities and Social Action Programme along with summaries of the research findings, please consult http://www.identities.org.uk/

Index